Internet of Things, Embedded Solutions, and Edge Intelligence for Smart Health

Internet of Things, Embedded Solutions, and Edge Intelligence for Smart Health

Guest Editors

Ilaria Sergi
Teodoro Montanaro

Basel • Beijing • Wuhan • Barcelona • Belgrade • Novi Sad • Cluj • Manchester

Guest Editors

Ilaria Sergi
Department of Engineering
for Innovation
Università del Salento
Lecce
Italy

Teodoro Montanaro
Department of Engineering
for Innovation
Università del Salento
Lecce
Italy

Editorial Office
MDPI AG
Grosspeteranlage 5
4052 Basel, Switzerland

This is a reprint of the Special Issue, published open access by the journal *Electronics* (ISSN 2079-9292), freely accessible at: www.mdpi.com/journal/electronics/special_issues/EB84XA56LV.

For citation purposes, cite each article independently as indicated on the article page online and using the guide below:

Lastname, A.A.; Lastname, B.B. Article Title. *Journal Name* **Year**, *Volume Number*, Page Range.

ISBN 978-3-7258-2614-8 (Hbk)
ISBN 978-3-7258-2613-1 (PDF)
https://doi.org/10.3390/books978-3-7258-2613-1

© 2024 by the authors. Articles in this book are Open Access and distributed under the Creative Commons Attribution (CC BY) license. The book as a whole is distributed by MDPI under the terms and conditions of the Creative Commons Attribution-NonCommercial-NoDerivs (CC BY-NC-ND) license (https://creativecommons.org/licenses/by-nc-nd/4.0/).

Contents

About the Editors vii

Preface ix

Elena Casabona, Sara Campagna, Lorena Charrier, Dante Viotti, Angela Castello and Paola Di Giulio et al.
Evaluation of a Telemergency Service for Older People Living at Home: A Cross-Sectional Study
Reprinted from: *Electronics* **2023**, *12*, 4786, https://doi.org/10.3390/electronics12234786 1

Francesco Mercaldo, Myriam Giusy Tibaldi, Lucia Lombardi, Luca Brunese, Antonella Santone and Mario Cesarelli
An Explainable Method for Lung Cancer Detection and Localisation from Tissue Images through Convolutional Neural Networks
Reprinted from: *Electronics* **2024**, *13*, 1393, https://doi.org/10.3390/electronics13071393 14

Antonio Vincenzo Radogna, Luca Francioso, Elisa Sciurti, Daniele Bellisario, Vanessa Esposito and Giuseppe Grassi
A Low-cost Wearable Potentiostat for-time Monitoring of Glucose Level
Reprinted from: *Electronics* **2024**, *13*, 1128, https://doi.org/10.3390/electronics13061128 34

Emi Yuda, Aoi Otani, Atsushi Yamada and Yutaka Yoshida
An Evaluation of the Autonomic Nervous Activity and Psychomotor Vigilance Level for Smells in the Work Booth
Reprinted from: *Electronics* **2024**, *13*, 3576, https://doi.org/10.3390/electronics13173576 46

Minh Long Hoang, Guido Matrella and Paolo Ciampolini
Artificial Intelligence Implementation in Internet of Things Embedded System for Real-Time Person Presence in Bed Detection and Sleep Behaviour Monitor
Reprinted from: *Electronics* **2024**, *13*, 2210, https://doi.org/10.3390/electronics13112210 60

Yutaka Yoshida, Kohei Kowata, Ryotaro Abe and Emi Yuda
Evaluation of Fatigue in Older Drivers Using a Multimodal Medical Sensor and Driving Simulator
Reprinted from: *Electronics* **2024**, *13*, 1126, https://doi.org/10.3390/electronics13061126 75

Min-Jung Kim, Ji-Hun Han, Woo-Chul Shin and Youn-Sik Hong
Gait Pattern Identification Using Gait Features
Reprinted from: *Electronics* **2024**, *13*, 1956, https://doi.org/10.3390/electronics13101956 87

Mario Cvetković and Bruno Sučić
Analysis of Magnetotherapy Device-Induced Fields Using Cylindrical Human Body Model
Reprinted from: *Electronics* **2024**, *13*, 849, https://doi.org/10.3390/electronics13050849 101

Paola Picozzi, Umberto Nocco, Andrea Pezzillo, Adriana De Cosmo and Veronica Cimolin
The Use of Business Intelligence Software to Monitor Key Performance Indicators (KPIs) for the Evaluation of a Computerized Maintenance Management System (CMMS)
Reprinted from: *Electronics* **2024**, *13*, 2286, https://doi.org/10.3390/electronics13122286 120

Woo-Chul Shin, Min-Jung Kim, Ji-Hun Han, Hyun-Sang Cho and Youn-Sik Hong
Feature-Based Gait Pattern Modeling on a Treadmill
Reprinted from: *Electronics* **2023**, *12*, 4201, https://doi.org/10.3390/electronics12204201 143

About the Editors

Ilaria Sergi

Ilaria Sergi received the master's degree in Automation Engineering from the University of Salento, Lecce, Italy, in 2012. Her thesis focused on the tracking of small laboratory animals, based on passive UHF RFID technology. Since 2012, she collaborates with the Identification Automation Laboratory (IDA Lab) of the Department of Engineering for Innovation, University of Salento. In 2019 she received the PhD in Engineering of Complex Systems from the University of Salento, Italy. Her research interests include RFID, Bluetooth, Internet of Things, smart environments, and homecare solutions. She has authored several papers on international journals and conferences. She has co-chaired some tracks, workshops, and symposia within the IEEE COMPSAC and the IEEE Splitech conferences. She has chaired a Special Session on the MDPI Electronics Journal titled "Internet of Things, Embedded Solutions, and Edge Intelligence for Smart Health".

Teodoro Montanaro

Teodoro Montanaro received the M.S. degree in Computer Engineering in 2014 and the Ph.D. degree in Computer and Control Engineering in 2018 from the Politecnico di Torino, Turin, Italy. From 2017 to 2020 he collaborated with the Istituto Superiore Mario Boella (ISMB) and LINKS Foundation by cooperating to different researches funded by the European Commission like IoF2020, S4G, MONICA, MAESTRI that brought innovations in different fields (e.g., food and farm, grid, city, health). Since 2020, he collaborates with the IDentification Automation Laboratory (IDA Lab), Department of Innovation Engineering, Università del Salento. His current research interests include IoT applications specifically focused on the exploitation of fog computing, DLT, blockchain, and AI in different domains like smart grids, smart homes, smart cities, industrial processes, food traceability, and smart health. He has authored different papers on international journals and conferences. He has co-chaired some tracks, workshops, and symposia within the IEEE COMPSAC, the IEEE WF-IoT, and the IEEE Splitech conferences. He has chaired a Special Session on the MDPI Electronics Journal titled "Internet of Things, Embedded Solutions, and Edge Intelligence for Smart Health". He also contributed to review some papers in some important Journals: IEEE Internet of Things Journal (41), IEEE Access Journal (24), MDPI Sensors Journal (5), MDPI Electronics Journal (3), Journal of Communications Software and Systems (3), ACM Computing Surveys (2), MDPI Future Internet Journal (2), Elsevier Future Generation Computer Systems (1), IEEE Transactions on Mobile Computing (1), MDPI Healthcare Journal (1), MDPI IoT Journal (1).

Preface

The Internet of Things (IoT) solutions are becoming increasingly popular in the healthcare domain due to their ability to monitor patients' health status remotely in real-time. Moreover, integrating IoT with edge intelligence solutions allows the devices to process and analyze the data locally instead of sending it to a central server. This is particularly important in applications where real-time decision-making or low latency is required. In the field of smart health, IoT solutions can play a crucial role in the monitoring and management of the individuals' health. This can also include wearable/embedded devices that track vital signs, medical devices that monitor chronic conditions, and even smart home devices that can assist users with medication management. By collecting and analyzing data from multiple sources, these solutions can provide a more complete picture of an individual's health and allow for more personalized and proactive healthcare.

This Special Issue aimed at presenting interesting papers focused on the exploitation of the IoT and edge intelligence in the healthcare domain. Topics of interest included Innovative healthcare architectures to improve patients' conditions; proposals to save costs, and consumption, and improve the efficiency of healthcare systems; Innovations for personalized healthcare; Improved data collection and analysis; Solutions that exploit real-time decision-making in the healthcare domain; Home-based healthcare assistance to reduce healthcare professionals' workload; Edge intelligent solutions for the early detection of potential health issues; IoT systems to promote the collection of more detailed and accurate information about patient's health; Solutions to improve the communication and coordination among healthcare professionals in critical scenarios; Innovative healthcare systems for providing prompt reactions and interventions in cases of emergency; Innovative healthcare systems for specific chronic diseases; The exploitation of energy-efficient designs and developments of devices for healthcare.

Ilaria Sergi and Teodoro Montanaro
Guest Editors

Article

Evaluation of a Telemergency Service for Older People Living at Home: A Cross-Sectional Study

Elena Casabona [1,*], Sara Campagna [1], Lorena Charrier [1], Dante Viotti [2], Angela Castello [1], Paola Di Giulio [1] and Valerio Dimonte [1]

1. Department of Public Health and Pediatrics, University of Torino, 10100 Torino, Italy; sara.campagna@unito.it (S.C.); lorena.charrier@unito.it (L.C.); angela.castello@edu.unito.it (A.C.); paola.digiulio@unito.it (P.D.G.); valerio.dimonte@unito.it (V.D.)
2. Ass.I.S.Te Company Scs, 10100 Torino, Italy; d.viotti@assiste.it
* Correspondence: elena.casabona@unito.it

Abstract: Personal Emergency Response Systems (PERSs) are fall-detection devices supporting users in any situation. No previous studies have investigated the differences in events and the use of PERS between users financially supported by public authorities (public users) and those who privately afford the PERS cost (private users). More than two years of data collected by the Telemergency Operation Centre (TOC) were downloaded. All users who sent at least one real alert to request support were included. No differences were found for falls (37, 16.7% vs. 95, 13.4%) and medical problems (46, 20.7% vs. 122, 17.2%). The dispatch of an ambulance was necessary for all medical problems, while for falls, this was only in half of cases. Public users significantly asked more for service demand, while private users asked for support calls. The TOC staff directly managed most of the service demands (398, 97.3%) and support calls. PERS could be a valid instrument for promoting independent living and helping manage chronic conditions in older adults. The results suggest that PERSs might improve in-home care services, facilitating the connection to in-home services.

Keywords: fall detection device; Personal Emergency Response System; older people; independent living; home care

Citation: Casabona, E.; Campagna, S.; Charrier, L.; Viotti, D.; Castello, A.; Di Giulio, P.; Dimonte, V. Evaluation of a Telemergency Service for Older People Living at Home: A Cross-Sectional Study. *Electronics* 2023, 12, 4786. https://doi.org/10.3390/electronics12234786

Academic Editors: Ilaria Sergi, Teodoro Montanaro and Antoni Morell

Received: 27 October 2023
Revised: 20 November 2023
Accepted: 24 November 2023
Published: 26 November 2023

Copyright: © 2023 by the authors. Licensee MDPI, Basel, Switzerland. This article is an open access article distributed under the terms and conditions of the Creative Commons Attribution (CC BY) license (https://creativecommons.org/licenses/by/4.0/).

1. Introduction

Personal Emergency Response Systems (PERSs) are fall-detection devices born at the end of the 1970s. These devices can be worn around the neck or wrist and, besides distinguishing falls from the activities of daily living, they can activate rescue systems that can quickly intervene in case of falls [1–3]. In this study, PERSs are characterised by three essential elements: (a) a red button to call to, (b) a 24 h emergency response centre, and (c) a home communication system [2,3]. The alert can also be directly sent to a nominated contact, such as a caregiver [2,3]. PERSs can be purchased, leased, or rented; in many cases, the costs of the service are not covered by health insurance [2,3].

Over the years, these devices have been integrated with numerous features, including vital signs detection or machine learning systems, making it possible to detect information on gait, gait speed, and acceleration, which are all predictors of falling [4]. Compared with other technologies, PERS remains the most marketed fall detection device due to its reliability, ease of use, ease of control, and affordability [5,6]. Some evidence has reported that PERSs increase older adults' confidence [7], feelings of safety [5–7], and independence [5,8], which contributes to the well-accepted use of this technology [5,6]. One possible explanation for their use is the balance they provide between maintaining the person's freedom and the early identification of falls. In fact, according to the guidelines of the Ontario Registered Nurses Association [1], family members, caregivers, and health care providers can inadvertently limit the person's independence when focusing on fall-prevention measures [9].

Few studies have underlined the capacity of PERS to provide a rapid rescue, with positive outcomes on ED admissions, hospitalisations, and hospital stay [10–12]. Moreover, PERS contributes to avoiding ambulance intervention, with a potential annual cost of AUD 76.8 per person per year [13]. Two cost-saving mechanisms exist: an intermediate assessment by the operations centre of the user's conditions and the possibility of contacting a reference person. Thus, the operation centre may quickly identify minor events, activating the caregiver or, whether not present, district services to treat the person at home, also avoiding an ambulance intervention [13].

Technology in the real world is often used differently and for different purposes than originally intended [14]. Even if PERSs were initially developed for the rapid detection of falls, observational studies showed that almost half of the alerts involved physical or psychological symptoms (medical alerts), such as dyspnoea, severe pain, or heart problems [12,15,16]. Medical alerts ranged from 41% to 45.7% of the total alerts sent by users, requiring, more often than falls, an ambulance [12,15–17]. PERSs are also used by older adults for requests of transportation, medications, and nursing care (non-medical alerts) [7,16]. However, published studies often do not report on these alerts [7,12,15–19].

The analysis of non-medical alerts would allow a more in-depth understanding of the needs of users and their caregivers, fostering a reflection upon the best future strategies to further develop PERSs and integrate them into community care [14]. The necessity to integrate technologies in home-care services, allowing distance monitoring and care, was well underlined during the COVID-19 pandemic. After an initial use of telemedicine or telenursing systems primarily to minimise the transmission of the virus during the pandemic [20], the role of telecare was exploited in the care and treatment of people in rural areas and those with limited access to health facilities [20,21]. Evidence was produced of a reduction in resources used in health facilities, yet with improved access to care, especially in older adults, through electronic devices [20,22,23].

A better shaping of users' profiles is another important aspect for PERSs' improved use in home-care services. PERS users may not share the same characteristics, as we may identify those who receive the service from a public authority or financial support to partially or fully cover its costs (public users) or those who privately sustained the cost of the PERS (private users) or those who do not use the PERS (non-purchasers) [7,12,15,16]. Most studies focus only on one of these groups of users.

Despite the numerous benefits, the main reasons not to purchase a PERS are the cost and the lack of a caregiver for contact in case of emergencies. The cost of the device is rarely reported but amounts to approximately AUD 600 for equipment and installation, with a monthly fee of AUD 19 [15]. Health insurance often does not cover these costs. The main users of PERS are women older than 85, living alone but with family support, with one or more comorbidities [12,18,24]. Offering the device only to those who live alone or lack health insurance coverage excludes a portion of the population that could benefit from this device but who either cannot afford the cost or, although frail, do not live alone.

To our knowledge, no article highlighted the differences in the need and use of the device between public and private users. These elements would help policymakers develop policies to promote equitable access to obtaining a PERS for older adults, or those with difficulties in accessing health services. The acknowledgement of the benefits of PERS could promote a revision of the criteria for the subsidy of these devices, possibly expanding their provision and broadening the coverage of the costs of the service [15].

The present study aims to highlight the differences in the use of PERSs (type and number of user requests, supportive calls, and medical alerts) between those who privately afford the cost of the telemergency system offered by Ass.I.S.Te Cooperative (Ass.I.S.Te from now on) (private users) and those who are financially supported by a public authority (public users).

2. Materials and Methods

This is a cross-sectional study conducted at the Telemergency Operation Centre (TOC), located at Ville Roddolo Nursing Home (Moncalieri, Northern Italy), between 1 December 2020 and 31 March 2023.

2.1. Setting of the Study

The telemergency service offered by for-profit agency Ass.I.S.Te aims to promote independent living at home to aged or frail people using PERSs. Users can be monitored in and out of the house, and the service is active for over twenty-four hours.

The service can be purchased by single users or public authorities, such as social services.

The public authority sustains the cost of device installation and the monthly fee for users with special health and non-health conditions (i.e., depression, loneliness, grief, etc.) with an income not exceeding EUR 850 per month or may ask for a partial contribution if the income is up to EUR 1100 per month. For private purchasers, the cost of the Telemergency service includes a monthly fee of EUR 25, plus the cost of activation and installation of the PERS (EUR 50 to 100 according to indoor-only monitoring, outdoor monitoring, or both) and a deposit (EUR 100). The user purchases the SIM card.

The user may choose between two types of PERS: indoor devices equipped with radio transmitters and connected to wearable devices around the neck or wrist; an outdoor device equipped with a Global Positioning System (GPS), which can be clipped to the belt or watch. All the PERSs are of the third generation: they are embedded with sensors (i.e., an accelerometer and a gyroscope) designed to automatically identify a fall or a high impact with a hard surface. Following an impact, the fall detection system evaluates the change in height and rotation of the device, as well as if the user is on the ground. The remote control, wearable on the wrist or neck, has a survival control function and a micro-movement sensor. It can send an automatic alert in cases of no motion for a pre-defined time (in days or hours), allowing the system to know whether the user is wearing it.

An alert can be automatically generated by the device (i.e., in case of a fall) or by the user by pressing a button. Each PERS is equipped with a small radio transmitter that allows easy communication with the TOC staff after activating an alert: if the user is on the floor after a fall, the PERS allows the user to talk with the staff. In cases of false alerts, the automatic call forwarding system can be turned off in indoor devices by pressing the green button within 15 s, while in outdoor devices, this occurs if the fallen person rises within 15 s from the impact.

All alerts are managed by the lay staff of the TOC (Figure 1).

Figure 1. Alert management of the Telemergency Operation Centre.

The staff can display the user's data on the screen (including the type of device), the date and time of alert dispatch, and the PERS code. The device can assign up to 31 codes (i.e., general alert, fall, medical alert, etc.). The TOC lay staff conducts a brief interview to assess the user's health conditions and to confirm or re-code the alert. Any other relevant information is reported in the software's free field 'Notes'. In the "closing code", the staff reports if the public safety answering point (112), the first aid station, the General Practitioner (GP), or the caregiver were contacted or if no action was needed.

2.2. Participants and Data Collection

All public and private users who sent a service demand, a support call, or a medical alert during the study period and consented to the processing of the information collected by the telemergency system for research purposes were included. The following baseline information from those regularly collected by the TOC are reported: service information (ID code, private/public user, date of start and end of the service use, reason for service interruption, and device type), demographics (sex, age, marital status, living condition, caregiver presence, dependence level), and health information (comorbidities, use of a walking aid, visual and hearing impairment, lower limb disabilities, alcohol or drugs abuse, and medications). Information on the number and type of drugs was collected, and on drugs that increase the risk of falling (anticoagulants, antihypertensives, diuretics, analgesics, antidepressants, anxiolytics, hypnotics, antiparkinsonians, and neuroleptics) [25,26]. The study was approved by the Ethics Committee of the University of Torino (Prot. n. 0339442).

Alerts sent for 28 months were downloaded from the software in use in the TOC, and between April and May 2023, and researchers created the dataset (the system did not allow for the downloading of longer periods). All the alerts received by the TOC were considered, whether sent by the user or automatically generated by the device. Each alert included the date and hour of dispatch, the date and hour of alert closure by the TOC staff, the PERS code, the TOC lay staff code, the free field note, and the closing code. Two researchers (E.C. and A.C.) independently reviewed all the alerts, comparing the PERS code and the TOC code (Table 1).

All the medical alerts identified by the TOC were re-coded as falls or medical problems based on the information reported in the free field notes and any fall or event that required a medical rescue, even if not coded as a medical alert. Researchers also reviewed the closing code, classifying the alert outcome into four categories: no action needed (if the TOC lay staff managed the alert), ambulance (if the TOC lay staff called a public safety answering point and an ambulance attended the scene), GP (if the TOC contacted the General Practitioner), first aid station (if the TOC reached the emergency medical service), and caregiver (if a relative or a friend was called by the TOC). Since users may send multiple alerts for the same event, alerts reporting the same activation and closure date and the same description in the free field were considered one event. Only support calls, service demands, and emergencies (falls and medical problems) were considered real events and included in the final analysis. Each event was associated with the user through the ID code. Only users who sent at least one real alert were included in the analyses.

Table 1. Process of re-coding performed by researchers.

TOC Codes	Researchers' Codes	Definition
Device test Watch test Remote control test Tracker test	Test alert	Recurrent alert from the user, to check the device's functioning.
Blackout Service activation Device installation Technical intervention Low battery Technical notification No data from the watch	Technical alert	Alert sent automatically from the PERS or by the user, caregiver, or the technical staff to notify of the device's malfunctioning, low battery, no data from the device, service activation, or lighting system failure.

Table 1. Cont.

TOC Codes	Researchers' Codes	Definition
User error False alert	False alert	Alerts due to an accidental button press, to device dropout, or automatically sent without any apparent reason.
Information from user/User request	• Information from user • Service demand	Alerts sent from the user or a caregiver to convey information or ask for additional services were classified as user requests. These alerts were still divided into the following: • Information from user: users' communications involving any information transmitted from them or caregivers to the TOC. (i.e., absence from home for holidays or due to hospitalisation) • Service demand: request for additional services offered by the company (i.e., ambulance transportation for planned medical exams)
Support calls	Support calls	Alert sent by the user to talk with the TOC staff; these calls are in addition to the ones performed two times per week by the TOC.
Emergency	• Medical alert • Fall • Medical problem	Alerts considered emergencies; all the alerts sent due to a (Falls), or for cardiovascular, respiratory symptoms, etc. (Medical problems)
No code assigned	Not-coded	Alerts without the TOC code and without information in the free field "Note" on the reason for alert activation.

2.3. Statistical Analyses

Descriptive data are reported as absolute frequencies and percentages for categorical variables. The normality of the distribution of continuous variables was assessed with the Shapiro–Wilk normality test. Continuous variables with a normal distribution were presented as mean and standard deviation (SD), otherwise median and interquartile range (IQR) were used. Differences between groups (private vs. public users) were assessed using the Chi-squared test for categorical variables and t-test or the non-parametric Wilcoxon rank-sum test, as appropriate, for continuous variables.

Statistical analyses were performed using Jamovi Version 2.3.26.0 [27–30].

3. Results

Out of the 720 users who sent at least one alert (total number of alerts = 48,871) from December 2020 to March 2023, 315 were included in the final analysis. At the end of March 2023, 308 patients (42.7%) had suspended the service for notice of termination (109, 35.4%), death (103, 33.4%), admission to a nursing home (73, 23.4%), cohabitation with a caregiver (16, 5.5%), and moving home (2, 0.6%); five (1.6%) did not specify the reason. Users who experienced real events were more dependent ($p = 0.049$) and presented a higher period of overall service use ($p < 0.001$) and of service use during the study period ($p < 0.001$). Moreover, they suffered more from respiratory diseases ($p = 0.009$) and visual impairment ($p < 0.001$). However, people who had not experienced a real event took more fall-risk-increasing drugs than those who experienced one ($p < 0.001$).

3.1. Users' Characteristics

Users' characteristics are shown in Table 2. Most were widowed women who lived alone with a family network. Private users were significantly older than public users but were comparable for gender, living condition, marital status, and time of service use during the study period (28 months). However, only seven (2.2%) private users lived alone and without a family network, compared with forty public users (12.6%). Private users were significantly more independent and more supported by a caregiver.

Table 2. Demographic characteristics of participants.

Variable	Total (n = 315)	Private Users (n = 101, 32.1%)	Public Users (n = 214, 67.9%)	Test Statistic
Gender n (%)				$X^2_1 = 0.31, 0.578$ [1]
Female	237 (75.2%)	74 (73.3%)	163 (76.2%)	
Age *				
Median (IQR)	86.6 (78.6; 91.5)	89.1 (80.8; 92.9)	84.8 (78.0; 90.2)	$F_{1,312} = 8.85, 0.003$ [2]
Range	30.5–100.9	30.5–99.7	44.2–100.9	
Caregiver n (%) Yes	265 (84.1%)	92 (91.1%)	173 (80.8%)	$X^2_1 = 5.40, 0.020$ [1]
Living condition n (%)				$X^2_1 = 0.01, 0.931$ [1]
Alone	258 (81.9%)	83 (82.2%)	175 (81.8%)	
Marital status n (%)				
Widowed	196 (62.2%)	68 (67.3%)	128 (59.8%)	
Unmarried	62 (19.7%)	17 (16.8%)	45 (21%)	$X^2_3 = 1.66, 0.645$ [1]
Married	35 (11.1%)	10 (9.9%)	25 (11.7%)	
Divorced	22 (7%)	6 (5.9%)	16 (7.5%)	
Dependence level n (%)				
Independent	126 (40%)	60 (59.4%)	66 (30.8%)	
Partially independent	163 (51.7%)	36 (35.6%)	127 (59.3%)	$X^2_2 = 23.41, <0.001$ [1]
Dependent	26 (8.3%)	5 (5%)	21 (9.8%)	
Walking aid n (%)				$X^2_1 = 11.50, <0.001$ [1]
Yes	137 (43.5%)	30 (29.7%)	107 (50%)	
Type of walking aid n (%)				
Cane	55 (17.5%)	13 (12.9%)	42 (19.6%)	
Walker	53 (16.8%)	12 (11.9%)	41 (19.2%)	$X^2_4 = 12.28, 0.015$ [2]
Wheelchair	26 (8.3%)	4 (4%)	22 (10.3%)	
Time of overall service use n (%)				
<1	9 (2.9%)	7 (6.9%)	2 (0.9%)	
1–5	146 (46.3%)	46 (45.5%)	100 (46.7%)	$F_{1,313} = 5.17, p = 0.003$ [2]
6–10	99 (31.4%)	36 (35.6%)	63 (29.4%)	
>10	61 (19.4%)	12 (11.9%)	49 (22.9%)	
Time of service use in the study period n (%)				$F_{1,313} = 0.15, 0.718$ [2]
Median (IQR)	2.3 (1.4; 2.3)	2.3 (1.3; 2.3)	2.3 (1.5; 2.3)	
Range	0.1–2.3	0.3–2.3	0.1–2.3	
PERS n (%)				
Indoor device	291 (92.4%)	85 (84.2%)	206 (96.3%)	$X^2_2 = 14.37, < 0.001$ [1]
Outdoor device	24 (7.6%)	16 (15.8%)	8 (3.8%)	

* Age was not available for one user. [1] Pearson Chi-squared test; [2] Wilcoxon rank-sum test.

Overall, the median time of use of the telemergency service was 4.6 years, 4.4 years for private users and 4.8 years for public ones. Nearly 50% of the participants used the service for between one and five years, with longer use by public users. However, the two groups were comparable for length of use during the study period: the median time of service use was 2.3 years for both groups.

3.2. Users' Health Status

Overall, the users had a median of two comorbidities (IQR 2; 3), with a statistically significant difference, between public (median three, IQR 2; 4) and private (median two, IQR 1; 3) users ($p = 0.02$). The two groups were comparable for hearing and visual impairment, number of drugs, and fall-risk-increasing drugs (Table 3). More than 60% (n = 237) of all users took at least one drug that may increase the risk of falling. The public users suffered significantly more from mental diseases.

Table 3. Users' health conditions and medication.

Variable	Total (n = 315)	Private Users (n = 101, 32.1%)	Public Users (n = 214, 67.9%)	Test Statistic
Weight *				
Median (IQR)	68 (58; 80)	65 (56; 77)	70 (58; 80)	$F_{1,301} = 3.92, 0.05$ [2]
Range	34–125	34–105	35–125	
Caregiver n (%)				
Yes	265 (84.1%)	92 (91.1%)	173 (80.8%)	$X^2_1 = 5.40, 0.020$ [1]
Comorbidities (Yes) n (%)				
Heart diseases	237 (75.2%)	75 (74.3%)	162 (75.7%)	$X^2_1 = 0.08, 0.782$ [1]
Endocrine diseases	103 (32.7%)	26 (25.7%)	77 (36%)	$X^2_1 = 3.27, 0.071$ [1]
CNS diseases	89 (28.3%)	24 (23.8%)	65 (30.4%)	$X^2_1 = 1.48, 0.224$ [1]
Respiratory diseases	80 (25.4%)	23 (22.8%)	57 (26.6%)	$X^2_1 = 0.54, 0.462$ [1]
Mental diseases	78 (24.8%)	16 (15.8%)	62 (29%)	$X^2_1 = 6.35, 0.012$ [1]
Vascular diseases	78 (24.8%)	23 (22.8%)	55 (25.7%)	$X^2_1 = 0.32, 0.574$ [1]
Musculoskeletal diseases	62 (19.7%)	22 (21.8%)	40 (18.7%)	$X^2_1 = 0.41, 0.520$ [1]
Abdominal diseases	61 (19.4%)	17 (16.8%)	44 (20.6%)	$X^2_1 = 0.61, 0.434$ [1]
Urinary diseases	43 (13.7%)	12 (11.9%)	31 (14.5%)	$X^2_1 = 0.39, 0.530$ [1]
Hearing impairment n (%)				
None	170 (54%)	58 (57.4%)	112 (52.3%)	
Partially not corrected	135 (42.9%)	40 (39.6%)	95 (44.4%)	$X^2_1 = 0.72, 0.398$ [1]
Partially corrected	9 (2.9%)	3 (3%)	6 (2.8%)	
Complete	1 (0.3%)	0 (0%)	1 (0.5%)	
Visual impairment n (%)				
None	154 (48.9%)	54 (53.5%)	100 (46.7%)	
Partially not corrected	41 (13%)	12 (11.9%)	29 (13.6%)	$X^2_1 = 1.25, 0.264$ [1]
Partially corrected	112 (35.6%)	31 (30.7%)	81 (37.9%)	
Complete	8 (2.5%)	4 (4%)	4 (1.9%)	
Lower limb disability n (%)				
Yes	118 (37.5%)	24 (23.8%)	94 (43.9%)	$X^2_1 = 11.91, <0.001$ [1]
Drugs n (%)				
None	76 (24.1%)	32 (31.7%)	44 (20.6%)	
1–5	190 (60.3%)	54 (53.5%)	136 (63.6%)	$X^2_3 = 4.79, 0.188$ [1]
5–10	45 (14.3%)	14 (13.9%)	31 (14.5%)	
>10	4 (1.3%)	1 (1%)	3 (1.4%)	
Fall-risk-increasing drugs n (%)				
Yes	189 (60%)	57 (56.4%)	132 (61.7%)	$X^2_1 = 0.79, 0.375$ [1]

* Weight was not available for twelve users. [1] Pearson Chi-squared test, [2] Wilcoxon rank-sum test.

3.3. PERS Activation

A significantly higher number of public users sent a request for service demand, but no differences were observed for the proportion of users that asked for a support call, or sent an alert for health emergencies (medical problems and falls) (Table 4). Moreover, during the study period, users experienced a median of two events, with a significant difference between private and public users (Table 4).

Table 4. Number of users with at least one real event (service demand, support call, medical problem or fall).

Event	Total (n = 315)	Private Users (n = 101, 32.1%)	Public Users (n = 214, 67.9%)	Test Statistic
Service demand n (%)	173 (54.9%)	39 (38.6%)	134 (62.6%)	$X^2_1 = 15.97, <0.001$ [1]
Support call n (%)	112 (35.6%)	39 (38.6%)	73 (34.1%)	$X^2_1 = 0.61, 0.436$ [1]
Medical problem n (%)	93 (29.5%)	31 (30.7%)	62 (29%)	$X^2_1 = 0.10, 0.755$ [1]
Fall n (%)	89 (28.3%)	27 (26.7%)	62 (29%)	$X^2_1 = 0.17, 0.680$ [1]
Median number of events				$F_{1,313} = 14.00, <0.001$ [2]
Median (IQR)	2 (1;3)	1 (1;2)	2 (1;4)	

[1] Pearson Chi-squared test; [2] Wilcoxon rank-sum test.

Over the observation time, 300 health emergencies were reported, 168 medical problems (i.e., cardiovascular symptoms, malaise, and tremors, etc.), and 132 falls (Table 5).

Table 5. Number and types of real events experienced by users.

Event	Total (n = 932)	Private Users (n = 222, 23.8%)	Public Users (n = 710, 76.2%)	Test Statistic
Service demand	409 (43.9%)	49 (22.1%)	360 (50.7%)	
Transportation	285 (69.7%)	15 (30.6%)	270 (75%)	
Request to talk with the caregiver	33 (8.1%)	13 (26.5%)	20 (5.5%)	$X^2_1 = 56.30, <0.001$ [1]
Information (payment, alert management)	23 (5.6%)	5 (10.2%)	18 (5%)	
Health support	13 (3.2%)	2 (4.1%)	11 (3%)	
Not specified	60 (14.7%)	15 (30.6%)	45 (12.5%)	
Support call *	223 (23.9%)	90 (40.5%)	133 (18.7%)	
Desire to talk with someone	212 (95.1%)	85 (94.4%)	127 (95.6%)	$X^2_1 = 44.19, <0.001$ [1]
Call for greetings	6 (2.7%)	3 (3.3%)	3 (2.2%)	
Anxiety-loneliness	5 (2.2%)	2 (2.2%)	3 (2.2%)	
Medical problem	168 (18.0%)	46 (20.7%)	122 (17.2%)	
Cardiovascular symptoms (hypertension, hypotension, fibrillation, hearth attack, tachycardia, hearth failure, holter malfunctioning)	29 (17.3%)	5 (10.9%)	24 (19.7%)	
Malaise and tremors	29 (17.3%)	14 (30.4%)	15 (12.3%)	
Respiratory symptoms (asthma, dyspnoea, aspiration, pneumonia)	25 (14.9%)	5 (10.9%)	20 (16.4%)	
Pain (back, legs, headache)	17 (10.1%)	4 (8.7%)	13 (10.6%)	$X^2_1 = 1.43, 0.231$ [1]
Disorientation	16 (9.5%)	4 (8.7%)	12 (9.8%)	
Gastro-intestinal symptoms (bowel occlusion, stoma occlusion, nausea, emesis)	14 (8.3%)	0 (0%)	14 (11.5%)	
Syncope	14 (8.3%)	6 (13%)	8 (6.5%)	
Bleeding	6 (3.6%)	3 (6.5%)	3 (2.4%)	
Medication overdose (insulin, analgesic)	6 (3.6%)	1 (2.2%)	5 (4.1%)	
Fever	4 (2.4%)	3 (6.5%)	1 (0.8%)	
Other (kidney colic, burn)	3 (1.8%)	0 (0%)	3 (2.4%)	

Table 5. *Cont.*

Event	Total (n = 932)	Private Users (n = 222, 23.8%)	Public Users (n = 710, 76.2%)	Test Statistic
Falls	132 (14.2%)	37 (16.7%)	95 (13.4%)	
Fall without trauma	99 (75%)	29 (78.4%)	70 (73.7%)	$X^2_1 = 1.50, 0.220$ [1]
Fall with trauma (head trauma, femur, arm, maxillofacial fracture, hip dislocation)	27 (20.4%)	6 (16.2%)	21 (22.1%)	
Fall automatically detected from the device	6 (4.6%)	2 (5.4%)	4 (4.2%)	

* Compared with the other participants, one public user sent 335 alerts for support calls, for a total of 312 events in the study time and was considered as an outlier. [1] Pearson Chi-squared test

No significant differences were observed between private and public users for falls, medical problems, and the dispatch of an ambulance. Health emergencies (falls and medical problems) were managed by the caregiver more in private than in public users, and by the first-aid station, significantly more in public than in private users.

Public users experienced more traumatic falls, mainly resulting in head trauma and hip fracture (Table 5). In two cases, the fall caused the death of the user. In the majority of cases, falls occurred when the user was alone (89, 67.4%) and only in in 1/3 of cases, the caregiver activated the alert (43, 32.6%), without differences between the two groups ($p = 0.983$). Only in six cases was the alert automatically activated by the device.

Of the 168 medical problems, the majority were due to cardiovascular symptoms (i.e., hypotension, heart attack, heart failure, etc.) and malaise and tremors (Table 5). As for falls, most medical problems were directly communicated by the user (141, 83.9%), while only in a small percentage of cases was the alert sent by a caregiver (27, 16.1%), without any differences between the two groups ($p = 0.101$).

Almost all medical problems (118, 70%) required the dispatch of an ambulance, while only half of the fall cases did so (71, 53.8%). Hospital admission was required in eight cases for medical problems (four in both groups) and two for falls; however, hospitalisations were not always reported, with possible underestimation.

Public users significantly asked for more service demands, while private users significantly sent more support calls (Table 5). Among those who used the service, private users sent, on average, 2.3 calls vs. 1.8 of public users. The main reason for service demands was the need for transportation for medical examinations. The majority of service demands were directly managed by the TOC staff (398, 97.3%), except for 11 cases where the staff asked for the support of a caregiver. The totality of support calls was managed by the TOC staff.

4. Discussion

To our knowledge, this is the first study which aimed at underlining the differences in the use of a PERS and at describing the reasons for alert activation between two different groups of users of a telemergency service. Previous studies focused on describing the characteristics and factors associated with using the PERS [24], focusing on a specific population [12,16,17], or comparing health outcomes (i.e., number of falls, emergency department admissions, or hospitalizations, etc.) between purchasers and non-purchasers [7,15,18,19]. Extending the analysis of alarms to include non-medical alarms may obtain a broader overview of how PERSs are actually used.

Even if PERSs were developed as a fall detection device, our real-world data show a broader use for medical and non-medical needs. Most activations during the study period regarded demands for services and the need to talk to someone (support calls). Only a small part of the alerts involved medical problems and falls, in contrast with previous studies [12,16,17]. A possible explanation for these discrepancies is related to the differences in the number of alerts and real events. In fact, more than one alert can be sent to manage a single fall or an event [12]. Analysing only the events may offer a clearer picture of reasons for using PERS, thereby avoiding overestimations, particularly those related to emergencies (falls and medical problems).

A significantly larger number of public users requested more assistance and sent demands for services compared with private users. A possible explanation for this difference is related to the possibility for public users to request additional services, such as transportation for health exams or health and social workers (i.e., nurses, nurse assistants, etc.) as part of an agreement with public authorities. In contrast, the same services are directly billed to private users. A second explanation was reported by Nyman et al. [24]: frail older people living alone and without the support of a caregiver declared a higher use of a PERS than those who cohabit. These results are consistent with ours, as public users, who were frailer, less independent, and less supported by a caregiver, sent a larger number of requests. These people may have unmet health and non-health needs due to the lack of a caregiver who can identify or solve them promptly [24].

While only 1/3 of users in both groups asked for support, private users needed it more (2.3 vs. 1.8 calls on average). The main reason for support calls was the need to talk to someone to alleviate the sense of loneliness, not mitigated by the two-week routine calls made by the TOC staff to check users' health status. Though a higher proportion of private users may rely on a caregiver, this may not alleviate the sense of loneliness. The availability of a caregiver does not imply a greater presence at home nor a reduced need for support calls [31]. When scheduling support calls, the sense of loneliness experienced should be considered.

Our findings regarding the characteristics of public and private users and the number of emergencies are consistent with the literature. The characteristics of our participants were very similar to other published studies: most users were women, living alone, and almost one in five users had no family support [18,24]. Similarities were found, particularly, between public users and non-purchasers, except for the independence level. Non-purchasers were younger, less functionally dependent, with less support from family members and they had a personal referred health lower than purchasers [15,19]. Moreover, even though they were younger and more independent, they had a higher risk of in-home emergencies than purchasers, underlining the advantages of using a PERS. Since, as reported by De San Miguel et al. [15], the main barriers in not purchasing a PERS are social isolation and the cost, the availability of all-inclusive services that include a PERS, could provide more equitable access for people at risk for home emergencies [15]. In our study, public authorities sustained the cost of the device (installation and monthly fee) for users with special health and non-health conditions. Compared with previous studies [12,17], the criteria for access to funding are broader. In fact, not only frail people who lived alone, had disabilities, and were at higher risk of falling or already falling were considered but so were those frail people (i.e., with cognitive impairment, lower limb disabilities, which highly limit the movements, etc.) who lived with a caregiver (child, elder spouse, etc.).

As in other studies [7,15,19], despite public users being more dependent and with a larger use of walking aids, no significant differences were observed in the number of falls and medical problems. One possible explanation for this lack of difference could be related to the additional services public users receive. The telemergency service is offered on top of home care services; thus, some health needs may have been detected in advance and treated promptly (i.e., home assessment and environmental hazard modification for fall prevention) [32]. Since data on hospitalisations for emergencies were possibly underestimated, differently from other studies [10,33], any differences between public and private users were not observed.

The presence of a single centralised point of contact which managed all the alerts made response faster, particularly in emergencies [17], and also performed a filter function, with the advantages of managing false alerts, thus alleviating the caregiver's stress [8,16,18]. In our study, in most cases, the minor health emergencies were managed by a caregiver more in private than public users, and conversely, by the first-aid station, significantly more in public users, who were almost entirely responsible for minor health events. The user was, therefore, treated at home, assuming a reduction not only in costs but also in the stress associated with avoidable transportation to the emergency department [13,18].

Compared with other published studies [7,12,15–17], it was possible to also highlight the use of the PERS by the caregiver. In fact, in 32.6% of falls and 16.1% of medical problems, a caregiver sent the alert, requesting the support of the TOC, instead of directly calling an ambulance. This is in contrast to other two other two studies, which reported that the main reason reported by users for not activating the alert is the presence of a caregiver when the emergency occurs, who directly manage the situation or call for rescue [7,18]. Thus, it seems that the PERS is useful not only for the user but also for the caregiver. Moreover, the notification to the TOC allowed the staff to assess the situation and activate the most relevant rescue service.

Moreover, the TOC is particularly relevant for people who live alone, representing the majority of our sample, without any family support, or for those living in rural areas with greater difficulty accessing health or social services. The TOC could further expand its intervention area by connecting the user to other services for health and social needs. A potential further expansion of the service may include the provision of health promotion, education, prevention, and disease management services or information [21]. The integration between telemergency and home care management services has already been described [12,17,24]. However, details on how the two services were integrated and interact are sometimes lacking.

In conclusion, our study presents some limitations. Firstly, data were analysed cross-sectionally, not allowing for the highlighting of the characteristics which may influence the alert sending. More prospective studies are necessary to understand these factors (i.e., age, living conditions, level of ADL/IADL, etc.). Another limit is related to health information, such as the number and type of comorbidities and drugs, as they were only sometimes fully collected at the start of the service; the hospitalisations were not regularly reported. This may have underestimated the number of medical conditions and medications taken by users and the possible benefits of the service in preventing hospitalisations by having a clearer picture of the severity of the events dealt with by the TOC.

5. Conclusions

Compared with other marketed and the newest technologies, PERSs still remain widely used due to their ease of use and affordable cost. Integrating a PERS in a telemergency service, with a single centralised point of contact, allows users to receive broader support, not only for health but also for social needs. Where the telemergency service is integrated into home care services, a broader population who may benefit from the service can be reached, i.e., persons living alone and without a caregiver or a social network. The support from public authorities allows us to overcome one of the principal barriers to adopting PERS, which is the cost of the service. The PERS represents a valid instrument to promote independent living, help manage chronic conditions, and facilitate access to other social and health services.

The TOC also plays a fundamental role during emergencies. The trained lay staff triages the person and activates the most appropriate service acting as a filter between users and health services, thus potentially reducing inappropriate transportation to emergency rooms and promoting the person's treatment at home.

The future integration of PERS with the newest forms of AI, such as Chat-GPT, in telemergency services may promote interesting developments, such as the refinement of algorithms to guide the phone interview by TOC staff, to better identify and answer to patients requests for help, and also by integrating medical patient history, symptoms, triage, and conditions [34]. The integration of requests for help with the health and social characteristics of users could better shape the characteristics of subgroups with the same needs for surveillance [34,35].

Further studies are needed to better understand how PERS could further promote the management of chronic conditions and to improve strategies adopted by public authorities to integrate private telemergency and homecare services.

Author Contributions: Conceptualization, data curation, methodology, supervision, validation, visualization, and writing original and editing draft of the manuscript E.C. and P.D.G.; data analysis, formal analysis E.C. and L.C.; conceptualization, formal analysis, validation, and visualization A.C.; validation, supervision, writing—review and editing L.C., D.V., S.C. and V.D. All authors have read and agreed to the published version of the manuscript.

Funding: This research received no external funding.

Institutional Review Board Statement: This study was approved by the Ethical Committee of the University of Torino, on 23 May 2023 with protocol number 0339442-[UOR: SI000045-Classif. III/11]. When signing the contract with Ass.I.S.Te scs company, users also provided their consent for data processing for research purposes. To further protect users' privacy, the data were provided to the researchers totally anonymized.

Data Availability Statement: Data that support the finding of our study are available from Ass.I.S.Te scs company, but restrictions are applied to the availability of these data, which were used thanks to an agreement with the company. The data are not available to the public without the consent of the PI Elena Casabona and the Ass.I.S.Te.

Acknowledgments: We would thank the staff of the Telemergency Operation Centre of the Ass.I.S.Te scs company for their support in the research and for providing anonymized data. We would thank the Ministry of University and Research for the founding of the doctoral programs on Innovation and Green topic. We also thank the REACtion research Group (Interreg Project 2014–2020) for their contribution.

Conflicts of Interest: Dante Viotti (D.V.) is the Director of Ville Roddolo Nursing Home (Ass.I.S.Te company), where the telemergency service is located. The remaining authors declare that the research was conducted in the absence of any commercial or financial relationships that could be construed as a potential conflict of interest.

References

1. Registered Nurses' Association of Ontario. *Preventing Falls and Reducing Injury from Falls*, 4th ed.; Registered Nurses' Association of Ontario: Toronto, ON, USA, 2017.
2. Hessels, V.; Le Prell, G.S.; Mann, W.C. Advances in Personal Emergency Response and Detection Systems. *Assist. Technol.* **2011**, *23*, 152–161. [CrossRef]
3. Mann, W.C.; Belchior, P.; Tomita, M.R.; Kemp, B.J. Use of Personal Emergency Response Systems by Older Individuals with Disabilities. *Assist. Technol.* **2005**, *17*, 82–88. [CrossRef] [PubMed]
4. Yu, L.; Wang, H.; Zhao, Y.; Sun, T.; Murphy, T.E.; Tsui, K. Assessing Elderly's Functional Balance and Mobility via Analyzing Data from Waist-Mounted Tri-Axial Wearable Accelerometers in Timed up and Go Tests. *BMC Med. Inform. Decis. Mak.* **2021**, *21*, 108. [CrossRef] [PubMed]
5. Hawley-Hague, H.; Boulton, E.; Hall, A.; Pfeiffer, K.; Todd, C. Older Adults' Perceptions of Technologies Aimed at Falls Prevention, Detection or Monitoring: A Systematic Review. *Int. J. Med. Inf.* **2014**, *83*, 416–426. [CrossRef] [PubMed]
6. Pietrzak, E.; Cotea, C.; Pullman, S. Does Smart Home Technology Prevent Falls in Community-Dwelling Older Adults: A Literature Review. *J. Innov. Health Inform.* **2014**, *21*, 105–112. [CrossRef]
7. De San Miguel, K.; Lewin, G.; Burton, E.L.; Howat, P.; Boldy, D.; Toye, C. Personal Emergency Alarms: Do Health Outcomes Differ for Purchasers and Nonpurchasers? *Home Health Care Serv. Q.* **2017**, *36*, 164–177. [CrossRef]
8. Moore, K.; O'Shea, E.; Kenny, L.; Barton, J.; Tedesco, S.; Sica, M.; Crowe, C.; Alamäki, A.; Condell, J.; Nordström, A.; et al. Older Adults' Experiences With Using Wearable Devices: Qualitative Systematic Review and Meta-Synthesis. *JMIR MHealth UHealth* **2021**, *9*, 204–211. [CrossRef]
9. Miake-Lye, I.M.; Hempel, S.; Ganz, D.A.; Shekelle, P.G. Inpatient Fall Prevention Programs as a Patient Safety Strategy: A Systematic Review. *Ann. Intern. Med.* **2013**, *158*, 390–396. [CrossRef]
10. Ong, N.W.R.; Ho, A.F.W.; Chakraborty, B.; Fook-Chong, S.; Yogeswary, P.; Lian, S.; Xin, X.; Poh, J.; Chiew, K.K.Y.; Ong, M.E.H. Utility of a Medical Alert Protection System Compared to Telephone Follow-up Only for Home-Alone Elderly Presenting to the ED—A Randomized Controlled Trial. *Am. J. Emerg. Med.* **2018**, *36*, 594–601. [CrossRef]
11. Roush, R.; Teasdale, T.A.; Murphy, J.N.; Kirk, S.M. Impact of a Personal Emergency Response System on Hospital Utilization by Community-Residing Elders. *South Med. J.* **1995**, *88*, 917–922. [CrossRef]

12. Soh, S.-E.; Ayton, D.; Morello, R.; Natora, A.; Yallop, S.; Barker, A. Understanding the Profile of Personal Alert Victoria Clients Who Fall. *Health Soc. Care Community* **2018**, *26*, 759–767. [CrossRef] [PubMed]
13. Wang, Y.; Srikanth, V.; Snowdon, D.A.; Ellmers, S.; Beare, R.; Moran, C.; Richardson, D.; Lotz, P.; Andrew, N.E. Quantifying the Economic Benefit of the Personal Alarm and Emergency Response System in Australia: A Cost Analysis of the Reduction in Ambulance Attendances. *Aust. Health Rev.* **2020**, *45*, 51–58. [CrossRef] [PubMed]
14. Stokke, R. The Personal Emergency Response System as a Technology Innovation in Primary Health Care Services: An Integrative Review. *J. Med. Internet Res.* **2016**, *18*, e187. [CrossRef] [PubMed]
15. De San Miguel, K.; Lewin, G.; Burton, E.; Toye, C.; Boldy, D.; Howat, P. Exploring Risk Profiles and Emergency Frequency of Purchasers and Non-Purchasers of Personal Emergency Alarms: A Prospective Cohort Study. *BMC Geriatr.* **2015**, *15*, 140. [CrossRef] [PubMed]
16. Agboola, S.; Golas, S.; Fischer, N.; Nikolova-Simons, M.; Op Den Buijs, J.; Schertzer, L.; Kvedar, J.; Jethwani, K. Healthcare Utilization in Older Patients Using Personal Emergency Response Systems: An Analysis of Electronic Health Records and Medical Alert Data: Brief Description: A Longitudinal Retrospective Analyses of Healthcare Utilization Rates in Older Patients Using Personal Emergency Response Systems from 2011 to 2015. *BMC Health Serv. Res.* **2017**, *17*, 282. [CrossRef]
17. Andrew, N.E.; Wang, Y.; Teo, K.; Callisaya, M.L.; Moran, C.; Snowdon, D.A.; Ellmers, S.; Beare, R.; Richardson, D.; Srikanth, V. Exploring Patterns of Personal Alarm System Use and Impacts on Outcomes. *Australas. J. Ageing* **2021**, *40*, 252–260. [CrossRef] [PubMed]
18. Johnston, K.; Worley, A.; Grimmer-Somers, K.; Sutherland, M.; Amos, L. Personal Alarm Use to Call the Ambulance after a Fall in Older People: Characteristics of Clients and Falls. *Australas. J. Paramed.* **2010**, *8*, 1–9. [CrossRef]
19. Bloch, F.; Lundy, J.-E.; Rigaud, A.-S. Profile Differences of Purchasers, Non-Purchasers, and Users and Non-Users of Personal Emergency Response Systems: Results of a Prospective Cohort Study. *Disabil. Health J.* **2017**, *10*, 607–610. [CrossRef]
20. Bouabida, K.; Lebouché, B.; Pomey, M.-P. Telehealth and COVID-19 Pandemic: An Overview of the Telehealth Use, Advantages, Challenges, and Opportunities during COVID-19 Pandemic. *Healthcare* **2022**, *2293*, 10. [CrossRef]
21. Rush, K.L.; Singh, S.; Seaton, C.L.; Burton, L.; Li, E.; Jones, C.; Davis, J.C.; Hasan, K.; Kern, B.; Janke, R. Telehealth Use for Enhancing the Health of Rural Older Adults: A Systematic Mixed Studies Review. *Gerontologist* **2022**, *62*, e564–e577. [CrossRef]
22. Khoshrounejad, F.; Hamednia, M.; Mehrjerd, A.; Pichaghsaz, S.; Jamalirad, H.; Sargolzaei, M.; Hoseini, B.; Aalaei, S. Telehealth-Based Services During the COVID-19 Pandemic: A Systematic Review of Features and Challenges. *Front. Public Health* **2021**, *9*, 711762. [CrossRef] [PubMed]
23. Monaghesh, E.; Hajizadeh, A. The Role of Telehealth during COVID-19 Outbreak: A Systematic Review Based on Current Evidence. *BMC Public Health* **2020**, *20*, 1193. [CrossRef] [PubMed]
24. Nyman, S.R.; Victor, C.R. Use of Personal Call Alarms among Community-Dwelling Older People. *Ageing Soc.* **2014**, *34*, 67–89. [CrossRef]
25. De Vries, M.; Seppala, L.J.; Daams, J.G.; Van De Glind, E.M.M.; Masud, T.; Van Der Velde, N.; Blain, H.; Bousquet, J.; Bucht, G.; Caballero-Mora, M.A.; et al. Fall-Risk-Increasing Drugs: A Systematic Review and Meta-Analysis: I. Cardiovascular Drugs. *J. Am. Med. Dir. Assoc.* **2018**, *19*, 371.e1–371.e9. [CrossRef] [PubMed]
26. Woolcott, J.C. Meta-Analysis of the Impact of 9 Medication Classes on Falls in Elderly Persons. *Arch. Intern. Med.* **2009**, *169*, 1952–1960. [CrossRef] [PubMed]
27. Jamovi The Jamovi Project 2022. Available online: https://www.jamovi.org/ (accessed on 1 September 2023).
28. R Core Team. *R: A Language and Environment for Statistical Computing*; R Core Team: Vienna, Austria, 2021.
29. Heinzen, E.; Sinnwell, J.; Atkinson, E.; Gunderson, T.; Dougherty, G. An Arsenal of "R" Functions for Large-Scale Statistical Summaries. [Computer Software]. 2018.
30. Serdar, B. *ClinicoPath Jamovi Module, Version 0.0.2.0038, [R Package]*; Zenodo: Genève, Switzerland, 2022. [CrossRef]
31. Johnston, K. Perspectives on Use of Personal Alarms by Older Fallers. *Int. J. Gen. Med.* **2010**, *2010*, 231–237. [CrossRef]
32. Stevens, M.; Holman, C.D.J.; Bennett, N. Preventing Falls in Older People: Impact of an Intervention to Reduce Environmental Hazards in the Home. *J. Am. Geriatr. Soc.* **2001**, *49*, 1442–1447. [CrossRef]
33. Lee, J.S.; Hurley, M.J.; Carew, D.; Fisher, R.; Kiss, A.; Drummond, N. A Randomized Clinical Trial to Assess the Impact on an Emergency Response System on Anxiety and Health Care Use among Older Emergency Patients after a Fall. *Acad. Emerg. Med.* **2007**, *14*, 301–308. [CrossRef]
34. Bugaj, M.; Kliestik, T.; Lizaroiu, G. Generative Artificial Intelligence-Based Diagnostic Algorithms in Disease Risk Detection, in Personalized and Targeted Healthcare Procedures, and in Patient Care Safety and Quality. *Contemp. Read. Law Soc. Justice* **2023**, *15*, 9. [CrossRef]
35. Grupa, M.; Zauskova, A.; Nica, E. Generative Artificial Intelligence-Based Treatment Planning in Clinical Decision-Making, in Precision Medicine, and in Personalized Healthcare. *Contemp. Read. Law Soc. Justice* **2023**, *15*, 45. [CrossRef]

Disclaimer/Publisher's Note: The statements, opinions and data contained in all publications are solely those of the individual author(s) and contributor(s) and not of MDPI and/or the editor(s). MDPI and/or the editor(s) disclaim responsibility for any injury to people or property resulting from any ideas, methods, instructions or products referred to in the content.

Article

An Explainable Method for Lung Cancer Detection and Localisation from Tissue Images through Convolutional Neural Networks

Francesco Mercaldo [1,2,*], Myriam Giusy Tibaldi [1,*], Lucia Lombardi [1,*], Luca Brunese [1], Antonella Santone [1] and Mario Cesarelli [3]

1. Department of Medicine and Health Sciences "Vincenzo Tiberio", University of Molise, 86100 Campobasso, Italy; luca.brunese@unimol.it (L.B.); antonella.santone@unimol.it (A.S.)
2. Institute for Informatics and Telematics, National Research Council of Italy, 56124 Pisa, Italy
3. Department of Engineering, University of Sannio, 82100 Benevento, Italy; mcesarelli@unisannio.it
* Correspondence: francesco.mercaldo@unimol.it or francesco.mercaldo@iit.cnr.it (F.M.); m.tibaldi@studenti.unimol.it (M.G.T.); l.lombardi12@studenti.unimol.it (L.L.)

Abstract: Lung cancer, a prevalent and life-threatening condition, necessitates early detection for effective intervention. Considering the recent advancements in deep learning techniques, particularly in medical image analysis, which offer unparalleled accuracy and efficiency, in this paper, we propose a method for the automated identification of cancerous cells in lung tissue images. We explore various deep learning architectures with the objective of identifying the most effective one based on both quantitative and qualitative assessments. In particular, we assess qualitative outcomes by incorporating the concept of prediction explainability, enabling the visualization of areas within tissue images deemed relevant to the presence of lung cancer by the model. The experimental analysis, conducted on a dataset comprising 15,000 lung tissue images, demonstrates the effectiveness of our proposed method, yielding an accuracy rate of 0.99.

Keywords: lung; cell; deep learning; machine learning; explainability; artificial intelligence

Citation: Mercaldo, F.; Tibaldi, M.G.; Lombardi, L.; Brunese, L.; Santone, A.; Cesarelli, M. An Explainable Method for Lung Cancer Detection and Localisation from Tissue Images through Convolutional Neural Networks. *Electronics* **2024**, *13*, 1393. https://doi.org/10.3390/electronics13071393

Academic Editors: George Angelos Papadopoulos, Ilaria Sergi and Teodoro Montanaro

Received: 12 February 2024
Revised: 25 March 2024
Accepted: 3 April 2024
Published: 7 April 2024

Copyright: © 2024 by the authors. Licensee MDPI, Basel, Switzerland. This article is an open access article distributed under the terms and conditions of the Creative Commons Attribution (CC BY) license (https://creativecommons.org/licenses/by/4.0/).

1. Introduction

Lung cancer (LC) is one of the leading causes of death worldwide, accounting for more than 20% of cancer deaths in Europe [1]. LC currently represents the most common cause of major cancer incidence and mortality in men, whereas in women it is the third most common cause of cancer incidence and the second most common cause of cancer mortality [2]. The poor prognosis (5-year survival rate of about 15%) is due to the limited curative options available for the vast majority of cases, as approximately 70% of patients suffer from advanced disease at the time of diagnosis [3,4]. Indeed, LC is an insidious disease with symptoms occurring mostly at advanced stages of disease and being absent or non-specific at early phases. In 2024, the American Cancer Society estimates that there will be 238,340 new cases of LC, and 127,070 people will die from LC, accounting for approximately 20% of all cancer deaths [5].

Smoking is the leading risk factor for LC, with 80% of LC mortality estimated to be attributable to tobacco consumption. Other risk factors include exposure to radon, asbestos, and some cancer-causing agents such as chromium, cadmium, arsenic, radioactivity, and coal products. Because these risk factors are highly reversible by smoking cessation, occupational protection, and clean air initiatives, evidence-based preventive measures could be implemented to reduce its disease burden. Therefore, evaluating its updated distribution, especially for the temporal trends by age, sex, and region, is important [6].

The recommended histopathological classification is that of the World Health Organization, in collaboration with the International Association for the Study of Lung Cancer. LC is a heterogeneous disease, mainly classified as non-small cell lung carcinoma (NSCLC) and small cell lung carcinoma (SCLC) [7]. NSCLC constitutes the majority of lung cancer cases (85%) and is further classified into adenocarcinoma (ADC), squamous cell carcinoma (SCC), and large cell carcinoma (LCC), while the remaining 15% accounts for SCLC, which is characterised by neuroendocrine differentiation. In the era of personalised medicine, lung cancer diagnosis and accurate classification strongly rely on cytological and histological subtyping by microscopic evaluation with standard histochemical stains and ancillary immunohistochemical staining [8].

The microscopic examination of LC cells is typically part of the process of diagnosing cancer through a biopsy. Pathologists analyse tissue samples to determine the type of cancer, its stage, and other important characteristics. This information is crucial for developing an appropriate treatment plan. In the last decade, deep learning (DL) approaches, including mostly convolutional neural networks (CNNs) [9–12], have become increasingly valuable in pathology. Limitations concerning the shortage of pathologists worldwide, subjectivity in diagnosis, and intra- and inter-observer variability could be overcome with the aid of DL models. Recent advances in lung cancer pathology leverage image analysis potential for cancer diagnosis from hematoxylin and eosin (H&E) whole slide images (WSIs) [13,14]. Considering that small biopsy and cytology specimens are the available material for 70% of lung cancer patients with advanced unresectable disease, DL methods could guide the diagnosis with high accuracy, minimizing the need for additional special stains required for differential diagnosis and preserving the already limited material for molecular testing [15,16].

Starting from these considerations, in this paper, we propose a method aimed to automatically detect the presence of LC automatically from histological tissue images. We consider several deep learning networks aimed at classifying a tissue image as benign or cancerous. Moreover, with the aim to provide a kind of explainability behind the model prediction, we consider a way to automatically highlight the area of the tissue image that is symptomatic of the cancer presence from the network point of view. For this purpose, we resort to Gradient-weighted Class Activation Mapping (i.e., Grad-CAM), a technique used in computer vision to visualise the regions of an input image that contribute the most to the predictions made by a CNN [17,18]. In a nutshell, it helps in understanding which parts of the input image are crucial for the network's decision, providing insights into the model's decision-making process.

The experiments carried out to test and prove the functioning of the proposed method were performed on a dataset of 15,000 images, 5000 of which were labelled as adenocarcinoma, 5000 as squamous cell carcinoma and 5000 as benign tissue. The results obtained are very promising: as a matter of fact, the model that obtained the best performance results is able to correctly classify images with an accuracy of 99.2%. This aspect is symptomatic such that during the new era of digital pathology, DL offers the potential for lung cancer interpretation to assist pathologists' routine practice. In this paper, the DL method used for the recognition of lung carcinoma by using histological images shows that it can guide lung cancer diagnosis with high accuracy rates, offering valuable information to researchers for further study. From the encouraging results obtained, we believe that the proposed method can be innovative and clinically applicable for a predictive and accurate histo-pathological diagnosis. In fact, it significantly reduces the analysis and reporting time for the pathologist. Early identification of the disease anticipates the therapeutic approach in treating the disease for the benefit of patient's health. For possible improvements, the network performance could be evaluated on a much larger dataset. Although the dataset used is substantial, a further increase in the number of images available could further limit any kind of inherent system bias. This and other learning methods developed offer enormous potential for improving clinical care, also based on the re-use and processing of big data from lung cancer patients, especially in view of the increasingly common use of electronic medical records. However, there is a need for a more open approach to such methods, as only in this way will it be possible to create comprehensive decision support for the clinical pathologists of the future.

The remaining of the paper proceeds as follows: in the next section, the proposed method is presented; the experimental results are discussed in Section 3; the state-of-the-art literature is provided in Section 4; and, finally, in the last section, the conclusion and future research lines are drawn.

2. A Method for Lung Cancer Detection and Localisation

This section shows the method we propose for LC detection and localisation starting from tissue images. We aim to find a model capable of classifying histological images as positive or negative for LC.

In detail, this is a multi-class classification problem because there are three classes to assign to a tissue image under analysis. Based on supervised learning, clearly all the images in the training are already labelled. As shown in Figure 1, the method adopted uses five main steps: composition of the dataset, selection of deep learning models, execution of the experiments, generation of a heatmap through Grad-CAMs, and analysis of the results.

Figure 1. The main steps of the proposed method.

2.1. Dataset and Preprocessing

The dataset plays a crucial role in the field of machine learning, influencing the performance, generalisation, and reliability of models. A dataset serves as the foundation for training machine learning models. The model learns patterns, features, and relationships from the examples provided in the dataset.

In the context of LC detection from tissue images, the dataset is of paramount importance for developing accurate and reliable machine learning models. Here are specific considerations for the importance of the dataset in LC detection:

- Representation of Variability: The dataset should encompass a diverse range of tissue images that accurately represent the variability in LC types, stages, and histopathological features. This ensures that the model learns to generalise well across different manifestations of LC.
- Inclusion of Normal Tissue: Alongside cancerous tissues, including samples of normal lung tissue is crucial. This helps the model distinguish between healthy and cancerous regions, promoting a more accurate diagnosis.
- Annotation Quality: High-quality annotations are essential for supervised learning in healthcare applications. The accurate labelling of cancerous and non-cancerous regions ensures that the model learns the correct patterns.
- Imbalance and Rarity: Due to the relative rarity of certain LC types or specific stages, the dataset should be carefully curated to address class imbalances. Strategies like oversampling, undersampling, or generating synthetic data can be employed to mitigate this issue.

From these aspects, it emerges that a well-curated and diverse dataset is essential for the development of accurate and clinically relevant machine learning models for LC detection from tissue images. The dataset's characteristics directly influence the model's ability to generalise, detect various cancer types, and contribute to the overall success of the diagnostic tool.

2.2. The CNN Models

In this paper, we exploit the following CNNs: Standard_CNN, AlexNet, VGG-16, VGG-19, and MobileNet.

In the following, a brief description of the CNNs we considered is given:

- Standard_CNN: This is a network characterised by 13 layers developed by authors. The convolutional block has three Conv2D layers based on the application of 32, 64 and 128 3×3 size filters and ReLu activation respectively, alternating with three MaxPooling2D layers. The classification block has three Dense layers of 512, 256, respectively, with ReLu activation and three neurons with SoftMax activation, alternating with 0.5 Dropout layers, used to regularise the network. This network leverages the categorical_crossentropy loss function, as it is a multi-class classification.
- AlexNet [19]: AlexNet was the first convolutional network which used GPU to boost performance. The AlexNet architecture consists of 5 convolutional layers, 3 max-pooling layers, 2 normalisation layers, 2 fully connected layers, and 1 softmax layer. The input size is $224 \times 224 \times 3$.
- VGG [20]: VGG-16 is a neural network architecture designed by Visual Geometry Group, the engineering sciences department of the University of Oxford. The most used versions of VGG are VGG-16 and VGG-19, which are distinguished by the number of layers. The network is inspired by the previous AlexNet but has smaller convolutional filters. The network architecture features 5 blocks of 3×3 convolutional layers. There are 2 convolutional layers in the first 2 blocks and 3 (in VGG-16) or 4 (in VGG-19) in the last 3. Maxpooling layers are inserted between one block and the other. Lastly, there is a block with 3 fully connected layers. The input image has dimensions of $224 \times 224 \times 3$. We consider two different variants of this network in this paper, i.e., VGG-16 and VGG-19: the difference between these two networks is the number of layers. As a matter of fact, VGG-16 consists of 16 layers, including 13 convolutional layers and 3 fully connected layers, while the VGG-19 model has 19 layers, by including 16 convolutional layers and 3 fully connected layers. The additional layers in VGG-19 are achieved by inserting more convolutional layers in the middle of the network.
- MobileNet [21]: This network primarily uses depthwise separable convolutions in place of the standard convolutions used in earlier architectures to build lighter models. Each depthwise separable convolution layer consists of a depthwise convolution and a pointwise convolution. Counting depthwise and pointwise convolutions as separate layers, a MobileNet has 28 layers, and the size of the input image is $224 \times 224 \times 3$.

2.3. Training

These models were inserted into the tool and trained on the dataset considered, selecting specific hyperparameters. These hyperparameters include the number of epochs, batch size and learning rate. The values that led to obtaining better results selected during the training phase are summarised in Table 1.

Table 1. The table shows the hyperparameters selected during the experimentation.

Model	Epochs	Batch	Learning Rate	Ex. Time
Standard CNN	50	32	0.001	3:06:09
MobileNet	20	32	0.001	2:10:55
AlexNet	20	32	0.001	1:53:55
VGG-16	24	32	0.001	5:54:36
VGG-19	20	32	0.001	7:38:46

During the training phase, other experiments were carried out by changing the number of epochs, learning rate, and batch size, but they all brought lower results than those in Table 1.

In this table, we can visualise hyperparameters such as epochs, batch size, and learning rate:

- The number of epochs is a hyperparameter that defines the number of times an algorithm will work on the entire dataset. The number of epochs is usually high; this is to allow the model to learn as much as possible. You must pay close attention to the number of epochs because too high a number could lead to the onset of overfitting.
- The number of examples contained in each batch is called the batch size. In this case, selecting a batch of 32 and having a training set of 12,000 examples means to have 32 batches with 375 examples each. We will therefore have that an epoch is made up of 32 iterations. Also in this case, you must pay attention to the value selected since a batch size that is too small (<10) does not allow for performance optimisation, and if it is too large, you could have a problem of running out of memory or a greater tendency towards overfitting. Usually, the most used values are 16, 32, 64 or 128.
- This hyperparameter indicates the frequency with which the neural network updates the notions learned. Model parameters may be updated too quickly if the learning rate is too high, which may cause the model to exceed the ideal solution. Model parameters may be updated too slowly if the learning rate is too low, which may hinder convergence and require multiple training iterations to achieve the best result. Values of 0.01, 0.001 and 0.0001 are usually used.

2.4. Grad-CAM

Explainability refers to the ability to understand and interpret the decisions made by machine learning models that analyse visual data, such as images or videos. A technique exploited for explainability is the so-called Class Activation Maps (CAMs), aimed to highlight the regions of an image that are most influential in the model's prediction. This helps users understand which parts of the input image contribute to the model's decision for a particular class. Using architectures designed for explainability, such as interpretable deep learning models, ensures that the network's inner workings are more transparent. These architectures are specifically crafted to provide clearer insights into the decision-making process.

In the field of CAM techniques, one of the most adopted techniques is the Grad-CAM, a technique used in the field of computer vision, particularly in the interpretation of deep neural networks, such as CNNs. It helps visualise and understand which parts of an input image were crucial in making a certain prediction by highlighting the regions that contributed the most to the final decision.

Below, there is an overview of how Grad-CAM works:

- Feedforward Pass: The input image is fed through the CNN, and the forward pass is performed to obtain the final convolutional feature maps just before the global average pooling layer.
- Compute Class Score: The class score is computed by applying the final fully connected layer to the global average pooled feature maps. This score represents the likelihood of the image belonging to a particular class.
- Compute Gradient of Class Score with Respect to Feature Maps: The gradients of the class score with respect to the feature maps are computed. These gradients highlight how much each feature map contributes to the final classification score for the predicted class.
- Global Average Pooling of Gradients: The gradients are global average pooled to obtain a weight for each feature map, representing the importance of that feature map for the predicted class. This pooling operation ensures that the importance weights have the same spatial dimensions as the original feature maps.

- Weighted Sum of Feature Maps: The weighted sum of the original feature maps is computed using the importance weights obtained from the global average pooling. This weighted sum represents the Grad-CAM heatmap.
- Rectified Linear Unit (ReLU): A ReLU operation is applied to ensure that only positive contributions are considered. This rectification helps in focusing on the regions where the class activation is positive.
- Heatmap Generation: The final Grad-CAM heatmap is obtained by overlaying the rectified weighted sum on the input image. The heatmap visually indicates which regions of the input image are crucial for the model's decision regarding the predicted class.

By generating these heatmaps, Grad-CAM provides a visual explanation of where the CNN is focusing its attention when making predictions. This helps in understanding which parts of the input image contribute the most to the final classification decision, offering insights into the model's decision-making process. Grad-CAM is a widely used interpretability tool in computer vision and has applications in various domains, including medical imaging and object recognition.

The primary benefits of Grad-CAM include its ability to provide insights into the decision-making process of deep neural networks, particularly in image classification tasks. This interpretability is valuable for understanding why a model made a certain prediction, especially in critical applications like medical diagnosis.

Grad-CAM has found applications in various domains, including healthcare (interpreting medical images), autonomous vehicles (understanding visual cues for decision-making), and other image-related tasks where transparency in model decisions is important.

We exploit Grad-CAM to extract the gradients of convolutional layers to produce a heatmap, a localisation map that highlights the most relevant regions of the image. These regions of the image describe which areas of the input image have most influenced the model's output decision; in particular, the most significant areas are identified by yellow and green, and the less significant by blue.

To better understand how Grad-CAM works, in the following we provide a step-by-step mathematical implementation:

Forward Pass: Let x be the input image, y_i be the predicted class score for class i, and $f_k(x)$ be the output of the last convolutional layer for feature map k.

Compute Gradients: The gradient of the predicted class score y_c with respect to the feature maps $f_k(x)$ is computed using backpropagation:

$$\frac{\partial y_c}{\partial f_k}$$

This gradient reflects how much the predicted class score would change with a small change in each feature map.

Global Average Pooling (GAP): The gradients are then globally averaged to obtain a weight for each feature map:

$$\alpha_k = \frac{1}{Z} \sum_i \sum_j \frac{\partial y_c}{\partial f_k^{ij}}$$

Here, Z is the spatial size of the feature maps, and f_k^{ij} represents the activation at position (i, j) in the k-th feature map.

Weighted Sum of Feature Maps: The weighted sum of the feature maps is computed to create the Class Activation Map (CAM):

$$L_{Grad-CAM}^c = ReLU\left(\sum_k \alpha_k f_k(x)\right)$$

Here, $L_{Grad-CAM}^c$ is the CAM for class c, and $ReLU$ is the rectified linear unit function.

Upsample CAM: The CAM is often upsampled to the size of the original input image for better visualisation.

Normalise and Create Heatmap: The CAM is normalised to the range [0, 1] and can be used as a heatmap:

$$H(x) = \frac{L^c_{Grad-CAM} - \min(L^c_{Grad-CAM})}{\max(L^c_{Grad-CAM}) - \min(L^c_{Grad-CAM})}$$

Overlay Heatmap on the Original Image: The heatmap is then overlaid onto the original image to visualise the regions that contribute most to the predicted class.

In a nutshell, the Grad-CAM provides a way to highlight important regions in an input image based on the gradients of the predicted class score with respect to the feature maps of the last convolutional layer.

3. Experimental Analysis

In this section, we present the results we obtained from the experimental analysis of the proposed method for LC detection and localisation.

In the following section, we will present the results obtained from the experimentation. Specifically, we will analyse the metrics obtained from the classification phase, and subsequently, we will examine the Grad-CAM to understand the basis on which the model drew its conclusions.

To demonstrate the effectiveness of the proposed method, the histological image dataset (LC25000) was considered [22]. This dataset contains 25,000 colour images, of which 10,000 relate to adenocarcinomas (marked with the *lung_aca* label) and 15,000 relate to squamous cell lung carcinomas (marked with the *lung_scc* label) and benign lung tissues (marked with the *lung_n* label). Based on the purpose of the following study, only images relating to lung tissue were selected. To create this dataset, 750 images of lung tissue were acquired, in particular, 250 of healthy lung tissue, 250 of lung adenocarcinomas, and 250 of squamous cell carcinomas, respecting the HIPAA regulation. All images were then cropped, using a script developed by authors with the Python programming language, resulting in square dimensions of 768 × 768 pixels from the original 1024 × 768 pixels. Subsequently, the images were augmented using the Augmentor software package, which allowed an expansion of the dataset to 15,000 images, through the following augmentations: left and right rotations (up to 25 degrees, probability 1.0) and horizontal and vertical flips (probability 0.5). The dataset contains 15,000 colour images, all with a size of 768 × 768 pixels and in .jpeg file format. Following the pre-processing phase, the elements of the dataset are divided into images relating to the training set, validation set, and test set, respectively, in 80%, 10% and 10%:

- Training Set composed of 12,000 images divided into 3 folders of 4000 images, relating to squamous cell carcinoma (lung_scc), adenocarcinoma (lung_aca), and healthy tissue (lung_n);
- Validation Set composed of 1497 images divided into three folders of 499 elements relating to squamous cell carcinoma, adenocarcinoma, and healthy tissue;
- Test Set composed of 1500 images of which 500 are adenocarcinoma, 500 are squamous cell carcinoma, and 500 are healthy tissue.

The experiments we conducted were carried out using the following hardware and software specifications: Intel Xeon Gold 6140 M, CPU 2.30 GHz, 64 GB RAM, with the Ubuntu 22.04.01 LTS operating system.

3.1. Quantitative Analysis

Table 2 shows the results of the experimental analysis by showing the values obtained for the computed metrics.

To determine which model achieved better results, it is essential to ensure that the values related to accuracy, precision, recall, F-measure, and AUC are close to 1. As for the loss, its value should approach as close to 0 as possible. Taking these considerations into account and examining Table 2, it is evident that the VGG-16 model outperforms others, followed by the Standard_CNN.

Table 2. Experimental analysis results.

Model	Accuracy	Loss	Precision	Recall	F-Measure	AUC
Standard_CNN	0.985	0.094	0.985	0.985	0.985	0.994
MobileNet	0.983	0.067	0.983	0.983	0.983	0.993
AlexNet	0.817	0.337	0.820	0.809	0.815	0.965
VGG-16	0.992	0.021	0.992	0.992	0.992	0.999
VGG-19	0.960	0.099	0.960	0.960	0.960	0.960

The differences in performance between these models can be attributed to factors such as network depth, architecture, kernel size, and parameter efficiency. MobileNet, in particular, focuses on efficiency and is well suited for applications where computational resources are limited, while VGG-16 benefits from a balance between depth and computational complexity.

Thus, considering that the model that obtained the best performance results is the VGG-16 one, we show the confusion matrix related to this model to better understand its performance in LC detection.

A confusion matrix is a table used in machine learning and classification tasks to evaluate the performance of a classification algorithm. It provides a summary of the predicted and actual classes for a set of instances. The matrix is particularly useful when dealing with binary or multi-class classification problems.

Here are the key components of a confusion matrix:

- True Positive (TP): Instances that are actually positive and are correctly predicted as positive by the model.
- True Negative (TN): Instances that are actually negative and are correctly predicted as negative by the model.
- False Positive (FP): Instances that are actually negative but are incorrectly predicted as positive by the model (Type I error).
- False Negative (FN): Instances that are actually positive but are incorrectly predicted as negative by the model (Type II error).

Concerning the confusion matrix shown in Figure 2, the VGG-16 model shows interesting performance:

- True Positive (TP): 1000 (patients truly positive), with 500 affected by adenocarcinoma and 500 by squamous cell carcinoma;
- True Negative (TN): 500 (patients truly negative);
- False Positive (FP): 0 (patients negative but classified as positive);
- False Negative (FN): 0 (patients positive but classified as negative).

Figure 3 shows the confusion matrix related to the Standard_CNN model.

From the confusion matrix shown in Figure 3, we can note that also the Standard_CNN model is able to rightly classify most of the patients in the right category, but we note that the VGG-16 is able to obtain better performance, in fact:

- With regard to the *lung_aca* class, the VGG-16 model rightly classifies 491 patients, while the Standard_CNN one rightly classifies 488 patients;
- With regard to the *lung_n* class, the VGG-16 model rightly classifies 500 patients, while the Standard_CNN one rightly classifies 499 patients;
- With regard to the *lung_scc* class, the VGG-16 model rightly classifies 497 patients, while the Standard_CNN one rightly classifies 490 patients.

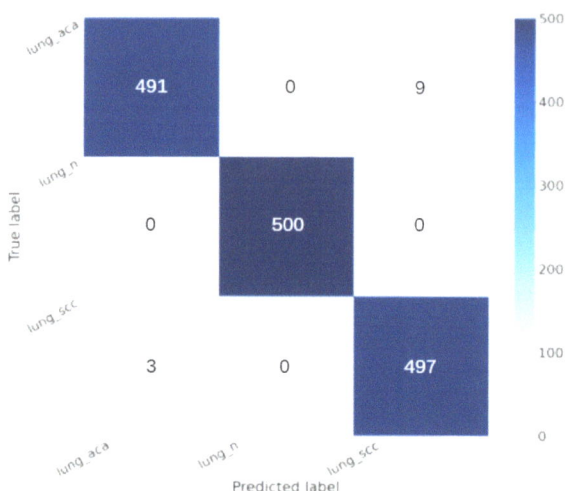

Figure 2. The confusion matrix obtained with the VGG-16 model.

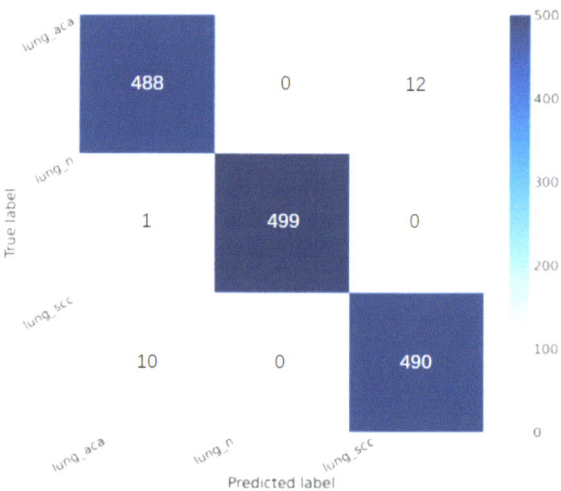

Figure 3. The confusion matrix obtained with the Standard_CNN model.

Comparing the confusion matrix of the remaining three models, we observe the following:

- The VGG-19 confusion matrix (in Figure 4) shows the following:
    - True Positive (TP): 911 (patients truly positive), with 453 affected by adenocarcinoma and 458 by squamous cell carcinoma;
    - True Negative (TN): 43 (patients truly negative);
    - False Positive (FP): 457 (patients negative but classified as positive);
    - False Negative (FN): 89 (patients positive but classified as negative).
- The AlexNet confusion matrix (in Figure 5) shows the following:
    - True Positive (TP): 987 (patients truly positive), with 487 affected by adenocarcinoma and 500 by squamous cell carcinoma;
    - True Negative (TN): 498 (patients truly negative);

- False Positive (FP): 2 (patients negative but classified as positive);
- False Negative (FN): 13 (patients positive but classified as negative).
- The MobileNet confusion matrix(in Figure 6) shows the following:
  - True Positive (TP): 1000 (patients truly positive), with 500 affected by adenocarcinoma and 500 by squamous cell carcinoma;
  - True Negative (TN): 500 (patients truly negative);
  - False Positive (FP): 0 (patients negative but classified as positive);
  - False Negative (FN): 0 (patients positive but classified as negative).

Having analysed the following results, the MobileNet confusion matrix presents a number of true positives, true negatives, false positives, and false negatives equal to those of VGG16; however, VGG16 presents higher values along the main diagonal, which allows us to consider the Standard_CNN and VGG16 better than others.

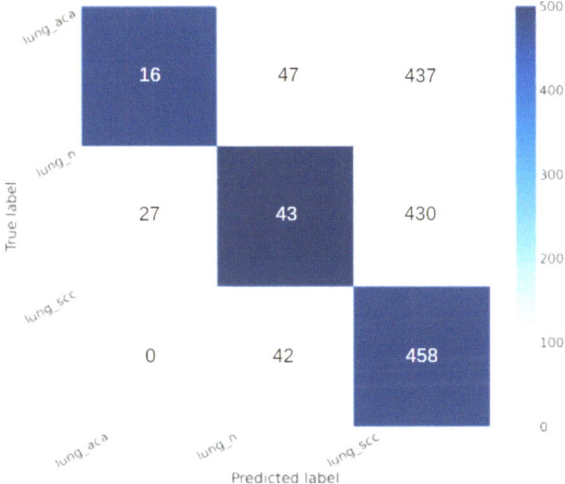

Figure 4. The confusion matrix obtained with the VGG-19 model.

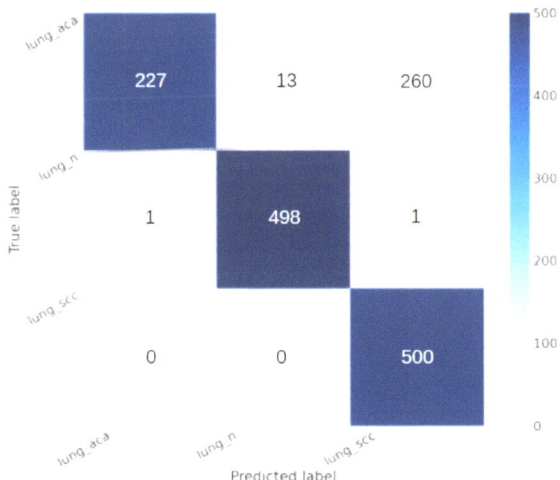

Figure 5. The confusion matrix obtained with the AlexNet model.

Figure 6. The confusion matrix obtained with the MobileNet model.

3.2. Qualitative Analysis

The Grad-CAM constitutes a valuable method for Explainable Artificial Intelligence (XAI). Explainability involves a set of tools and techniques aimed at aiding individuals in better understanding why an artificial intelligence model makes specific decisions. It addresses a common critique that machine learning and deep learning models operate as 'black boxes', concealing their underlying functioning. The generated Grad-CAMs for Standard_CNN and VGG-16 models are presented below, utilizing heatmaps to visually highlight the most relevant areas contributing to the model's decisions. Typically, information is encoded using colours, where significant regions are represented by colours like yellow, and less crucial areas are depicted in colours such as blue or green.

Below are the Grad-CAMs obtained from the VGG-16 model (shown in Figures 7–9):

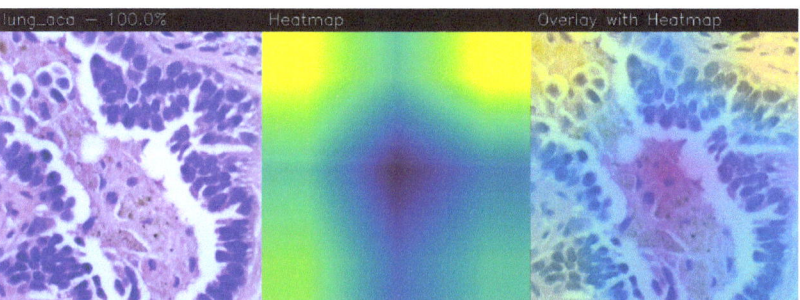

Figure 7. Heatmap related to lung adenocarcinoma, classified as 100% positive.

Lung adenocarcinoma is a tumour of epithelial origin that usually develops in the peripheral portion of the lung. It originates from the mucus-secreting cells that make up the mucus glands. The cuboidal and/or columnar cells of the neoplastic tissue come together to form a glandular structure. The neural network bases its decision on the geometry of the structures and the number and shape of the cells. In the central figure, the neural network recognises the most significant areas of the tumour (shown in yellow), which are actually those characterised by Pleiomorphism (increased number and size of cells), Hyperbasophilia (intensely bluish colour of the cytoplasm of the cells), and those with a higher nucleus/cytoplasm ratio (the nucleus occupies more space within the cytoplasm), which is a clear histological criterion of malignancy.

Squamous cell carcinoma originates from the squamous cells of the epithelium lining the bronchi. It is classified as such on the basis of the fish-scale appearance of the cells under the microscope, with the presence of keratinisation and intercellular bridges. From the cell membrane emerge 'spines' that form bridges between cell and cell. The intercellular bridges are desmosomes that, together with keratinisation, demonstrate the conversion of the cylindrical bronchial epithelium into an epithelium much more similar to skin. Keratinisation is clearly visible due to the presence of eosinophilic spindle-shaped cells without nuclei. In the central figure, the neural network recognises the most significant areas of the tumour (shown in yellow) characterised precisely by an intense proliferation of cells around a point, leading to the formation of concentric areas of high keratinisation. Indeed, one of the fundamental characteristics of cancer is uncontrolled cell proliferation.

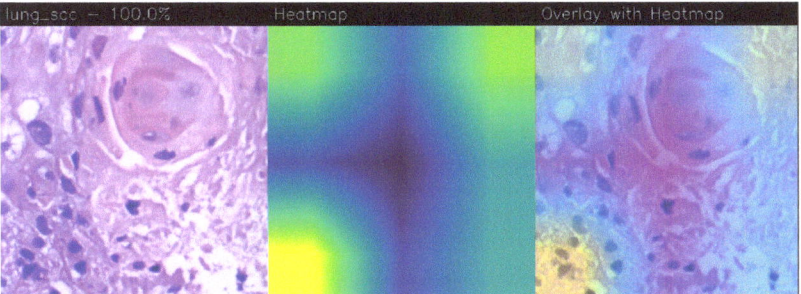

Figure 8. Heatmap related to squamous cell lung carcinoma, classified as 100% positive.

Figure 9. Heatmap related to healthy lung tissue, classified as 100% healthy.

The healthy lung parenchyma consists of the pulmonary alveoli. The pulmonary alveoli are lined by a simple pavement epithelium, beneath which is the basement membrane and a thin layer of interstitial connective tissue. The epithelium consists of 95% type I pneumocytes (small cells, thin cytoplasm, and small nucleus) and type II pneumocytes (cuboidal cells and granular cytoplasm). The neural network, which bases its decision on the geometry of the structures and the number and shape of the cells, recognises the area characterised by cells with a normal nucleus/cytoplasm ratio and a normal shape and size (shown in yellow).

In the following are the Grad-CAMs obtained from the Standard_CNN model:

Below is presented the only false positive case, meaning the only healthy patient misclassified as diseased, identified with the Standard_CNN.

Comparing the VGG-16 and Standard_CNN models from a qualitative point of view, i.e., from the heatmaps obtained from the Grad-CAM, it is evident that the Standard_CNN tends to focus on certain areas more than others based on the presence or absence of lung carcinoma:

- In the presence of adenocarcinoma (Figure 10), the classifier relies on cells near the white portions representing mucosa or connective tissue as a distinguishing element for this class. This is because adenocarcinoma typically affects more peripheral areas, such as smaller airways like alveoli, which are surrounded by connective tissue.
- In the presence of squamous cell carcinoma (Figure 11), the classifier utilises areas with concentrations of dark or irregularly shaped cells as a distinguishing element for this class. This is explained by the fact that squamous cell carcinoma affects the squamous cells of lung tissue.
- In the case of healthy lung tissue (Figure 12), the classifier relies on red cells, specifically red blood cells, as a distinguishing element for this class.

These differentiations can be considered accurate, as lung tumours involve the uncontrolled growth of malignant cells, compromising the lungs' function to transfer and cleanse oxygen and carbon dioxide. These functions are also related to the concentration of erythrocytes in lung tissue, as they are responsible for transporting oxygen and carbon dioxide through the hemoglobin they contain.

Therefore, a low concentration of red blood cells in lung tissue is a clear indicator of cancer.

In the case of misclassification as shown in Figure 13, the pathologist can detect it by reading the term 'WRONG' present in the image's top left corner. This prompts a more careful analysis of those samples as is the case for heatmaps with a low classification percentage.

With regard to the qualitative analysis of the heatmaps obtained from the application of the Grad-CAM on the VGG-16 model, the following hold:

- In the case of adenocarcinoma (as shown in Figure 10) and squamous cell carcinoma (as shown in Figure 11), the model focuses on large areas of the image, particularly near the four corners. This suggests that the model is capturing broad patterns associated with these types of LC.
- For images of healthy patients (as shown in Figure 12), the model directs more attention to one corner of the image and the centre. This may indicate that the model recognises distinctive features specific to healthy lung tissue, possibly related to the absence of irregular cell patterns seen in cancerous conditions.

Given these observations, it can be asserted that despite VGG-16 demonstrating superior overall performance, the Grad-CAMs generated using Standard_CNN appear to be more precise in identifying lung carcinoma and offer enhanced explainability. With Standard_CNN, its focus on localised patterns might contribute to its effectiveness in pinpointing specific regions associated with different lung conditions.

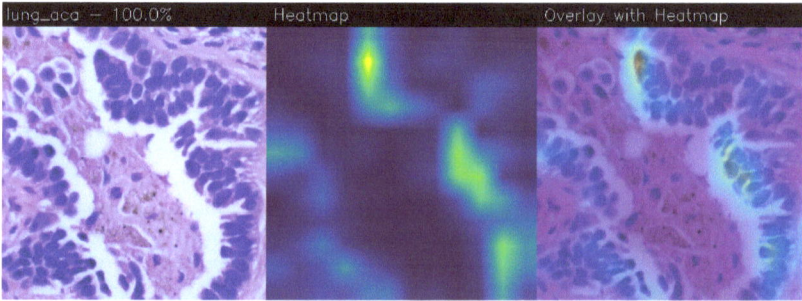

Figure 10. Heatmap related to lung adenocarcinoma, classified as 100% positive.

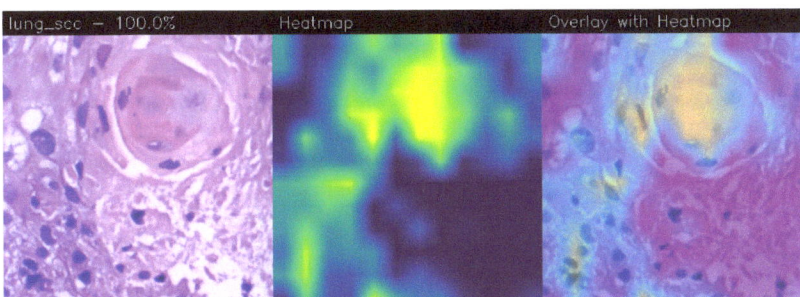

Figure 11. Heatmap related to squamous cell lung carcinoma, classified as 100% positive.

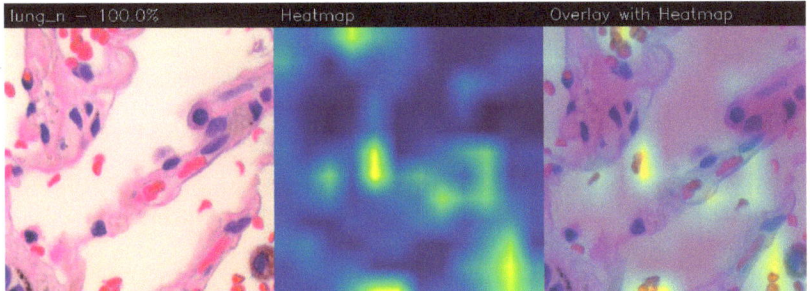

Figure 12. Heatmap related to healthy lung tissue, classified as 100% healthy.

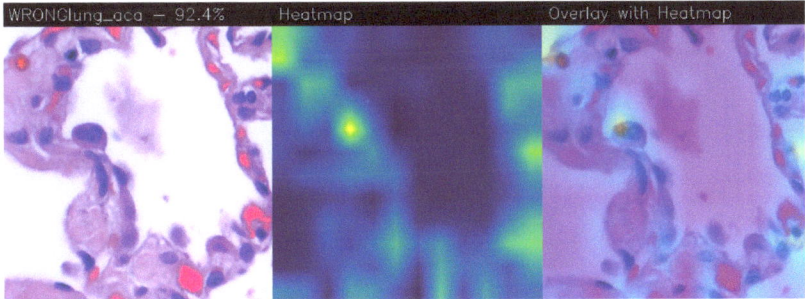

Figure 13. Heatmap related to healthy lung tissue, mistakenly classified as adenocarcinoma with a confidence level of 92.4%.

4. Related Work

The field in which the most progress has been made in terms of the use of artificial intelligence as a support for doctors is certainly the diagnostic one, on which there is also a series of scientific evidence present in the literature. In particular, in the oncology, respiratory, or cardiology area, thanks to the availability of images provided via X-rays, ultrasounds or CT scans, it is possible to identify, with a good degree of reliability, pathologies, both tumoural and non-tumorous, at the initial stage, even before they become important. Deep learning systems have shown their usefulness in the development of new drugs, in the analysis of radiographic images, up to the search for tumours. Deep learning allows you to analyse specific factors and cases in quantities much higher than those manageable by a human being, allowing faster decisions [23].

This section discusses the various state-of-the-art methods in lung carcinoma detection employing deep learning techniques.

One of the studies on LC classification through deep learning is that of Siddharth Bhatia et al., in which ResNet neural networks are used to detect LC from CT scans. In this study, images in DICOM format are pre-processed to extract the central region of interest of the lungs, from which features are then extracted, using deep networks inserted into classifiers for supervised learning. The results predict an accuracy of 80% [24].

Another study by Atsushi Teramoto et al. [25] proposes an automated classification scheme for lung tumours presented in microscopic images, using a deep convolutional neural network (DCNN). The evaluation results showed an accuracy of 71.1%.

Many studies also performed experiments on the same dataset used in this study, LC25000. For instance, using the LC25000 dataset, authors Mehedi Masud et al. [26] have automated the detection of colon and LC. Preprocessing of the channel-separated images included wavelet decomposition and 2D Fourier transform. They achieved an accuracy of 96.33% using a CNN model.

Neha Baranwal et al. [27] used this dataset, considering histopathological images of lung tissue, subjected to a classification into three categories: normal, adenocarcinoma and squamous cell carcinoma. This classification was carried out using ResNet 50, VGG-19, Inception-ResNet-V2, the latter being found to be better than the others with an accuracy of 99.7%, the best result among those mentioned.

Finally, the study by Daria Hlavcheva et al. [28] was based on the implementation of four different CNN models for LC classification, always using the LC25000 dataset. The input images were considered in three distinct dimensions. The maximum accuracy on the test dataset was 96.6%, using an input size of 768 × 768 pixels and a CNN model with four convolutional layers and maximum pooling layers. It was found that the accuracy increased as the size of the input image and the number of convolutional layers increased. In the study by Shankara et al. [29], a computer-aided system for detecting lung cancer using a convolution neural network (CNN) was proposed. The proposed model includes preprocessing, image segmentation model training, and tumour classification. The model was based on the Lung Image Database Consortium (LIDC), which contains 5200 lung images in which 3400 cancer lung images and 1800 non-cancer images. The proposed model classified the lung CT images as cancerous or normal image accurately with 92.96% accuracy.

In order to accurately and effectively diagnose lung cancer, the authors I. Naseer et al., presented the LungNet-SVM model for automated module identification technique in CT scans. On the LUNA16 dataset, the model demonstrated outstanding performance with 97.64% accuracy [30]. In the study by M Pradhan et al., a unique approach was constructed to automatically classify the LC25000 lung histology image collection. The accuracy rating for the EGOA (Enhanced Grasshopper Optimisation Algorithm) with random forest model was 98.50%. EffcientNetV2 big, medium, and small models are a deep learning architecture built on the concepts of compound scaling and progressive learning [31].

As shown from the comparison of the state-of-the-art literature shown in Table 3, to the best of the authors' knowledge, this paper represents the first attempt considering the prediction explainability in LC detection from tissue images by exploiting CNNs. In fact, in all these studies, the explicability of the prediction in the detection of lung cancer from both CT, cytological and histological images is not considered, leading to a major limitation in considering the results reliable.

We discuss the model effectiveness for the diagnosis of cancer lung not only on the basis of quantitative results (i.e., how many pathological images they can correctly classify) but also on the basis of qualitative results, by considering the quality of explainability and on the robustness of predictions. We use an explainable deep learning method, with the aim of providing a stronger descriptive approach to the algorithm, thus improving the understanding of the data. We have not found other papers using the explainable convolutional neural networks CNN model to classify only the given three different histopathological images and the given model's accuracy. For all these reasons, we believe that our study adds new knowledge to the already existing literature.

Table 3. State-of-the-art comparison.

Reference	Year	Method	Images	XAI	Accuracy
Atsushi Teramoto et al. [25]	2017	DCNN	cytological	No	0.711
Siddharth Bhatia et al. [24]	2019	ResNet	TC	No	0.80
Neal Joshua et al. [32]	2021	3D-CNN	TC	No	0.972
Neha Baranwal et al. [27]	2021	CNN	LC2500	No	0.997
Mehedi Masud et al. [26]	2021	CNN	LC2500	No	0.963
Daria Hlavcheva et al. [28]	2021	CNN	LC2500	No	0.966
C Shankara et al. [29]	2023	CNN	TC	No	0.929
I. Naseer et al. [30]	2023	Net-SVM	TC	No	0.976
M. Pradhan et al. [31]	2023	Net-V2	LC2500	No	0.985
Our method	2023	CNN	LC2500	Yes	0.992

This research work presents lung cancer detection using histopathological images. A convolutional neural network (CNN) was implemented to classify an image of three different categories: benign, adenocarcinoma, and squamous cell carcinoma. The model was able to achieve 92% of validation accuracy. Medical professionals use histopathological images of biopsied tissue from potentially infected areas of lungs for diagnosis. Most of the time, the diagnosis regarding the types of lung cancer are error-prone and time-consuming. The main contribution of the work shows that convolutional neural networks (CNNs), one of the deep learning techniques, can identify and classify lung cancer types with greater accuracy in a shorter period, which is crucial for determining patients' right treatment procedure and their survival rate. AI is playing a significant role in medical imaging researches. It has changed the way people process an enormous number of images.

Advances and the successful application of artificial intelligence (AI)-based diagnosis in clinical practice, especially in the field of radiology, dermatology, and pathology, is reflected with the speed of diagnosis exceeding that of experts in the medical field. Moreover, the accuracy of diagnosis through implementation of AI technologies is very high, paralleling that of medical experts [33].

The analysis of medical images, viz. X-rays, ultrasounds, MRI, computerised tomography scans and dual-energy X-ray absorptiometry, can be performed through AI algorithms. This provides assistance to healthcare professionals for the identification and diagnosis of diseases rapidly with more accuracy. The analysis of large amount of patient data can be performed by AI. These data may be related to 2D/3D imaging in the medical field, bio signals (viz., electrocardiography, electroencephalography, and electromyography), vital signs like temperature of the body, pulse rate, rate of respiration and blood pressure, information related to demography, medical history, and results of laboratory tests.

In this way, the decision-making process may be supported, and the provision of prediction results with accuracy is possible. The diversity of the data of patients in terms of multimodal data is a smart solution (optimal) that can facilitate diagnostic decisions in a better way on the basis of more than one finding, in images, signals, representation in text form, etc. Through the integration of more than one data source, the diagnosticians can gain a better understanding of the health of the patient in a comprehensive manner, and the underlying root causes in relation to the symptoms of the diseases can also be understood. The chances of misdiagnosis are also minimised in that way. Healthcare providers can be helped by multimodal data which help them in better diagnosis and the monitoring of the progress of a clinical condition over time.

This allows the therapeutic management of chronic illnesses in a more effective way. By the use of medical data (multimodal), the explainable AI (XAI)-based diagnosticians can determine potential problems of health at an early stage before the condition becomes grave and threatens the life of the patient. Further, Clinical Decision Support Systems (CDSSs) (AI-powered) provide assistance in real-time and ensure support to make informed decisions about the care of the patient in a better way. The automation of routine tasks is possible through the application of XAI tools. This frees the healthcare professionals for focusing on more complex care of patients [34,35].

Several AI-based techniques, viz. machine as well as deep learning models, are being used by researchers for detecting diseases of the heart, skin, and liver, and Alzheimer's disease, which requires early diagnosis [36].

Machine learning has an added value for the processing of images where the identification of early signs of disease through classical tools is not possible. This is especially true for cancer, the diagnosis of which frequently requires the assistance of AI approaches [37]. It is applicable for developing nations too, where resources, cost of healthcare, and other shortcomings resist the provision of care optimally.

The Food and Drug Administration (FDA) has given a breakthrough status to AI for an algorithm (AI-based) which has the ability of diagnosing cancer in computational histopathology with tremendous precision. This facilitates pathologists with obtaining time for focusing on important slides. It is possible to develop cost-effective point-of-care diagnostics for lymphoma on the basis of basic imaging along with deep learning [38,39].

By the application of the fuzzy clustering method and neural network, successful classification and detection of people at greater risk of influenza have been performed by using rate of respiration, heart rate, and facial temperature. It is to be noted here that there is difference between fuzzy clustering methods and k-means clustering because of the addition of fuzzifier and membership values. Thus, in contrast to the non-fuzzy clustering methods, each point can belong to more than one cluster. This in turn reflects the capability of developing efficacious methods for the identification of populations at risk. In more sophisticated contexts, the application of methods of machine learning can be carried out. For example, when the support vector machine (SVM) learning algorithm, Matlab, leave-one-out cross-validation method, and nested one-versus-one SVM are used in combination, the sequences of the genes of the bacteria can be separated in a better way, thereby aiding in diagnosis more efficiently. Interestingly, there exists an artificial immune recognition system for the diagnosis of various diseases by using the properties of the immune system, such as immunological memory, which is in line with the development of AI tools on the basis of the cognitive function of humans. The artificial immune recognition system that utilises supervised methods of machine learning is found to be more accurate. Another pandemic infection that puts the life of the patient at risk is malaria. The diagnosis of malaria takes much time, and intervention of various health services may become essential. The development of machine learning algorithms has been performed for detection of red blood cells infected with the parasite from in-line holographic microscopy (digital) data, which is a relatively cost-effective technology. Various machine learning algorithms have been tried for improvement of the diagnostic capacity for malaria. The best accuracy has been shown by the model trained by SVM [40].

5. Conclusions and Future Work

In this paper, an automatic algorithm for the recognition of lung carcinoma in histological images has been proposed and developed. The developed method serves as a supportive tool for pathologists, offering a second opinion on lung biopsy diagnoses, significantly reducing analysis times, and alleviating the workload of medical professionals. This paper focuses on utilizing a deep learning algorithm, specifically, CNNs. Various CNN architectures, including MobileNet, AlexNet, VGG-19, Standard_CNN, and VGG-16, were tested. The performance results of the Standard_CNN and VGG-16 models proved to be the best, with accuracies of 98.5% and 99.2%, and AUC values of 99.4% and 99.9%, respectively. The confusion matrix analysis revealed zero misclassified patterns with VGG-16 and only one false positive with Standard_CNN, consistent with the high AUC values. These results characterise these models as highly accurate classifiers with good generalisation capabilities. The identified potentials in terms of reliability and speed could serve as an excellent foundation for future developments.

We analysed the proposed models not only from a quantitative point of view but also from a qualitative one by resorting to the Grad-CAM to have a visual explainability behind the model prediction. From the qualitative analysis, it emerged that the best model, in terms of explainability, is the Standard_CNN one. This is the reason why, considering both the quantitative and the qualitative points of view, we conclude that the Standard_CNN model is the best one for LC classification starting from tissue image analysis.

From the future work point of view, we will explore the possibility of considering other models, for instance, related to object detection, to understand whether it is possible to improve the performance obtained in terms of LC localisation. Moreover, we will investigate whether it is possible to classify other kinds of diseases related to other organs with the Standard_CNN model, for instance, by analysing tissue images related to colon tissue. In this research, a deep learning model for the localisation of lung cancer from tissue images has been proposed. In future research, artificial intelligence solutions can be leveraged for 3D lung tumour reconstruction by CT images through a novel model based on generative adversarial networks (GANs). The generative adversarial network (GAN) is a class of neural networks developed for semi-supervised and unsupervised learning. In GAN, the model learns the distribution function of the data, and then it is possible to generate new desired data by sampling it. GANs can be used to find the structure and distribution of medical imaging data and generate new images [41]. While 2D images can be valuable for many applications, 3D images provide more detail about tumour shape and geometry. Therefore, understanding the 2D/3D geometry of the tumour is necessary to show its growth behaviour and help in better surgery and drug delivery. In clinical practice, the application of AI for the purpose of diagnosis holds promise of further developments and has evolved rapidly in combination with other modern fields of tele-consultation and genomics. It is mandatory for the progress in science to remain extremely thorough and careful along with transparency for development of new solutions for improvement of healthcare in modern times. But it must not be forgotten that the focus of the health policies should be to tackle the financial issues in association with the development of various AI tools for the progress of clinical medicine. Last but not least, the experts in the medical field should understand in a better way how exactly AI should be used for the diagnosis of different diseases and illnesses. This will lead to fruitful proposals and formulating action pans in a more appropriate manner in the future for developing and exploring highly beneficial AI-based techniques in the medical field.

Author Contributions: Conceptualization, F.M. and M.G.T.; methodology, F.M. and M.G.T.; software, F.M. and M.G.T.; validation, F.M., M.G.T., L.L. and A.S.; formal analysis, F.M., M.G.T., L.L., A.S. and M.C.; investigation, F.M., M.G.T., L.B. and A.S.; writing—original draft preparation, F.M., M.G.T., L.L., L.B. and A.S.; writing—review and editing, F.M., M.G.T., L.L., L.B., A.S. and M.C.; supervision, L.B., A.S. and M.C. All authors have read and agreed to the published version of the manuscript.

Funding: This work has been partially supported by MUR REASONING: foRmal mEthods for computAtional analySis for diagnOsis and progNosis in imagING PRIN, e-DAI (Digital ecosystem for integrated analysis of heterogeneous health data related to high-impact diseases: innovative model of care and research), Health Operational Plan, FSC 2014 2020, PRIN-MUR-Ministry of Health, the National Plan for NRRP Complementary Investments D^3 4 Health: Digital Driven Diagnostics, prognostics and therapeutics for sustainable Health care and Progetto MolisCTe, Ministero delle Imprese e del Made in Italy, Italy, CUP: D33B22000060001.

Data Availability Statement: The original contributions presented in the study are included in the article, further inquiries can be directed to the corresponding authors.

Conflicts of Interest: The authors declare no conflict of interest.

References

1. Silva, M.; Pastorino, U.; Sverzellati, N. Lung cancer screening with low-dose CT in Europe: Strength and weakness of diverse independent screening trials. *Clin. Radiol.* **2017**, *72*, 389–400. [CrossRef] [PubMed]
2. Jemal, A.; Bray, F.; Center, M.M.; Ferlay, J.; Ward, E.; Forman, D. Global cancer statistics. *CA: A Cancer J. Clin.* **2011**, *61*, 69–90. [CrossRef] [PubMed]
3. Wong, M.C.; Lao, X.Q.; Ho, K.F.; Goggins, W.B.; Tse, S.L. Incidence and mortality of lung cancer: Global trends and association with socioeconomic status. *Sci. Rep.* **2017**, *7*, 14300. [CrossRef] [PubMed]
4. Ferreira-Junior, J.R.; Koenigkam-Santos, M.; Magalhaes Tenorio, A.P.; Faleiros, M.C.; Garcia Cipriano, F.E.; Fabro, A.T.; Näppi, J.; Yoshida, H.; de Azevedo-Marques, P.M. CT-based radiomics for prediction of histologic subtype and metastatic disease in primary malignant lung neoplasms. *Int. J. Comput. Assist. Radiol. Surg.* **2020**, *15*, 163–172. [CrossRef] [PubMed]
5. Clancy, E. ACS Report Shows Prostate Cancer on the Rise, Cervical Cancer on the Decline. *Ren. Urol. News* **2023**.
6. Huang, J.; Deng, Y.; Tin, M.S.; Lok, V.; Ngai, C.H.; Zhang, L.; Lucero-Prisno, D.E., III; Xu, W.; Zheng, Z.J.; Elcarte, E.; et al. Distribution, risk factors, and temporal trends for lung cancer incidence and mortality: A global analysis. *Chest* **2022**, *161*, 1101–1111. [CrossRef] [PubMed]
7. Tsao, M.S.; Nicholson, A.G.; Maleszewski, J.J.; Marx, A.; Travis, W.D. Reprint of "Introduction to 2021 WHO Classification of Thoracic Tumors". *J. Thorac. Oncol.* **2022**, *17*, 337–340. [CrossRef]
8. Anand, K.; Phung, T.L.; Bernicker, E.H.; Cagle, P.T.; Olsen, R.J.; Thomas, J.S. Clinical utility of reflex ordered testing for molecular biomarkers in lung adenocarcinoma. *Clin. Lung Cancer* **2020**, *21*, 437–442. [CrossRef]
9. Mercaldo, F.; Martinelli, F.; Santone, A. A proposal to ensure social distancing with deep learning-based object detection. In Proceedings of the 2021 International Joint Conference on Neural Networks (IJCNN), Shenzhen, China, 18–22 July 2021; pp. 1–5.
10. Huang, P.; Xiao, H.; He, P.; Li, C.; Guo, X.; Tian, S.; Feng, P.; Chen, H.; Sun, Y.; Mercaldo, F.; et al. LA-ViT: A Network with Transformers Constrained by Learned-Parameter-Free Attention for Interpretable Grading in a New Laryngeal Histopathology Image Dataset. *IEEE J. Biomed. Health Inform.* **2024**, 1–13. [CrossRef]
11. Jiang, L.; Sun, X.; Mercaldo, F.; Santone, A. DECAB-LSTM: Deep Contextualized Attentional Bidirectional LSTM for cancer hallmark classification. *Knowl. Based Syst.* **2020**, *210*, 106486. [CrossRef]
12. Zhou, X.; Tang, C.; Huang, P.; Mercaldo, F.; Santone, A.; Shao, Y. LPCANet: Classification of laryngeal cancer histopathological images using a CNN with position attention and channel attention mechanisms. *Interdiscip. Sci. Comput. Life Sci.* **2021**, *13*, 666–682. [CrossRef]
13. Wang, S.; Yang, D.M.; Rong, R.; Zhan, X.; Fujimoto, J.; Liu, H.; Minna, J.; Wistuba, I.I.; Xie, Y.; Xiao, G. Artificial intelligence in lung cancer pathology image analysis. *Cancers* **2019**, *11*, 1673. [CrossRef]
14. Baxi, V.; Edwards, R.; Montalto, M.; Saha, S. Digital pathology and artificial intelligence in translational medicine and clinical practice. *Mod. Pathol.* **2022**, *35*, 23–32. [CrossRef] [PubMed]
15. Travis, W.D.; Brambilla, E.; Noguchi, M.; Nicholson, A.G.; Geisinger, K.R.; Yatabe, Y.; Beer, D.G.; Powell, C.A.; Riely, G.J.; Van Schil, P.E.; et al. International association for the study of lung cancer/american thoracic society/european respiratory society international multidisciplinary classification of lung adenocarcinoma. *J. Thorac. Oncol.* **2011**, *6*, 244–285. [CrossRef] [PubMed]
16. Bubendorf, L.; Lantuejoul, S.; de Langen, A.J.; Thunnissen, E. Nonsmall cell lung carcinoma: Diagnostic difficulties in small biopsies and cytological specimens: Number 2 in the Series "Pathology for the clinician" Edited by Peter Dorfmüller and Alberto Cavazza. *Eur. Respir. Rev.* **2017**, *26*. [CrossRef] [PubMed]
17. Selvaraju, R.R.; Cogswell, M.; Das, A.; Vedantam, R.; Parikh, D.; Batra, D. Grad-cam: Visual explanations from deep networks via gradient-based localization. In Proceedings of the IEEE International Conference on Computer Vision, Venice, Italy, 22–29 October 2017; pp. 618–626.
18. Huang, P.; He, P.; Tian, S.; Ma, M.; Feng, P.; Xiao, H.; Mercaldo, F.; Santone, A.; Qin, J. A ViT-AMC network with adaptive model fusion and multiobjective optimization for interpretable laryngeal tumor grading from histopathological images. *IEEE Trans. Med. Imaging* **2022**, *42*, 15–28. [CrossRef] [PubMed]
19. Krizhevsky, A.; Sutskever, I.; Hinton, G.E. Imagenet classification with deep convolutional neural networks. *Adv. Neural Inf. Process. Syst.* **2012**, *25*, 1–9.
20. Simonyan, K.; Zisserman, A. Very deep convolutional networks for large-scale image recognition. *arXiv* **2014**, arXiv:1409.1556.
21. Howard, A.G.; Zhu, M.; Chen, B.; Kalenichenko, D.; Wang, W.; Weyand, T.; Andreetto, M.; Adam, H. MobileNets: Efficient Convolutional Neural Networks for Mobile Vision Applications. *arXiv* **2017**, arXiv:1704.04861.
22. Borkowski, A.A.; Bui, M.M.; Thomas, L.B.; Wilson, C.P.; Del, L.A.; Mastorides, S.M. Lung and Colon Cancer Histopathological Image Dataset (LC25000). *arXiv* **2019**, arXiv:1912.12142.
23. Testolin, A.; Zorzi, M. The modern approach to artificial intelligence and the deep learning revolution. *Ital. J. Psychol.* **2021**, *48*, 313–334.
24. Bhatia, S.; Sinha, Y.; Goel, L. Lung Cancer Detection: A Deep Learning Approach. In *Soft Computing for Problem Solving*; Springer: Singapore, 2019; pp. 699–705.
25. Teramoto, A.; Tsukamoto, T.; Kiriyama, Y.; Fujita, H. Automated classification of lung cancer types from cytological images using deep convolutional neural networks. *BioMed Res. Int.* **2017**, *2017*, 4067832. [CrossRef] [PubMed]
26. Masud, M.; Sikder, N.; Nahid, A.A.; Bairagi, A.K.; AlZain, M.A. A machine learning approach to diagnosing lung and colon cancer using a deep learning-based classification framework. *Sensors* **2021**, *21*, 748. [CrossRef] [PubMed]

27. Baranwal, N.; Doravari, P.; Kachhoria, R. Classification of Histopathology Images of Lung Cancer Using Convolutional Neural Network (CNN). In *Disruptive Developments in Biomedical Applications*; CRC Press: Boca Raton, FL, USA, 2021.
28. Hlavcheva, D.; Yaloveha, V.; Podorozhniak, A.; Kuchuk, H. Comparison of CNNs for lung biopsy images classification. In Proceedings of the 2021 IEEE 3rd Ukraine Conference on Electrical and Computer Engineering (UKRCON), Lviv, Ukraine, 26–28 August 2021; pp. 1–5.
29. Shankara, C.; Hariprasad, S.; Latha, D. Detection of lung cancer using convolution neural network. *SN Comput. Sci.* **2023**, *4*, 225. [CrossRef]
30. Naseer, I.; Masood, T.; Akram, S.; Jaffar, A.; Rashid, M.; Iqbal, M.A. Lung Cancer Detection Using Modified AlexNet Architecture and Support Vector Machine. *Comput. Mater. Contin.* **2023**, *74*, 2039–2054. [CrossRef]
31. Pradhan, M.; Sahu, R.K. Automatic detection of lung cancer using the potential of artificial intelligence (ai). In *Machine Learning and AI Techniques in Interactive Medical Image Analysis*; IGI Global: Hershey, PA, USA, 2023; pp. 106–123.
32. Neal Joshua, E.S.; Bhattacharyya, D.; Chakkravarthy, M.; Byun, Y.C. 3D CNN with visual insights for early detection of lung cancer using gradient-weighted class activation. *J. Healthc. Eng.* **2021**, *2021*, 1–11. [CrossRef] [PubMed]
33. Miller, D.D.; Brown, E.W. Artificial intelligence in medical practice: The question to the answer? *Am. J. Med.* **2018**, *131*, 129–133. [CrossRef] [PubMed]
34. Ukwuoma, C.C.; Qin, Z.; Heyat, M.B.B.; Akhtar, F.; Bamisile, O.; Muaad, A.Y.; Addo, D.; Al-Antari, M.A. A hybrid explainable ensemble transformer encoder for pneumonia identification from chest X-ray images. *J. Adv. Res.* **2023**, *48*, 191–211. [CrossRef] [PubMed]
35. Al-Antari, M.A. Artificial intelligence for medical diagnostics—existing and future aI technology! *Diagnostics* **2023**, *13*, 688. [CrossRef] [PubMed]
36. Kumar, Y.; Koul, A.; Singla, R.; Ijaz, M.F. Artificial intelligence in disease diagnosis: A systematic literature review, synthesizing framework and future research agenda. *J. Ambient Intell. Humaniz. Comput.* **2023**, *14*, 8459–8486. [CrossRef]
37. Mercaldo, F.; Zhou, X.; Huang, P.; Martinelli, F.; Santone, A. Machine learning for uterine cervix screening. In Proceedings of the 2022 IEEE 22nd International Conference on Bioinformatics and Bioengineering (BIBE), Taichung, Taiwan, 7–9 November 2022; pp. 71–74.
38. Im, H.; Pathania, D.; McFarland, P.J.; Sohani, A.R.; Degani, I.; Allen, M.; Coble, B.; Kilcoyne, A.; Hong, S.; Rohrer, L.; et al. Design and clinical validation of a point-of-care device for the diagnosis of lymphoma via contrast-enhanced microholography and machine learning. *Nat. Biomed. Eng.* **2018**, *2*, 666–674. [CrossRef]
39. Huang, P.; Li, C.; He, P.; Xiao, H.; Ping, Y.; Feng, P.; Tian, S.; Chen, H.; Mercaldo, F.; Santone, A.; et al. MamlFormer: Priori-experience Guiding Transformer Network via Manifold Adversarial Multi-modal Learning for Laryngeal Histopathological Grading. *Inf. Fusion* **2024**, 102333. [CrossRef]
40. Agrebi, S.; Larbi, A. Use of artificial intelligence in infectious diseases. In *Artificial Intelligence in Precision Health*; Elsevier: Amsterdam, The Netherlands, 2020; pp. 415–438.
41. Brownlee, J. *Generative Adversarial Networks with Python: Deep Learning Generative Models for Image Synthesis and Image Translation*; Machine Learning Mastery: San Juan, PR, USA, 2019.

Disclaimer/Publisher's Note: The statements, opinions and data contained in all publications are solely those of the individual author(s) and contributor(s) and not of MDPI and/or the editor(s). MDPI and/or the editor(s) disclaim responsibility for any injury to people or property resulting from any ideas, methods, instructions or products referred to in the content.

Article

A Wireless Potentiostat Exploiting PWM-DAC for Interfacing of Wearable Electrochemical Biosensors in Non-Invasive Monitoring of Glucose Level

Antonio Vincenzo Radogna [1,*], Luca Francioso [2], Elisa Sciurti [2,*], Daniele Bellisario [2], Vanessa Esposito [2] and Giuseppe Grassi [3]

1. Department of Experimental Medicine, University of Salento, Campus Ecotekne, Via per Monteroni s.n., 73100 Lecce, Italy
2. Institute for Microelectronics and Microsystems, National Research Council of Italy (CNR-IMM), Campus Ecotekne, Via per Monteroni s.n., 73100 Lecce, Italy; lucanunzio.francioso@cnr.it (L.F.); daniele.bellisario@imm.cnr.it (D.B.); vanessa.esposito@imm.cnr.it (V.E.)
3. Department of Innovation Engineering, University of Salento, Campus Ecotekne, Via per Monteroni s.n., 73100 Lecce, Italy; giuseppe.grassi@unisalento.it
* Correspondence: antonio.radogna@unisalento.it (A.V.R.); elisa.sciurti@imm.cnr.it (E.S.)

Abstract: In this paper, a wireless potentiostat code-named ElectroSense, for interfacing of wearable electrochemical biosensors, will be presented. The system is devoted to non-invasive monitoring of glucose in wearable medical applications. Differently from other potentiostats in literature, which use digital-to-analog converters (DACs) as discrete components or integrated in high-end microcontrollers, in this work the pulse width modulation (PWM) technique is exploited through PWM-DAC approach to generate signals. The ubiquitous presence of integrated PWM peripherals in low-end microcontrollers, which generally also integrate analog-to-digital converters (ADCs), enables both the generation and acquisition of read-out signals on a single cheap electronic device without additional hardware. By this way, system's production costs, power consumption, and system's size are greatly reduced with respect to other solutions. All these features allow the system's adoption in wearable healthcare Internet-of-things (IoT) ecosystems. A description of both the sensing technology and the circuit will be discussed in detail, emphasizing advantages and drawbacks of the PWM-DAC approach. Experimental measurements will prove the efficacy of the proposed electronic system for non-invasive monitoring of glucose in wearable medical applications.

Keywords: potentiostat; wearable; glucose; electrochemical; analog front-end circuit; PWM-DAC

Citation: Radogna, A.V.; Francioso, L.; Sciurti, E.; Bellisario, D.; Esposito, V.; Grassi, G. A Wireless Potentiostat Exploiting PWM-DAC for Interfacing of Wearable Electrochemical Biosensors in Non-Invasive Monitoring of Glucose Level. *Electronics* **2024**, *13*, 1128. https://doi.org/10.3390/electronics13061128

Academic Editor: Maciej Ławryńczuk

Received: 27 February 2024
Revised: 17 March 2024
Accepted: 18 March 2024
Published: 20 March 2024

Copyright: © 2024 by the authors. Licensee MDPI, Basel, Switzerland. This article is an open access article distributed under the terms and conditions of the Creative Commons Attribution (CC BY) license (https://creativecommons.org/licenses/by/4.0/).

1. Introduction

Recent advances in smaller, lower-powered technologies are fueling the revolution of portable electronic products [1]. Many Internet-of-Things (IoT) applications, in both consumer and healthcare markets, enable an unmatched interaction with smart environments, providing the users with massive amount of information, changing and adapting it according to their needs and preferences. IoT products are supported by development and pervasive deployment of smart electronic devices equipped with a microcontroller (MCU), a communication interface (wired or wireless), a power supply, and a set of sensors and actuators that are used to interface with the environment. A key innovation, leading to modern portable products, has been the introduction of wearable sensors and devices. Their adoption in low-cost point-of-care devices permits to avoid the use of bulky and expensive laboratory equipment for healthcare monitoring. A prominent benefit of this could be the decreasing of the number of hospital visits while increasing the quality of patient life [2]. Many sensing principles, such as enzyme field effect transistors (ENFETs) [3] and resonator-based biosensors [4], can be exploited to develop affordable and accurate monitoring systems. However, their adoption in low-power wearable applications results unpractical since they require laboratory instrumentation which is not suitable for portable and low-power devices. In contrast, electrochemical biosensors are frequently adopted in wearable contexts as emerging technology for continuous and non-invasive monitoring of a wide range of analytes such as lactate, sodium, alcohol and glucose for diabetes monitoring [5,6]. An important application field is the therapeutic check through bodily fluids [6]. This correlates the pharmacokinetic properties of drugs with optimal outcomes by realizing customized dose regulations in real-time. Devices can track dynamic changes in pharmacokinetics behavior while assuring the medication of patients. Another field of application of wearable electrochemical biosensors is the abuse of drugs. Monitoring devices can serve as powerful screening tools in the hands of law enforcement agents to contrast drug trafficking and to support on-site forensic investigations. Regarding the glucose, the positive impact of real-time monitoring would concern the proper regulation of glucose homeostasis through correct insulin administration, eliminating the risk of patient's overdosing [7]. Research efforts over more than two decades were devoted for the development of non-invasive optical and electrochemical glucose monitoring [8]. However, despite of this, realizing a reliable and stable non-invasive sensing device for non-invasive glucose monitoring remains an elusive goal. The electronic systems for the interfacing and read-out of electrochemical sensors are called potentiostats. By considering a typical 3-electrodes electrochemical cell, a potentiostat operates by maintaining a potential on the working electrode (WE) with respect to the reference electrode (RE) and by measuring the current flowing between the WE and the counter electrode (CE).

Here, a low-cost wireless potentiostat, for interfacing of wearable electrochemical biosensors, is introduced. The device uses the PWM-DAC technique for the generation of excitation signal and it is adopted in the non-invasive monitoring of glucose level for wearable medical applications. The paper is organized as follows: Section 3 provides an overview the proposed system, emphasizing details on the circuit design, on the PWM-DAC technique, and on the sensing technology. The system is experimentally validated through the measurements reported in Section 4. Finally, Section 5 summarizes the findings.

2. Literature Review

Miniaturized potentiostats were adopted as monitoring devices for a multitude of analytes in the sweat [9]. For instance, in [10] a wireless and wearable potentiostat for cyclic voltammetry is described and tested with buffer solutions. The device shows a maximum read-out current of 500 µA and leverages on the Bluetooth wireless protocol for data communication. In addition to the Bluetooth MCU, the solution adopts a discrete digital-to-analog converter (DAC) for the signal generation. A similar solution is adopted in [11] where a portable potentiostat with USB communication is presented and tested with a dummy circuit. Another wireless potentiostat with discrete DAC is proposed in [12]. As an alternative approach, in [13] a monolithic solution is proposed by integrating the DAC in the same an ARM-Cortex-M4-based MCU. A different approach is used in the wearable solution presented in [5]. It leverages on the LMP91000, a well-known commercial integrated circuit acting as a programmable analog front-end (AFE) for electrochemical measurements. This component integrates all the useful circuits for the signal generation and acquisition from sensors. The mentioned works make use of high-end MCUs with integrated DAC or, alternatively, use a discrete DAC. These solutions account for high production costs of the system and for additional power consumption as well.

In this paper, a wireless potentiostat code-named ElectroSense, devoted to the interfacing of wearable electrochemical sensors for non-invasive detection of glucose, is described. As an extended version of [14], more details are provided on the system's design and implementation, both from the point of view of the circuit and the sensor. The device's key features lie in the technique for the generation of analog signals (current or voltage) responsible for the sensor's stimulation. A pulse-width-modulation-based digital-to-analog converter (PWM-DAC) technique is adopted instead of conventional voltage DAC. This approach aims to use a single low-end MCU to implement both the signal generation and acquisition. This is possible since, differently from DACs, which are not integrated in cheap MCUs, the PWM peripheral is always available on chip. By this way, it is possible to save resources in terms of cost for the system's realization, power consumption of the device, and area occupation on printed circuit board (PCB).

3. System Overview

3.1. Sensing Technology

Modern electrochemical sensors exhibit relevant advantages such as low detection limit, in the picomoles range, fast response, and simple equipment for measurement. Thanks to their sensing principle, they can be miniaturized for full integration in wearable devices [15]. Here, electrochemical sensors are selected since they deliver accurate and real-time data regarding the chemical composition of its surroundings. The electrochemical glucose sweat sensor was fabricated by a standard fabrication process on a silicon wafer substrate with a circular chromium/gold 5 nm/200 nm film thickness) working electrode (8 mm diameter) and a titanium/platinum thin film (10 nm/300 nm thickness) pseudo-reference electrode deposited by e-beam evaporation. A photo of the realized sensor is depicted in Figure 1. The working electrode was functionalized with three different layers: a first electroactive layer of Prussian Blue (PB) was electrodeposited on the gold surface of the electrode; then a polymer solution of chitosan mixed with 20 mg/mL of the enzyme glucose oxidase (GOx) and gold nanourchins (GNU) was drop-coated on the PB film. Finally, the electrode was covered with a 5% Nafion solution to form a protective layer. The response of the sensor to glucose is mediated by GOx, incorporated into the chitosan membrane in the presence of gold nanourchins to enhance the sensor sensitivity. GOx catalyzes the production of hydrogen peroxide (H_2O_2) in proportion to glucose concentration according to the following equation:

$$\text{glucose} + \text{oxygen} \longrightarrow \text{gluconic acid} + \text{hydrogen peroxide} \tag{1}$$

The amperometric detection of hydrogen peroxide usually take place at high potential (above 0.6 V vs. Ag/AgCl), but is interfered by many other substances present in the sample [16]. The PB layer acts as an "artificial peroxidase" allowing the reduction of H_2O_2 at low potential, avoiding the problem of interfering species. This produces an amperometric response which reflects the glucose concentration in the sample.

Figure 1. Fabricated electrochemical sensor.

3.2. Circuit Implementation

Figure 2 shows a diagram of the ElectroSense circuit schematic.

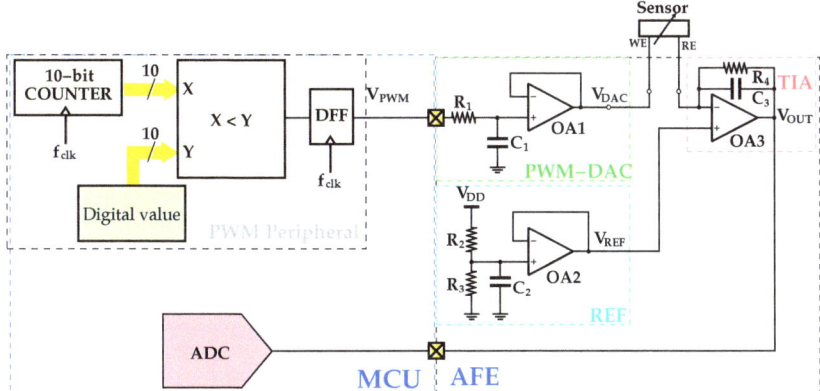

Figure 2. Simplified circuit schematic of the designed ElectroSense wireless potentiostat.

The circuit is composed by the MCU section (left) and the AFE section (right). The first is responsible for the Bluetooth communication, the generation of the excitation signal, the analog-to-digital conversion, and for the control of system's operation. An ATmega328 microcontroller, manufactured by Atmel, was selected thanks to its wide availability on the market and for its low cost. It exhibits the following specifications: advanced RISC architecture, operating frequency of 16 MHz, 32 k flash memory, 2 k RAM memory, and a 1 k EEPROM. Prominent features, useful to implement the desired functionality, are the 10-bit ADC and 6 PWM channels. Regarding the AFE section, it is responsible for the interfacing between the electrochemical sensor and the digital section. The excitation signal for the amperometry operation mode is generated through the PWM-DAC approach. This technique has been exploited in [17,18] in order to generate digitally controlled AC voltages with low requirements in terms of cost and hardware demand [19]. In brief, the PWM-DAC generates a desired analog voltage by filtering, with a low-pass filter, a PWM signal with a variable duty cycle (δ). In the recent years, this technique was exploited for high accuracy applications since modern chip manufacturers provide improved PWM modules with significantly high clock rates, thus enhancing the performance of the overall signal generation process [20]. The peripheral in the MCU, which is responsible for the pulse-width modulation, can be considered as an N_d-bit binary counter followed by an N_d-bit magnitude comparator [18]. A periodical digital ramp is available at the output of the counter with the following period:

$$T = \frac{2^{N_d}}{f_{clk}} \qquad (2)$$

The desired output waveform from the PWM-DAC is obtained by comparing the output of the comparator (X input) with a digital word (Y input). As a result, the pulse width of the comparator output signal is proportional to the digital value. Finally, a D flip-flop is used to eliminate the transition glitches. The δ is defined as the ratio between the high-value interval and the overall period. Figure 3 depicts a generic PWM signal with increasing δ, where V_H and V_L are the high and low voltage values, respectively, of the signal, T_H is the high-value interval of the signal, and T is its period. Regarding the choice of the PWM frequency, it was selected equal to 7.8 kHz.

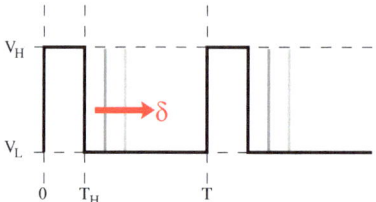

Figure 3. Generic PWM signal with increasing δ.

The PWM peripheral of the MCU provides a δ resolution of 10 bits. This means that the δ range from 0% to 100% is mapped in the integer range from 0 to 1023. The following expanded expression through Fourier analysis, for the V_{PWM} signal, is derived in [21]:

$$V_{PWM}(t) = [\delta \cdot V_{FS} - V_L] + \frac{2 \cdot V_{FS}}{\pi} \cdot \sin(\delta \cdot \pi) \cdot \cos\left(\frac{2\pi}{T} \cdot t - \delta \cdot \pi\right) \\ + \sum_{n=2}^{\infty} \frac{2 \cdot V_{FS}}{n \cdot \pi} \cdot \sin(\delta \cdot n \cdot \pi) \cdot \cos\left(\frac{2\pi \cdot n}{T} \cdot t - \delta \cdot \pi \cdot n\right) \quad (3)$$

where V_{FS} is equal to $V_H - V_L$. The V_{PWM} waveform is then filtered in order to preserve the first term in (3). Since this term is proportional to the duty cycle, δ, by varying the latter from 0 to 100%, a desired output voltage, V_{DAC}, with voltage values from V_L to V_H is obtained. As depicted in the PWM-DAC subcircuit in Figure 2, the PWM signal is filtered by a low-pass filter to obtain the desired V_{DAC} voltage for the sensor excitation. This voltage is obtained through the following expression:

$$V_{DAC} = \frac{N_i}{2^{N_d} - 1} \cdot V_{FS} - V_{REF} \quad (4)$$

where N_i is the integer δ range from 0 to 1023, N_d is the PWM resolution equal to 10 bits, $V_{FS} = V_H - V_L$ is the full-scale voltage of the PWM-DAC set to 5 V, and V_{REF} is the reference voltage set to $V_{DD}/2$. The output signal can be a triangular waveform, useful as the potentiostat is in voltammetry mode, or a constant voltage, useful in amperometry mode. In order to keep a low number on components on PCB, a first-order passive RC filter was chosen and its sizing was performed according to [19]. The resistor and capacitor values have been selected equal to 10 kΩ and 100 nF, respectively. The filter's time constant, equal to 1 ms, was chosen much larger than the period of the PWM, which is about 130 μs. This value is a trade-off between filtering efficacy, mandatory to obtain a small peak-to-peak ripple voltage, and settling time of the PWM-DAC. However, it can be specified that in the case of static excitation signal, the settling time does not really matter since the generated signal is constant. This is the case of the amperometry mode, whose measurements are described in Section 4.2. As already specified, the potentiostat was designed for the readout of a 2-terminal electrochemical sensor. Specifically, while the output of the PWM-DAC is connected to the WE of the sensor, the RE is connected to the transimpedance amplifier for the current read-out. The latter block is identified as TIA in Figure 2. Basically, the TIA acts as a current-to-voltage converter in order to convert the output current from the sensor in a voltage for the ADC. From basic circuit theory, the output voltage of the TIA, V_{OUT}, can be expressed as:

$$V_{OUT} = V_{REF} - R_4 \cdot I_S(t) \quad (5)$$

where $I_S(t)$ is the output current from the sensor. The feedback resistor, R_4, is selected in order to prevent the opamp saturation and depends on the sensor's maximum output current according to (5). By considering a maximum output current from the sensor, I_{MAX}, equal to 10 μA and a rail-to-ral opamp with maximum V_{OUT} equal to 5 V, a R_4 resistor equal to 250 kΩ was chosen. The C_4 capacitor, whose value is 1 nF, was added in feedback to the OA3 opamp in order to ensure its stability. The following expression is used to convert the output word from the ADC, N_o, to the sensor's output current, I_S:

$$I_S = \frac{V_{REF} - \frac{N_o \cdot V_{FS}}{2^{N_a} - 1}}{R_4} \qquad (6)$$

where N_a is the resolution of the used ADC, equal to 10 bits. Regarding the V_{REF} voltage generation, it has been obtained through a buffered voltage divider with the R_2 and R_3 resistor being both equal to 100 kΩ. The N_o digital words are processed through a basic moving average filter which was implemented on the MCU. This filter works as low-pass filter and it represents an efficient way to filter the sensor's signal from electronic noise, environmental interferences, non-idealities of electronic components, etc. This is also useful in order to attenuate the ripple contribution. Regarding the operational amplifier (opamp) selection, an OPA2344 has been selected since it satisfies the requirements in terms of gain, bandwidth and input/output rail-to-rail operation. The latter feature is useful in order to use the entire full-scale of the ADC.

The wireless communication is ensured through an HC-05 Bluetooth module. This is a widely adopted device for the easy wireless replacement of serial RS232 communications. It uses the 2.4 GHz frequency band with a data rate up to 1 Mbps and it can operate in a range of 10 m.

A photo of the realized system is depicted in Figure 4. The figure shows the UART connector for the HC-05 module and the screw terminal for the 2-electrodes electrochemical sensor. The realized module also features a power section for driving valves and pumps for other intended uses outside wearable systems [22].

Figure 4. Photo of the ElectroSense mainboard.

The portable operation of the wearable system is possible thanks to a battery.

4. Experimental Measurements

4.1. Potentiostat Electrical Test

A first electrical test was conducted on the wireless potentiostat in order to verify the correct signal generation and acquisition. A self-check for cyclic voltammetry mode was conducted by generating 3 periods of a triangular waveform with a 100 mV s^{-1} slope and a voltage range from −1 V to 1 V. The WE and RE electrodes were connected together with OA3 opamp connected as voltage follower.

The result of this self-check is then captured by a serial terminal software by means of Bluetooth communication. Figure 5 shows the desired triangular waveform for the cyclic voltammetry. The signal range goes from 1.5 V to 3.5 V and it corresponds to the +1 V ÷ −1 V by considering the V_{REF} (i.e., 2.5 V) as zero. A gaussian random process, with measured standard deviation equal to about 40 mV, can be used to describe the voltage ripple in the PWM-DAC signal. This voltage ripple is the main drawback of the PWM-DAC approach, resulting from the filtering of the PWM signal. A mean current consumption of 30 mA was measured during the read-out operation, corresponding to a power consumption of 150 mW at 5 V supply voltage. The reduced power consumption makes the system suitable for adoption in healthcare Internet-of-Things (IoT) ecosystems.

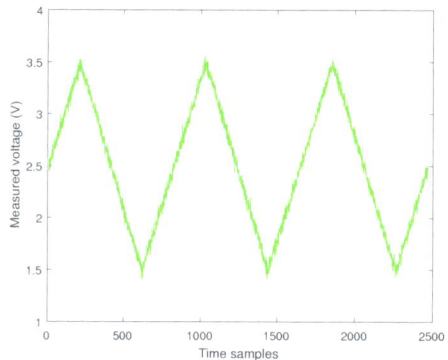

Figure 5. Self-check for signal generation and acquisition.

4.2. Amperometric Measurements with Electrochemical Sensor

The preliminary electrochemical measurements were performed using a commercial potentiostat/galvanostat (Ivium Vertex One, Ivium Technologies B.V., Eindhoven, The Netherlands). For electrochemical characterization of PB layer, cyclic voltammetry measurement were performed from 0.35 V to −0.05 V vs. Ag/AgCl in a solution containing 100 mM KCl and 100 mM HCl, and the typical oxidation/reduction peaks of PB are shown in Figure 6a. For the detection of glucose, chronoamperometric measurements were performed at −0.4 V vs. Pt with the two-electrode integrated sensor.

The measurement through the commercial instrument and with different glucose concentrations (0.3–9.37 mM in PBS, pH 7.4) are reported in Figure 6b. The enzymatic sensor exhibited a sensitive response to the addition of the analyte with a linear decrease in current as glucose concentrations increased. The linear relationship between the absolute current and the different glucose concentrations is described by the fitting equation $y = (0.68 \pm 0.02) \cdot x + (1.74 \pm 0.05)$ with a correlation coefficient of 0.99 (Figure 6c). The selectivity of the developed glucose electrochemical sensor was evaluated by performing chronoamperometric measurements in the presence of typical interfering species in sweat including NaCl (0.1 mM), KCl (0.1 mM), uric acid (1 mM) and lactic acid (3 mM). Figure 6d shows the excellent selectivity of the sensor, with a non-significant increase in the response (%) in the presence of lactic acid.

The sensor was also measured through ElectroSense potentiostat and the results are depicted in Figure 7. From the figure, it can be noted a very good accordance in the measurements between the commercial instrument and the ElectroSense potentiostat.

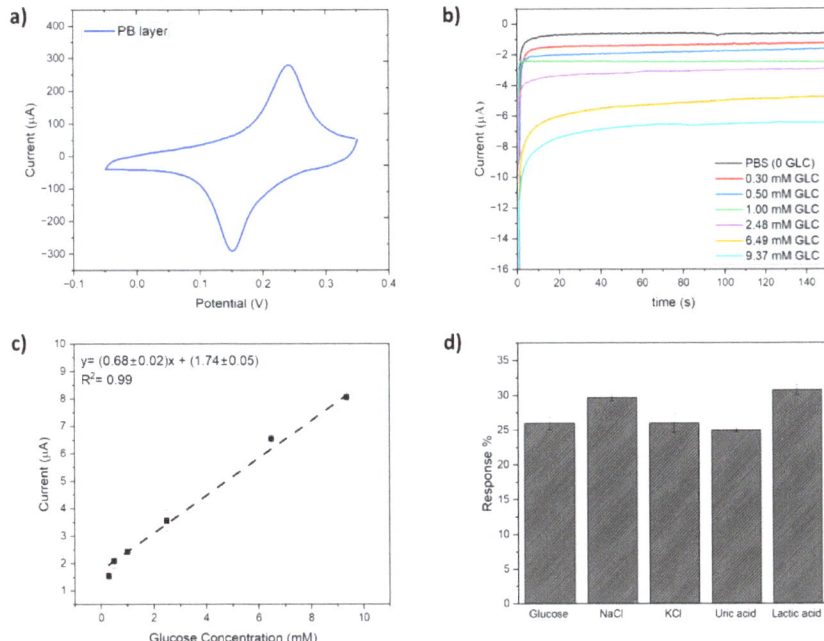

Figure 6. Electrochemical measurements: (**a**) cyclic voltammetry of the PB layer in KCl/HCl (0.1 M); (**b**) chronoamperometric response of the glucose sensor with different glucose (GLC) concentrations (0.3–9.37 mM through the commercial instrument); (**c**) calibration curve of the glucose sensor at increasing concentrations of glucose; (**d**) variation in amperometric response (%) for glucose (0.5 mM) and added interfering species (0.1 mM NaCl, 0.1 mM KCl, 1 mM uric acid, 3 mM lactic acid).

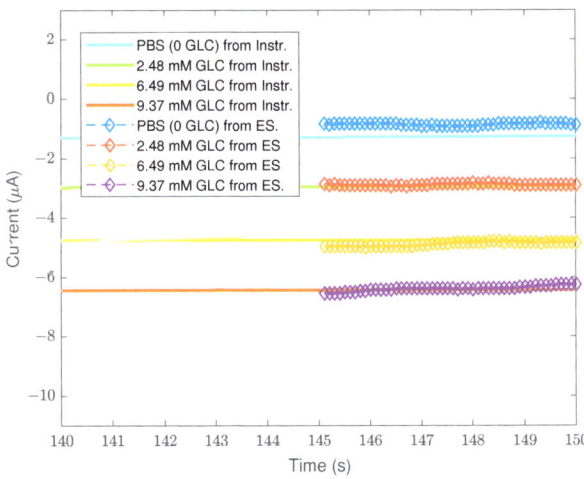

Figure 7. Real-time sensor measurements with different glucose (GLC) concentrations through the ElectroSense (ES) potentiostat. The measurement are compared with those from the commercial instrument.

4.3. Measurements in Real Conditions

The realized electrochemical sensor was integrated in a commercial patch used in medical practice, as depicted in Figure 8. Real wearable conditions were reproduced in laboratory environment by testing the system, composed by electrochemical sensor and ElectroSense wireless potentiostat, in artificial sweat. First, agarose-based hydrogels were developed as sweat collectors on which the glucose sensors performed the electrochemical measurements. An agarose hydrogel at a concentration of 2% was prepared by dissolving the agarose powder (Sigma-Aldrich, St. Louis, MO, USA) in water, boiled and poured in a petri dish. After gelling for 2 h at room temperature, the hydrogel was cut into 1 cm^2 sheets, about 1 mm thick. The remarkable hydrophilicity of the agarose hydrogel facilitates the absorption of aqueous solutions, allowing it to be used as a sweat reservoir. The captured sweat solution is then released onto the nanocomposite polymeric layer of the electrochemical sensor which is able to quantify the glucose. An artificial sweat solution was prepared as reported in [23] by dissolving NaCl (0.5 wt%), urea (0.1 wt%), lactic acid (0.1 wt%) and glucose at a concentration of 0.25 mM in distilled water. The agarose hydrogel sheets were immersed in the artificial sweat containing glucose for 1 h and then used for the sensing measurements, after a removal of excess solution by a gentle contact with filter paper to avoid measurements artifacts. A number of hydrogels were soaked in a sweat solution without glucose as negative control. Amperometric measurements were performed with both the commercial potentiostat and the ElectroSense potentiostat by applying the sweat-impregnated hydrogel to the sensor surface. Figure 9 shows the electrochemical response of the sensor from the artificial sweat impregnated hydrogel (blue plots) and the sweat containing glucose (red plots). The results also confirmed the response of the glucose sensor in sweat, showing an increased current change in the presence of glucose and the accordance between the measurements with the ElectroSense potentiostat and the commercial instrument. The obtained results demonstrate the ability of the electrochemical sensor to quantify glucose in artificial sweat and the possibility of combining it with the wireless potentiostat to set up a potential system for wearable glucose monitoring.

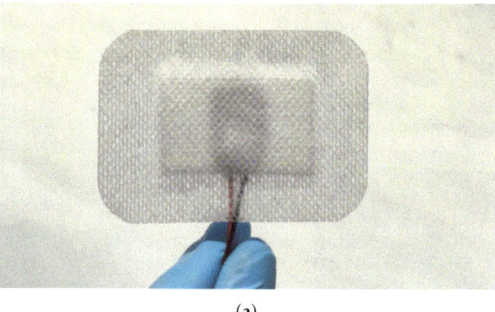

(a)

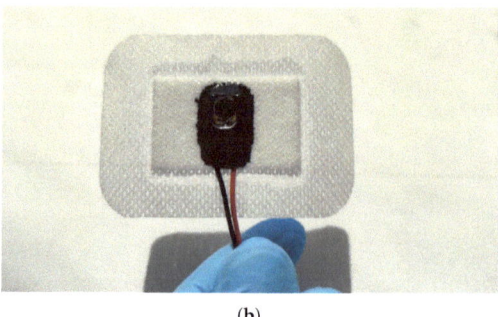

(b)

Figure 8. Realized adhesive patch with integrated sensor. (**a**) External side. (**b**) Internal side.

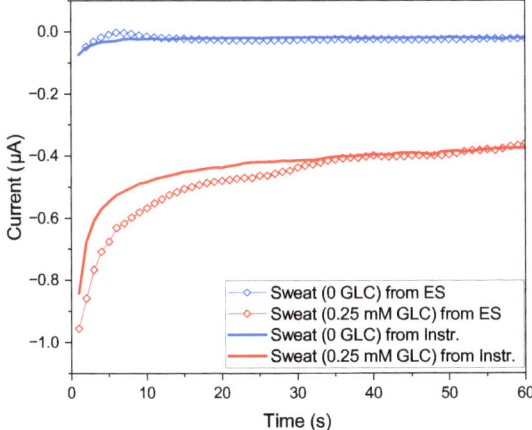

Figure 9. Amperometric responses of the electrochemical sensor to glucose (0.25 mM) in artificial sweat. The measurements were taken with both the ElectroSense potentiostat and the commercial instrument.

Table 1 shows a comparison between the proposed potentiostat and other works in literature.

Table 1. Comparison with the state-of-the-art.

	Meas. Approach	Terminals No.	Application	Signal Generation	Communication
[5]	Cyclic voltammetry, square wave voltammetry, chronoamperometry, and normal pulse voltammetry	3	Anti-cocaine aptamer	External AFE and DAC	USB (Wired)
[10]	Cyclic voltammetry and chronoamperometry	3	Healthcare	External 16-bit DAC	BLE
[11]	Cyclic voltammetry	3	Generic electroch. measurements	External 16-bit DAC	USB (Wired)
[12]	Cyclic voltammetry, chronoamperometry, and square wave voltammetry	3	Generic electroch. measurements	Integrated DAC into the MCU	BLE
[13]	Cyclic voltammetry, linear sweep voltammetry, chronoamperometry, chronocoulometry	2	Macroelectrode and ultramicroelectrode studies	Integrated DAC into the MCU	USB (Wired)
This work	CV and chronoamperometry	2	Wearable Healthc.	PWM-DAC	Bluetooth V2.0

5. Conclusions

In this paper, a low-cost wireless potentiostat, for interfacing of wearable electrochemical biosensors, was proposed. The device, code-named ElectroSense, is adopted in the non-invasive monitoring of glucose level and it is aimed to wearable medical applications. Differently from other wireless potentiostats in literature, which use high-end microcontrollers with integrated DACs, the ElectroSense potentiostat uses the PWM-DAC approach for signal generation. This design choice permits to save production costs since a low-end microcontroller with a PWM peripheral can be adopted for both the signal generation and acquisition. Moreover, power consumption of the circuit and area occupation on PCB are greatly reduced as well. All these features make the system suitable for the adoption in healthcare IoT ecosystems. The wireless potentiostat was coupled with a wearable electrochemical biosensor and the resulting amperometric measurements show a good accordance with those obtained by commercial laboratory equipment. Finally, measurements in artificial sweat were reported, proving the efficacy of the proposed device for non-invasive measurements of glucose in wearable medical applications. A future upgrade of the work will include a constant current generation circuit, on the ElectroSense board, for iontophoretic sweating stimulation.

Author Contributions: Conceptualization, A.V.R. and L.F.; methodology, A.V.R., L.F. and E.S. software, A.V.R. and D.B.; validation, A.V.R., E.S. and V.E.; formal analysis, A.V.R., E.S., D.B. and V.E.; investigation, A.V.R., L.F. and E.S.; resources, L.F.; data curation, G.G.; writing—original draft preparation, A.V.R.; writing—review and editing, A.V.R. and E.S.; visualization, V.E. and G.G.; supervision, L.F.; project administration, L.F.; funding acquisition, L.F. All authors have read and agreed to the published version of the manuscript.

Funding: This work was supported by the "ChAALenge" MiSE PON Project, CUP: B39J22003050005. We acknowledge co-funding from Next Generation EU, in the context of the National Recovery and Resilience Plan, Investment PE8—Project Age-It: "Ageing Well in an Ageing Society". This resource was co-financed by the Next Generation EU [DM 1557 11.10.2022]. The views and opinions expressed are only those of the authors and do not necessarily reflect those of the European Union or the European Commission. Neither the European Union nor the European Commission can be held responsible for them. The technical content of this manuscript will be adopted in the context of early diagnosis of pulmonary diseases. The authors acknowledge the Department of Engineering for Innovation of University of Salento for co-funding this research.

Institutional Review Board Statement: Not applicable.

Informed Consent Statement: Not applicable.

Data Availability Statement: No new data were created or analyzed in this study. Data sharing is not applicable to this article.

Conflicts of Interest: The authors declare no conflicts of interest.

Abbreviations

The following abbreviations are used in this manuscript:

ADC	analog-to-digital converter
AFE	analog front end
CE	counter electrode
DAC	digital-to-analog converter
GNU	gold nanourchins
GOx	glucose oxidase
IoT	Internet-of-things
MCU	microcontroller unit
PWM-DAC	pulse-width-modulation-based digital-to-analog converter
RE	reference electrode
PCB	printed circuit board
TIA	transimpedance amplifier
WE	working electrode

References

1. Shumba, A.T.; Montanaro, T.; Sergi, I.; Fachechi, L.; Vittorio, M.D.; Patrono, L. Leveraging IoT-Aware Technologies and AI Techniques for Real-Time Critical Healthcare Applications. *Sensors* **2022**, *22*, 7675. [CrossRef] [PubMed]
2. Xu, W.; Althumayri, M.; Mohammad, A.; Ceylan Koydemir, H. Foldable low-cost point-of-care device for testing blood coagulation using smartphones. *Biosens. Bioelectron.* **2023**, *242*, 115755. [CrossRef] [PubMed]
3. Ravariu, C.; Parvulescu, C.C.; Manea, E.; Tucureanu, V. Optimized Technologies for Cointegration of MOS Transistor and Glucose Oxidase Enzyme on a Si-Wafer. *Biosensors* **2021**, *11*, 497. [CrossRef] [PubMed]
4. Yue, W.; Kim, E.S.; Zhu, B.H.; Chen, J.; Liang, J.G.; Kim, N.Y. Permittivity-Inspired Microwave Resonator-Based Biosensor Based on Integrated Passive Device Technology for Glucose Identification. *Biosensors* **2021**, *11*, 508. [CrossRef] [PubMed]
5. Hoilett, O.S.; Walker, J.F.; Balash, B.M.; Jaras, N.J.; Boppana, S.; Linnes, J.C. KickStat: A Coin-Sized Potentiostat for High-Resolution Electrochemical Analysis. *Sensors* **2020**, *20*, 2407. [CrossRef] [PubMed]
6. Teymourian, H.; Parrilla, M.; Sempionatto, J.R.; Montiel, N.F.; Barfidokht, A.; Echelpoel, R.V.; Wael, K.D.; Wang, J. Wearable Electrochemical Sensors for the Monitoring and Screening of Drugs. *ACS Sens.* **2020**, *5*, 2679–2700. [CrossRef] [PubMed]

7. Lee, H.; Song, C.; Hong, Y.S.; Kim, M.S.; Cho, H.R.; Kang, T.; Shin, K.; Choi, S.H.; Hyeon, T.; Kim, D.H. Wearable/disposable sweat-based glucose monitoring device with multistage transdermal drug delivery module. *Sci. Adv.* **2017**, *3*, e1601314. [CrossRef] [PubMed]
8. Kim, J.; Campbell, A.S.; Wang, J. Wearable non-invasive epidermal glucose sensors: A review. *Talanta* **2018**, *177*, 163–170. [CrossRef] [PubMed]
9. Gao, W.; Emaminejad, S.; Nyein, H.Y.Y.; Challa, S.; Chen, K.; Peck, A.; Fahad, H.M.; Ota, H.; Shiraki, H.; Kiriya, D.; et al. Fully integrated wearable sensor arrays for multiplexed in situ perspiration analysis. *Nature* **2016**, *529*, 509–514. [CrossRef] [PubMed]
10. Ahmad, R.; Wolfbeis, O.S.; Alshareef, H.N.; Salama, K.N.; Surya, S.G.; Sales, J.B.; Mkaouar, H.; Catunda, S.Y.C.; Belfort, D.R.; Lei, Y.; et al. KAUSTat: A Wireless, Wearable, Open-Source Potentiostat for Electrochemical Measurements. In Proceedings of the 2019 IEEE SENSORS, Montreal, QC, Canada, 27–30 October 2019; IEEE: New York, NY, USA, 2019. [CrossRef]
11. Setiyono, R.; Lestari, T.F.H.; Anggraeni, A.; Hartati, Y.W.; Bahti, H.H. UnpadStat Design: Portable Potentiostat for Electrochemical Sensing Measurements Using Screen Printed Carbon Electrode. *Micromachines* **2023**, *14*, 268. [CrossRef] [PubMed]
12. Ainla, A.; Mousavi, M.P.S.; Tsaloglou, M.N.; Redston, J.; Bell, J.G.; Fernández-Abedul, M.T.; Whitesides, G.M. Open-Source Potentiostat for Wireless Electrochemical Detection with Smartphones. *Anal. Chem.* **2018**, *90*, 6240–6246. [CrossRef] [PubMed]
13. Glasscott, M.W.; Verber, M.D.; Hall, J.R.; Pendergast, A.D.; McKinney, C.J.; Dick, J.E. SweepStat: A Build-It-Yourself, Two-Electrode Potentiostat for Macroelectrode and Ultramicroelectrode Studies. *J. Chem. Educ.* **2019**, *97*, 265–270. [CrossRef]
14. Radogna, A.V.; Francioso, L.; Sciurti, E.; Bellisario, D.; Esposito, V.; Grassi, G. ElectroSense: A Low-cost Wearable Potentiostat for Real-time Monitoring of Glucose Level. In Proceedings of the 2023 8th International Conference on Smart and Sustainable Technologies (SpliTech), Split, Croatia, 20–23 June 2023; pp. 1–5. [CrossRef]
15. Baranwal, J.; Barse, B.; Gatto, G.; Broncova, G.; Kumar, A. Electrochemical Sensors and Their Applications: A Review. *Chemosensors* **2022**, *10*, 363. [CrossRef]
16. Vidal, J.C.; Espuelas, J.; Garcia-Ruiz, E.; Castillo, J.R. Amperometric cholesterol biosensors based on the electropolymerization of pyrrole and the electrocatalytic effect of Prussian-Blue layers helped with self-assembled monolayers. *Talanta* **2004**, *64*, 655–664. [CrossRef] [PubMed]
17. Wright, P.; Pickering, J. An AC voltage standard based on a PWM DAC. *IEEE Trans. Instrum. Meas.* **1999**, *48*, 457–461. [CrossRef]
18. Halper, C.; Heiss, M.; Brasseur, G. Digital-to-analog conversion by pulse-count modulation methods. *IEEE Trans. Instrum. Meas.* **1996**, *45*, 805–814. [CrossRef]
19. Pejovic, P. Output Voltage Filtering in Pulse Width Modulation Based D/A Converters. In Proceedings of the 2018 International Symposium on Industrial Electronics (INDEL), Banja Luka, Bosnia and Herzegovina, 1–3 November 2018; IEEE: New York, NY, USA, 2018. [CrossRef]
20. Thilakarathne, C.; Meegahapola, L.; Fernando, N.; Niakinezhad, M. PWM DAC based Input System for Synchrophasor Algorithm Testing. In Proceedings of the 2018 8th International Conference on Power and Energy Systems (ICPES), Colombo, Sri Lanka, 21–22 December 2018; pp. 93–97. [CrossRef]
21. Wang, Y.; Cheng, F.; Zhou, Y.; Xu, J. Analysis of double-T filter used for PWM circuit to D/A converter. In Proceedings of the 2012 24th Chinese Control and Decision Conference (CCDC), Taiyuan, China, 23–25 May 2012; pp. 2752–2756. [CrossRef]
22. Radogna, A.V.; Latino, M.E.; Menegoli, M.; Prontera, C.T.; Morgante, G.; Mongelli, D.; Giampetruzzi, L.; Corallo, A.; Bondavalli, A.; Francioso, L. A Monitoring Framework with Integrated Sensing Technologies for Enhanced Food Safety and Traceability. *Sensors* **2022**, *22*, 6509. [CrossRef] [PubMed]
23. Eldamak, A.R.; Thorson, S.; Fear, E.C. Study of the Dielectric Properties of Artificial Sweat Mixtures at Microwave Frequencies. *Biosensors* **2020**, *10*, 62. [CrossRef] [PubMed]

Disclaimer/Publisher's Note: The statements, opinions and data contained in all publications are solely those of the individual author(s) and contributor(s) and not of MDPI and/or the editor(s). MDPI and/or the editor(s) disclaim responsibility for any injury to people or property resulting from any ideas, methods, instructions or products referred to in the content.

Article

An Evaluation of the Autonomic Nervous Activity and Psychomotor Vigilance Level for Smells in the Work Booth

Emi Yuda [1], Aoi Otani [2], Atsushi Yamada [2] and Yutaka Yoshida [1,*]

[1] Graduate School of Information Sciences, Tohoku University, 6-3-09 Aoba, Aramaki-aza Aoba-ku, Sendai 980-8579, Japan; emi.a.yuda@tohoku.ac.jp

[2] Fuji Industrial Co., Ltd., 2-1-9 Fuchinobe, Chuo-ku, Sagamihara 252-0206, Japan; a-otani@fujioh.com (A.O.); a-yamada@fujioh.com (A.Y.)

* Correspondence: yutaka.yoshida.e3@tohoku.ac.jp

Abstract: In this study, we investigated the effects of the smell environment in the work booth on autonomic nervous activity (ANS) and psychomotor vigilance levels (PVLs) using linalool (LNL) and trans-2-nonenal (T2N). The subjects were six healthy males (31 ± 6 years old) and six healthy females (24 ± 5 years old). They sat in the work booth filled with the smells of LNL and T2N for 10 min, and their electrocardiograms (ECGs), skin conductance levels, pulse wave variabilities, skin temperatures, and seat pressure distributions were measured. In addition, the orthostatic load test (OLT) and psychomotor vigilance test (PVT) were performed before and after entering the work booth, and a subjective evaluation of the smell was also performed after the experiment. This paper focused on ECG and PVT data and analyzed changes in heart rate variability indices and PVT scores. Males felt slightly comfortable with the LNL smell and showed promoted sympathetic nerve activity in the OLT after the smell presentation. Females felt slightly uncomfortable with the T2N smell and showed promoted sympathetic nerve activity and a decrease in PVT scores in the OLT after the smell presentation. Gender differences were observed in ANS and PVLs, and it is possible that the comfort of LNL increased sympathetic nervous activity in males, while the uncomfortableness of T2N may have reduced work performance in females.

Keywords: work booth; linalool (LNL); trans-2-nonenal (T2N); autonomic nervous activity (ANS); psychomotor vigilance level (PVL)

Citation: Yuda, E.; Otani, A.; Yamada, A.; Yoshida, Y. An Evaluation of the Autonomic Nervous Activity and Psychomotor Vigilance Level for Smells in the Work Booth. *Electronics* **2024**, *13*, 3576. https://doi.org/10.3390/electronics13173576

Academic Editors: Gongping Yang, Ilaria Sergi and Teodoro Montanaro

Received: 22 June 2024
Revised: 30 August 2024
Accepted: 6 September 2024
Published: 9 September 2024

Copyright: © 2024 by the authors. Licensee MDPI, Basel, Switzerland. This article is an open access article distributed under the terms and conditions of the Creative Commons Attribution (CC BY) license (https:// creativecommons.org/licenses/by/ 4.0/).

1. Introduction

As the spread of COVID-19 has led to the widespread adoption of teleworking and online work around the world, the installation and use of work booths at train stations and airports have become common as part of work reforms to combat infectious diseases. Work booths are used not only when you want to concentrate on your work alone, but also for meetings and business negotiations with people outside the company, Zoom meetings, and so on. However, work booths are small spaces and are used by an unspecified number of people, which creates problems with smells lingering. Furthermore, people have different preferences when it comes to smells; it is possible that a disliked smell can cause discomfort or reduce work performance. Therefore, it is necessary to investigate the effects of smells inside work booths on the biological body.

Most studies on smells use essential oils and aromatic oils and include the calming effects of smells on mental stress [1], the synergistic effects of combining smells and music to reduce cognitive stress [2], recovery from physical stress [3], the improvement of work performance [4], and the physiological evaluation of bad smells [5]. Most of these studies involve objective evaluations of autonomic nervous activity (ANS) by analyzing biosignals such as heart rate variability (HRV), blood pressure, electrodermal activity, and salivary alpha amylase, or subjective evaluations through questionnaire surveys. However, such experiments have been performed in large spaces, and there are few studies that have examined the effects of smells by presenting them to humans in a small space, such as a work booth. Therefore, although it is difficult to compare the effects of biological condition to smell in the work booth with previous studies, there is a novelty in investigating the effects using similar biosignals as in previous studies.

We aim to evaluate the biological condition by the multimodal analysis of many biosignals in fields related to smells, such as industry, environmental design, and health management. The purpose of this study is to investigate whether comfortable and uncomfortable smells in a work booth affect the ANS and psychomotor vigilance levels (PVLs) using biosignals and subjective evaluation.

The smell focused on in this study were linalool (LNL) and trans-2-nonenal (T2N). LNL is said to have a relaxing effect and is a fragrance widely used in cosmetics and household products, and until recently, it was also shown to have low contact allergies. It is a valuable fragrance ingredient used in various cosmetics and is known as a valuable essential oil used as a fragrance alongside citrus fruits and lavender [6,7]. On the other hand, T2N is known as a malodorous compound that causes body odor associated with human aging. It may cause physiological changes such as stress responses, mood changes, increased skin conductance, and activation of the sympathetic nervous system, suggesting that sensing malodors may be a way to detect health hazards [8,9].

Since people have different preferences for these smells, it is not necessarily the case that LNL is comfortable and T2N is uncomfortable. Moreover, since this is an experiment on humans, strong smells are limited, so the subjects' psychology regarding smell was investigated through subjective evaluation. Biosignals were measured, including the electrocardiogram (ECG), skin conductance, pulse rate, skin temperature, and seat pressure. In this paper, ANS was evaluated by calculating the time domain and frequency domain indices of HRV from the ECG. In addition, the PVL can be measured by measuring the reaction time of the fingers using the psychomotor vigilance test (PVT) [10].

In a previous experiment, the authors have developed HRV analysis software with a PVT application implemented together with Crosswell Co., Ltd. (Yokohama, Japan) [11]. This software not only measures ECG, but also has the orthostatic load test (OLT) application installed, which allows the easy examination of the state of ANS from HRV indices when standing up from a sitting position. This paper focuses on physiological considerations when presenting LNL and T2N in a work booth using these applications.

2. Methods

2.1. Subjects

The subjects were 6 healthy males (31 ± 6 years old) and 6 healthy females (24 ± 5 years old). All subjects received an explanation from the experimenter in advance, and after being fully satisfied with the content, agreed to participate in the experiment. The selection criteria for the subjects were that they were healthy adults under 40 years old without any chronic diseases. In addition, the following five exclusion criteria were used to select subjects:

i. Within the past 3 months, there has been an acute illness requiring hospitalization or the appearance of new symptoms of a chronic illness.

ii. Are possibly pregnant, pregnant or breastfeeding.

iii. Person with a history of skin allergies to wristwatch-type wearable devices or medical electrocardiogram electrodes.

iv. Person with allergies or hypersensitivity to fragrances.

v. Person who is unable to make their own judgment about whether to participate, or whom the research physician deems inappropriate for any other reason.

2.2. Components of Fragrances and Work Booth

The fragrances used in the experiment were LNL and T2N. These fragrances were diluted with ethanol and pure water and sprayed using a diffuser. The mixing ratios of

LNL, ethanol, and pure water were 0.5%, 37.5%, and 62%, respectively. The mixing ratios of T2N, ethanol, and pure water were 0.5%, 50%, and 49.5%, respectively. Figure 1 shows the exterior and interior of the work booth (Law Partition C&L typeF, COMANY Corporation, Komatsu, Japan). The external dimensions of the work booth are 1000 mm (W) × 1200 mm (D) × 1940 mm (H), the internal dimensions of the work booth are 900 mm (W) × 1100 mm (D) × 1940 mm (H), the indoor volume is 1.92 m^3, and the ventilation volume is 10 m^3/h. A diffuser, temperature/humidity CO_2 sensor, table fan, and chair were set on the floor in the booth. During the experiment, the room temperature in the work booth was 22.1 ± 1.2 °C and the humidity was 41.3 ± 5.2%.

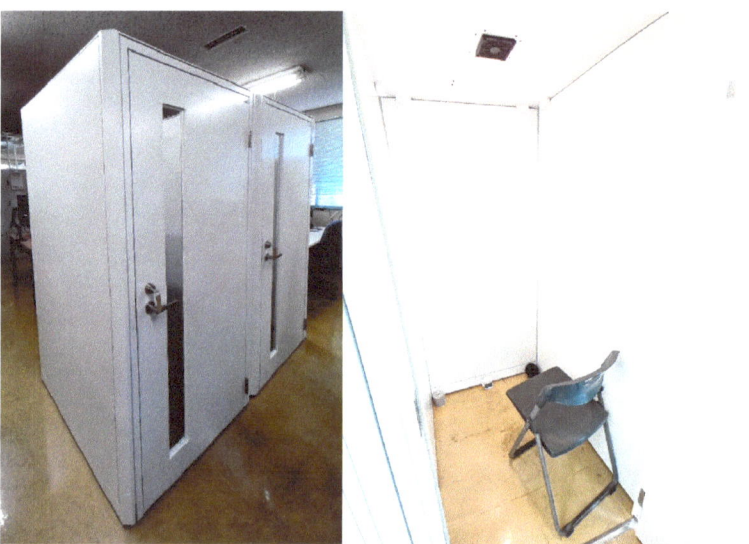

Figure 1. Exterior and interior of the work booth.

The airborne fragrance concentrations set in the booth were 24 ppb for LNL and 1.5 ppb for T2N. Figure 2 shows the diffuser (nebulizing diffuser orb, @aroma Corporation, Tokyo, Japan) used in the experiment. The fragrance was sprayed for 2 min using a nebulizer system, followed by a 1 min pause. Preliminary tests have confirmed that if the 2 min spray and 1 min pause are continued for more than 1 h with ventilation, the airborne fragrance concentration will remain almost constant. In the preliminary tests, the amount of fragrance sprayed was measured after 3 sets of 2 min sprays and 1 min pauses, and the required ventilation volume was calculated using the Seidel formula based on SHASE-S102, specified by the Society of Heating, Air-Conditioning and Sanitary Engineers of Japan [12]. Two work booths were set up on the floor: one was presented with LNL and the other with T2N.

The lighting equipment in the booth was an LED (LSEB9505KLB1, Panasonic Corporation, Tokyo, Japan). The illuminance in the booth was measured using a digital illuminometer (TLX-204, TRUSCO NAKAYAMA Corporation, Tokyo, Japan). The illuminance was measured in the center of the booth at a height of 700 mm and in the gaze direction at a height of 1200 mm. The illuminance was measured 5 times in each booth and the mean illuminance was calculated. Table 1 shows the mean illuminance and standard deviation in the booth. There is not much difference in illuminance between the two booths.

Figure 2. Diffuser used in the experiment. Body dimensions: 80 mm (diameter) × 152 mm (H); weight: 376 g; spray method: nebulizer; maximum diffusion capacity: 70 m^2.

Table 1. Mean illuminance and standard deviation in the work booth.

Booth No.	Measurement Position	Illuminance [lux]
Booth1	Center of the booth	802 ± 2
	Gaze direction	683 ± 8
Booth2	Center of the booth	805 ± 2
	Gaze direction	687 ± 9

2.3. Measurement Device of Biosignals

2.3.1. ECG and HRV Analysis

ECG was measured using the ECG/Heart Rate Measurement Amplifier (LRR-05, GMS Company Limited, Tokyo, Japan) with a detection sensitivity of 0.3 mV to 10 mV, dimensions of 114 mm (W) × 68 mm (H) × 19 mm (D), a weight of 118 g, and a power supply of two AAA batteries or USB [13]. The ECG was recorded with electrodes attached to the right arm and left ankle (2-lead ECG measurement) at a sampling frequency of 1 kHz. The measured ECG was sent to the PC via the USB port and the ECG was analyzed using the real-time monitoring of ANS (Reflex Meijin, Crosswell Corporation, Yokohama, Japan) [11]. All R waves (sharp deflections corresponding to electrical excitation of the ventricles) were detected, and RR intervals (RRI) were obtained for each beat. HRV was analyzed by separating the variability in the RRI time series into the time and frequency domains. The time domain indices used were the mean heart rate [MHR, bpm] and the coefficient of variation of RRI [CVRR %]. The CVRR was calculated by dividing the standard deviation of the RRI by its mean value. The frequency domain indices used were LFP (power of low frequency component; 0.04–0.15 Hz, [ms^2]), HFP (power of high frequency component; 0.15–0.45 Hz, [ms^2]), and LFP/HFP (LFP to HFP ratio). These indices were calculated beat-by-beat from the RRI over 30 s using the maximum entropy method (MEM). LFP reflects both sympathetic and parasympathetic activity and baroreceptor reflex sensitivity, and HFP reflects parasympathetic activity. LFP/HFP reflects sympathetic nerve activity [14,15].

In addition, OLT was performed using the same manufacturer's blood pressure and HRV analysis software [11]. This software calculates the mean HRV indices and other indices of ANS from posture changes during 2 min of sitting, 1 min immediately after standing, and 2 min of maintaining the standing position. Methods for power spectral density analysis of RRI time series include fast Fourier transform (FFT), coefficient estimation of autoregressive model (ARM), and MEM [16–18]. FFT and ARM are mainly used in stable states where body movement does not change significantly. On the other hand, MEM enables us to also analyze transient states where body movements change significantly in a short period of time [18]. Therefore, it is suitable for real-time frequency analysis even in a state where HRV fluctuates significantly during OLT.

2.3.2. Measurement of PVT

PVT is known internationally as a measure of sleepiness, fatigue, and PVL [19–21]. Using a computer and mouse, subjects repeatedly performed the simple task of clicking the mouse when a number (elapsed time) appeared on the display for several minutes. By measuring this reaction time and analyzing the variance, it is possible to objectively evaluate levels of sleep deprivation and fatigue. To investigate PVL before and after smell presentation, reaction times of the mouse click (RT, ms) and the number of times RT was between 500 ms and 1000 ms (minor lapse: ML, %) were measured using the PVT. The number of flying starts (FSs) was also measured. The measurement time was 300 s, the waiting time until the value was displayed on the screen was between 2 s and 10 s, and RTs exceeding 1000 ms were excluded. The PVT software used was the PVT Meijin (Crosswell Corporation, Yokohama, Japan) [11]. PVT was performed using a 15.6-inch laptop (Panasonic, Windows11, Let's note SV8). The distance from the subject's eyes to the screen was approximately 70 cm, and the PVT font size was 72 pt.

2.3.3. Measurement of Other Biosignals

In parallel to the ECG, the following biosignals were measured: skin conductance level (SCL, Electro Dermal Activity Sensors, PLUX wireless biosignals S.A., Lisbon, Portugal), pulse wave variability and skin temperature (SilmeeW22, TDK Corporation, Tokyo, Japan), and seat pressure distribution (SR Soft Vision Numeric Version, Sumitomo Riko Company Limited, Nagoya, Japan).

The performance specifications of the Electro Dermal Activity Sensors are as follows: a range of 0–24 µS, a bandwidth of 0–3 Hz, a consumption of 0–0.72 mA, and a sampling frequency of 1 kHz. The sensor was a 2-wire-type with polarity, with the positive and negative sensors attached to the index and middle fingers of the left hand, respectively.

The SilmeeW22 was a wristwatch-type pulse wave sensor and it was worn on the left wrist. For pulse wave detection, volume pulse waves were measured with a green LED at a sampling frequency of 20 Hz. The temperature sensor used was a digital semiconductor temperature sensor to measure the skin temperature of the wrist in the range of $-10\,°C$ to $45\,°C$. These biosignals were recorded every minute [22].

The seat pressure distribution was measured using SR Soft Vision Numeric Version. The seat size was 450 mm × 450 mm (detection area: 350 mm × 350 mm), there were 256 measurement points (16 × 16), the spatial resolution was 22 mm^2 square, the measurement range was 20–200 mmHg, and the screen update interval was approximately 0.2 s [23].

2.4. Subjective Evaluation of Smell

After the smell presentation, the subjects answered a subjective evaluation questionnaire of the smell (Table 2). The evaluation questions included smell intensity, comfort level, and liking. Smell intensity was rated on a scale of 6 levels, comfort level on a scale of 9 levels, and liking on a scale of 5 levels.

Table 2. Subjective evaluation of smell in the work booth.

Q1. How intense was the smell?	
0	Smell-less
1	Barely detectable smell
2	Weak smell
3	Easy to detect smell
4	Strong smell
5	Intense smell
Q2. How comfortable or uncomfortable did you find the smell?	
−4	Extremely uncomfortable
−3	Very uncomfortable
−2	Uncomfortable
−1	Slightly uncomfortable
0	Neither comfortable nor uncomfortable
1	Slightly comfortable
2	Comfortable
3	Very comfortable
4	Extremely comfortable
Q3. How much did you like the smell?	
−2	Disliked
−1	Slightly disliked
0	Neither liked nor disliked
1	Slightly liked
2	Liked

2.5. Experimental Protocol

The twelve subjects were divided into group A (N = 6, 3 females, 28 ± 5 years old) and group B (N = 6, 3 females, 27 ± 9 years old). The experiment was performed between 9:00 a.m. and 5:00 p.m. on 13 December 2023, and subjects were fully informed in advance. The experimental protocol adopted a crossover design to account for the order of smell presentation. In the morning, LNL was presented to group A and T2N was presented to group B. In the afternoon, T2N was presented to group A and LNL was presented to group B. First, the airborne fragrance concentration inside the booth was adjusted. Next, subjects were fitted with electrodes and sensors outside the booth and performed the OLT (5 min) and PVT (5 min). After sitting in a chair and resting for 5 min, they entered the booth and sat in the chair with their eyes open for 10 min. After that, subjects exited the booth and performed a sitting rest (5 min), the OLT (5 min), PVT (5 min), and subjective evaluation (5 min), at which point the morning experiment was concluded (Table 3).

Table 3. Timetable of experiment.

Events	OLT1	PVT1	Rest1	Smell presentation	Rest2	OLT1	PVT2	Subjective evaluation
Measurements	ECG	RT, ML	ECG, pulse, SCL	ECG, pulse, SCL, seat pressure	ECG, pulse, SCL	ECG	RT, ML	Psychology
Time [min]	5	10	15	25	30	35	40	45

The total experiment time was approximately 45 min per subject. While the subject was in the booth, the next subject performed the OLT and PVT. In the afternoon experiment, similar measurements were performed with different smell presentations. These experiments were performed simultaneously for both Group A and Group B. The washout period for the smell effect on each subject was approximately 3 h. The instructions given to the subjects were as follows: Get enough sleep the night before the experiment and avoid drinking alcohol. On the day of the experiment, avoid smoking and eating or drinking anything with a strong smell.

2.6. Statistical Analysis

In this study, we measured many biosignals to evaluate the effect of smell on biological conditions. This paper focused on the ECG, the PVT, and subjective evaluation data, and analyzed separately for both sexes to investigate whether the two types of smell significantly changed ANS and PVL. Data of the OLT were analyzed using univariate general linear models (UGLM) to investigate whether there were significant differences in HRV indices due to 2 factors: before and after smell presentation (factor 1: 2 levels) and posture change (factor 2: 3 levels). The mean of HRV indices during smell presentation and at rest before and after smell presentation were calculated for each subject, and HRV indices were analyzed using UGLM with 2 factors: smell presentation (factor 1: 2 levels) and event change (factor 2: 3 levels; rest1, smell, rest2). UGLM analysis was adjusted for age as a covariate. The RT and ML measured from the PVT were compared before and after smell presentation using paired t-tests. In the subjective evaluation, the questions about the two types of smells were compared using paired t-tests. The statistical software used was IBM SPSS Statistics (version 28.0.1.0, Armonk, NY, USA). The significance level was set at 5%, with $p < 0.05$ for significance and $p < 0.1$ for trends.

3. Results

Figures 3 and 4 show the results of the OLT before and after the presentation of the LNL smell in males and females, respectively. In males, LFP increased significantly after smell presentation compared with before ($p = 0.045$). Furthermore, all HRV indices showed significant differences for posture change ($p < 0.01$). In females, CVRR increased significantly after smell presentation compared with before ($p = 0.010$). MHR, CVRR, HFP, and LFP/HFP showed significant differences for posture change ($p < 0.05$). There was no interaction between the two factors in both males and females.

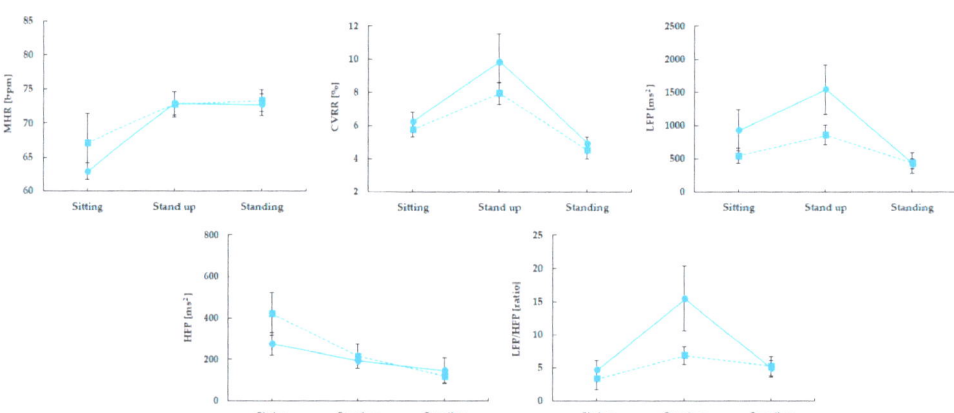

Figure 3. OLT before and after presentation of LNL smell in males. ●: after smell presentation; ■: before smell presentation; mean ± S.E. Factor 1 (before and after smell presentation): LFP ($p = 0.045$). Factor 2 (posture change): MHR ($p = 0.002$), CVRR ($p < 0.001$), LFP ($p = 0.003$), HFP ($p < 0.001$), LFP/HFP ($p = 0.010$). Interaction between the two factors: no interaction.

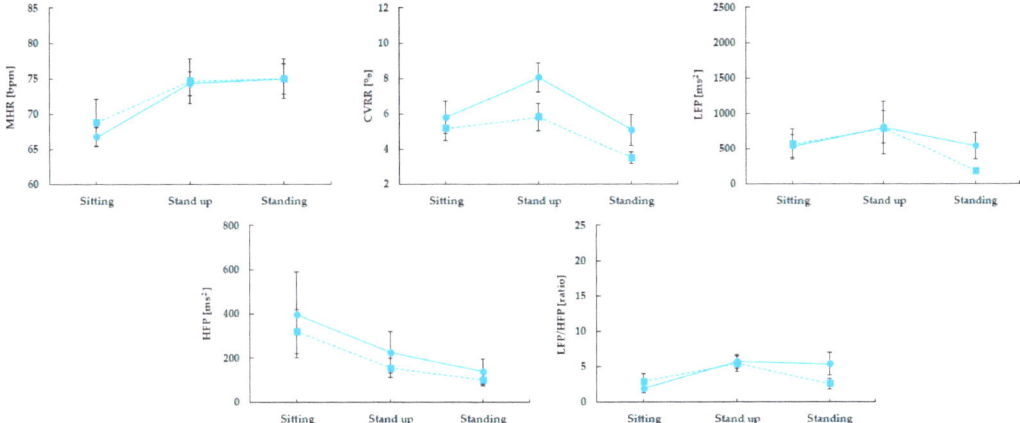

Figure 4. OLT before and after presentation of LNL smell in females. ●: after smell presentation; ■: before smell presentation; mean ± S.E. Factor 1 (before and after smell presentation): CVRR ($p = 0.010$). Factor 2 (posture change): MHR ($p < 0.001$), CVRR ($p = 0.002$), HFP ($p = 0.047$), LFP/HFP ($p = 0.016$). Interaction between the two factors: no interaction.

Figures 5 and 6 show the results of the OLT before and after the presentation of the T2N smell in males and females, respectively. In males, no significant differences were shown in any of the HRV indices before and after smell presentation. All HRV indices showed significant differences for posture change ($p < 0.01$). There was no interaction between the two factors. In females, CVRR and LFP/HFP showed increasing trends after smell presentation compared with before (CVRR: $p = 0.083$, LFP/HFP: $p = 0.055$). MHR, CVRR, HFP, and LFP/HFP showed significant or trend differences for posture change ($p < 0.1$). An interaction between the two factors was shown in LFP/HFP ($p = 0.050$).

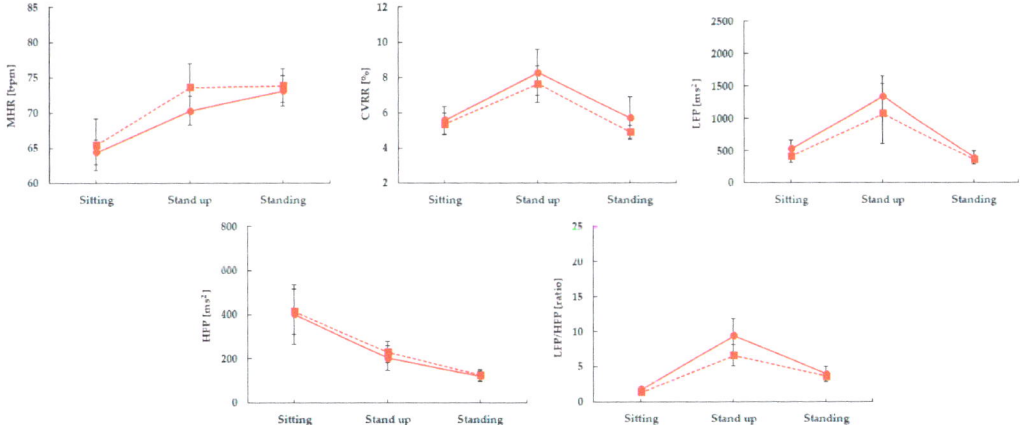

Figure 5. OLT before and after presentation of T2N smell in males. ●: after smell presentation; ■: before smell presentation; mean ± S.E. Factor 1 (before and after smell presentation): no significant difference. Factor 2 (posture change): MHR ($p = 0.006$), CVRR ($p = 0.005$), LFP ($p = 0.002$), HFP ($p = 0.001$), LFP/HFP ($p < 0.001$). Interaction between the two factors: no interaction.

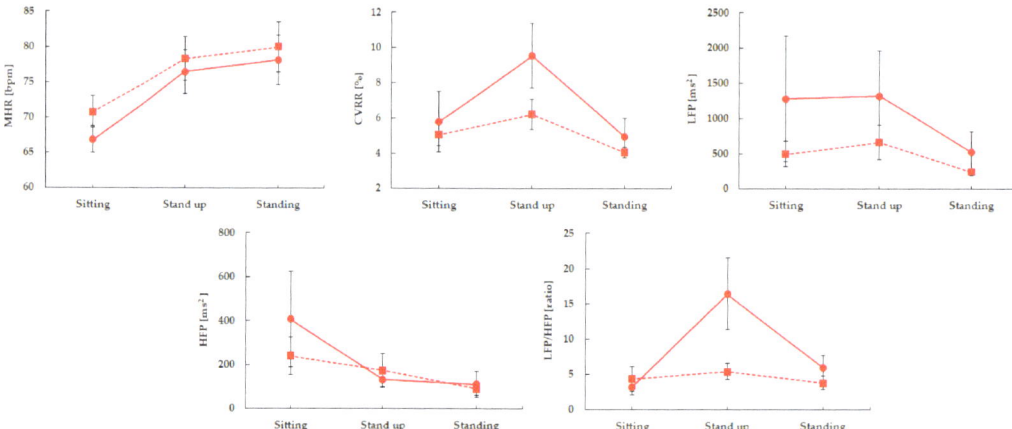

Figure 6. OLT before and after presentation of T2N smell in females. ●: after smell presentation; ■: before smell presentation; mean ± S.E. Factor 1 (before and after smell presentation): CVRR ($p = 0.083$), LFP/HFP ($p = 0.055$). Factor 2 (posture change): MHR ($p < 0.001$), CVRR ($p = 0.015$), HFP ($p = 0.087$), LFP/HFP ($p < 0.014$). Interaction between the two factors: LFP/HFP ($p = 0.050$).

Figures 7 and 8 show the changes in HRV indices during rest and smell presentation in males and females, respectively.

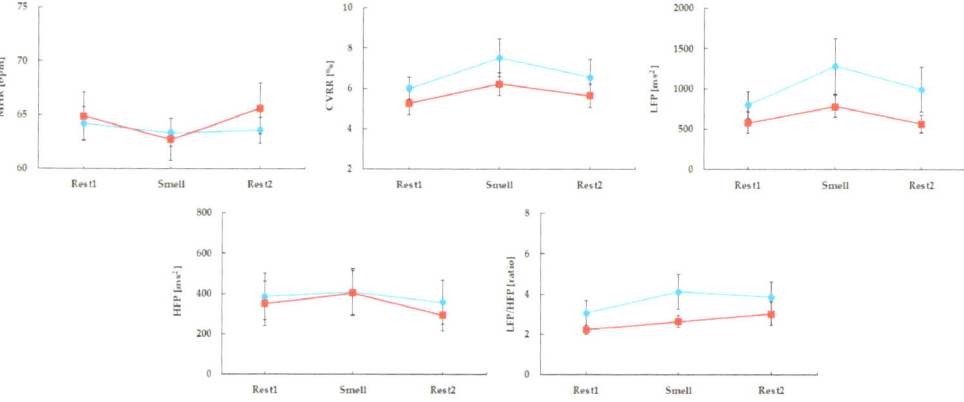

Figure 7. Changes in HRV indices during rest and smell presentation in males. ●: LNL; ■: T2N; mean ± S.E. Factor 1 (smell): CVRR ($p = 0.063$), LFP ($p = 0.024$), LFP/HFP ($p = 0.070$). Factor 2 (event change): no significant difference. Interaction between the two factors: no interaction.

In males, CVRR, LFP, and LFP/HFP were significantly increased or showed an increasing trend in LNL compared with T2N (CVRR: $p = 0.063$, LFP: $p = 0.024$, LFP/HFP: $p = 0.070$). No significant differences were shown in any of the HRV indices for event change. In females, MHR was significantly decreased in LNL compared with T2N ($p = 0.005$), and MHR showed a decreasing trend for event change. There was no interaction between the two factors in both males and females.

Figures 9 and 10 show the changes in PVT indices before and after smell presentation in males and females. In males, no significant differences were shown in any of the indices in both LNL and T2N. In females, RT increased significantly after smell presentation compared with before for T2N ($p = 0.049$), and ML showed an increasing trend after smell presentation compared with before for T2N ($p = 0.087$).

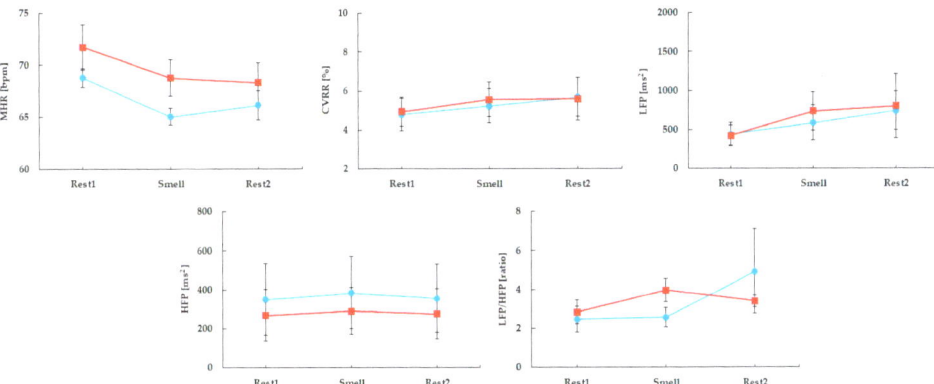

Figure 8. Changes in HRV indices during rest and smell presentation in females. ●: LNL; ■: T2N; mean ± S.E. Factor 1 (smell): MHR (p = 0.005). Factor 2 (event change): MHR (p = 0.060). Interaction between the two factors: no interaction.

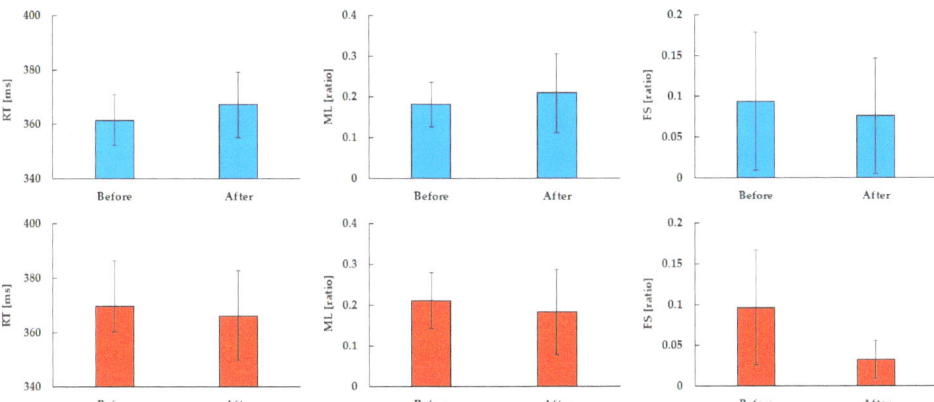

Figure 9. Changes in PVT indices before and after smell presentation in males. ■: LNL; ■: T2N; mean ± S.E., no significant difference.

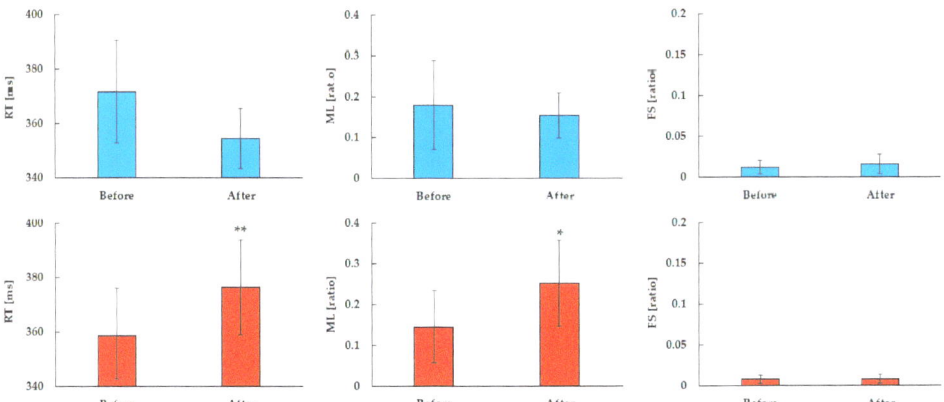

Figure 10. Changes in PVT indices before and after smell presentation in females. ■: LNL; ■: T2N; mean ± S.E. ** p = 0.049; * p = 0.087 vs. before.

Table 4 shows the results of the subjective evaluation for males and females. Values are shown as means and standard errors. The smell intensity tended to be stronger in T2N than LNL in females ($p = 0.093$). Males and females were more comfortable with LNL than T2N (males: $p < 0.001$, females: $p = 0.007$) and LNL was liked by them (males: $p = 0.025$, females: $p = 0.003$). Focusing on the mean values for each question, for LNL, the values in males were as follows: Q1, "Weak smell"; Q2, at a level ranging from "Neither comfortable nor uncomfortable" to "Slightly comfortable"; and Q3, "Neither liking nor disliking". For Q1, females were at a level ranging from "Barely detectable smell" to "Weak smell"; for Q2, "Slightly comfortable"; and for Q3, "Slightly liking". For T2N, males were as follows: Q1, "Weak smell"; Q2, at a level ranging from "Slightly uncomfortable" to "Uncomfortable"; and Q3, "Slightly disliking". For Q1, females were at a level ranging from "Weak smell" to "Easy to detect smell"; for Q2, "Slightly uncomfortable"; and for Q3, "Slightly disliking".

Table 4. Mean and standard error of subjective evaluation for males and females.

Question Items	Males			Females		
	LNL	T2N	p-Value	LNL	T2N	p-Value
Smell intensity	2.3 ± 0.2	2.5 ± 0.3	0.611	1.8 ± 0.4	2.7 ± 0.4	0.093
Comfortable/Uncomfortable	0.7 ± 0.4	−1.7 ± 0.3	<0.001	1.2 ± 0.5	−1.3 ± 0.4	0.007
Liking	0.2 ± 0.3	−1.2 ± 0.3	0.025	1.0 ± 0.4	−1.3 ± 0.4	0.003

4. Discussion

In this paper, we evaluated ANS and PVL when smell stimuli of LNL and T2N were presented in a work booth using HRV and PVT. First, the smells used in this experiment were LNL and T2N. The subjective evaluation of how these smells were felt by the subjects revealed that neither of the smells was extremely comfortable nor uncomfortable, but rather slightly comfortable or slightly uncomfortable.

LNL was slightly preferred by females compared to males, and T2N was slightly dislikable by both males and females. At a slight level, significant differences were observed between LNL and T2N in the comfortable/uncomfortable questions and preferences for both males and females. In questions of smell intensity, both males and females rated the smells as weak smells; however, they were easy to detect, which was roughly the middle level of the intensity scale. However, females felt the smell to be significantly stronger with T2N than with LNL.

In the OLT, immediately after active standing, peripheral vascular resistance decreases, and over time, venous return decreases and cardiac output decreases, resulting in a decrease in arterial pressure. To prevent a decrease in arterial pressure, the baroreceptor reflex is activated, promoting sympathetic nervous activity and keeping blood pressure by increasing vascular resistance and heart rate [24,25]. In the standing test, MHR, LFP, and LFP/HFP increased immediately after standing in both males and females regardless of the type of smell, revealing that the baroreceptor reflex was functioning normally. Comparing the OLT results before and after smell presentation, LFP increased after LNL presentation in males, and CVRR and LFP/HFP increased after T2N presentation in females. These results suggest that after LNL in males and T2N in females, the baroreflex sensitivity increases, and that RR interval variability is also increased, especially in females.

In the work booth, CVRR, LFP, and LFP/HFP increased in males with LNL compared to T2N. In addition to blood pressure variability, factors that cause the increase in LFP include respiratory sinus arrhythmia caused by slow respiration of 0.15 Hz or less [26,27]. Since there was no body movement and conversation in the work booth, and the subjects were sitting quietly in their chairs, it is unlikely that the rhythm of respiration was a factor in the increase in LFP. Therefore, it suggests that the cause of LFP increase is blood pressure variability due to LNL, and that LNL has the effect of promoting sympathetic nervous activity. It is considered that CVRR increased due to an increase in the LF component of HRV. MHR in females was higher with LNL compared to T2N. Because the baseline MHR was different from that at rest, it is unlikely that this difference was due to LNL or T2N; however, this suggests that MHR decreases regardless of the smell.

In the PVT, no difference was observed in PVL after the presentation of the two types of smells in males, but RT was significantly slower after the presentation of T2N in females, and ML tended to increase. Since increased sympathetic nervous activity was observed in females after T2N presentation, it is considered that the stress of the uncomfortable smell increased sympathetic nervous activity and reduced PVL. On the other hand, in females, although sympathetic nervous activity was promoted during and after LNL presentation, there was no difference in PVL between LNL and T2N. This suggests that the factors behind the changes in PVL due to the smell may involve not only ANS, but also the subjective perception of the smell.

There are many previous studies on ANS related to LNL. Lin H et al. (2017) reported that the aromatherapy group performed faster on a PC task than the control group, and there was a significant difference in HRV [28]. Eva H et al. (2004) reported on physiological parameters and subjective well-being after transdermal administration of LNL and found a decrease in systolic blood pressure and skin temperature, but no effect on well-being [29]. Kyoko K et al. (2005) reported the effect of the scent of jasmine tea, which contains LNL, on ANS and mood [30]. The concentration used in this experiment was at a level that did not cause psychological effects, and the promotion of parasympathetic nervous activity was confirmed.

On the other hand, there are no research papers on HRV analysis when T2N is presented, but there are research papers on uncomfortable smells. Croy I et al. (2013) reported that uncomfortable smells attract a lot of attention, but when presented repeatedly, only the emotional salience decreases, which is reflected in a decrease in neural activity [31]. Iordanis K et al. (2006) suggested that smells perceived as uncomfortable are age-invariant [32]. Mateus H et al. (2020) investigated the effect of uncomfortable vomit smells from fermented foods on subjects' emotions and found feelings of sadness [33]. Yukei H et al. (2019) suggested that the subjective uncomfortableness of smells itself can trigger emotions and stress responses in sympathetic nervous activity [5].

These previous studies results confirm that parasympathetic nervous activity is promoted by LNL, which improves PC task time. However, the results of this study showed that LNL did not significantly affect ANS or PVL in females, whereas sympathetic nervous activity was promoted in males. It has been reported that sympathetic nervous activity is promoted by negative psychological stress [34], but also by positive psychological stress [35]. The subjective evaluation by males showed slightly positive results from LNL, and it is possible that the comfort of LNL increased sympathetic nervous activity. On the other hand, previous studies have shown that uncomfortable smells induce negative emotions and stress, and sympathetic nervous activity is promoted. Both males and females found T2N mildly uncomfortable and did not like it, but the promotion of sympathetic nervous activity in females is consistent with previous studies. Gender differences were observed in ANS and PVL, and in particular, females may reduce work performance due to the uncomfortable smell.

In this experiment, the smell was sprayed using a diffuser in a work booth, which is a small space for one person, and the airborne fragrance concentration was different from that in previous studies, so it is not possible to simply compare the results with previous studies. Furthermore, because this was a large-scale experiment using a work booth, there is a limitation in that the number of subjects collected was relatively small. As work booths become more widespread in the future, it will be necessary to verify the reproducibility of the research results.

5. Conclusions

This study mainly focused on the practical application of medical electronic devices in daily life and the pursuit of spatial comfort. We investigated the effects of the smell environment in the work booth on ANS and PVL using LNL and T2N. These effects were clarified by analyzing gender differences. This analysis focused on HRV and PVT data, but we have also measured skin conductance level, seat pressure distribution, and skin temperature, and will aim to quantify the subjective perception of smells by clarifying human responses to comfortable and uncomfortable smells using a multimodal analysis. We believe that the insights gained from this research will provide the basis for potential future hardware innovations.

Author Contributions: E.Y. designed the main conceptual ideas, supervised the project, and wrote the manuscript. Y.Y. analyzed the data and wrote the manuscript. A.O. and A.Y. supported the design of experiment, data collection, and interpretation of the results. All authors have read and agreed to the published version of the manuscript.

Funding: This work was supported by the New Energy and Industrial Technology Development Organization (NEDO).

Institutional Review Board Statement: The studies involving human participants were reviewed and approved by the Graduate School of Information Sciences Tohoku University Institutional Review Board (No. 23A-06; approved 29 November 2023).

Informed Consent Statement: Informed consent was obtained from all subjects involved in this study.

Data Availability Statement: Data is contained within the article.

Conflicts of Interest: Authors A.O. and A.Y. were employed by the company Fuji Industrial Co., Ltd. The remaining authors declare that the research was conducted in the absence of any commercial or financial relationships that could be construed as a potential conflict of interest.

References

1. Tamaki, M.; Hiroyuki, A.; Tatsuya, H. Does lavender aromatherapy alleviate premenstrual emotional symptoms?: A randomized crossover trial. *Biopsychosoc. Med.* **2013**, *7*, 12.
2. Alessia, B.; Sophie, D.; Sonia, P.; Renaud, B. Relaxing effects of music and odors on physiological recovery after cognitive stress and unexpected absence of multisensory benefit. *Psychophysiology* **2023**, *60*, e14251.
3. Pin, H.L.; Yuan, P.L.; Kai, L.C.; Shang, Y.Y.; Yin, H.S.; Po, Y.W. Effect of aromatherapy on autonomic nervous system regulation with treadmill exercise-induced stress among adolescents. *PLoS ONE* **2021**, *16*, e0249795.
4. Reiko, S.; Kazuya, M.; Akira, U.; Yoshikazu, I.; Shigenobu, K. Effectiveness of aroma on work efficiency: Lavender aroma during recesses prevents deterioration of work performance. *Comp. Study Chem. Senses* **2005**, *30*, 683–691.
5. Yukei, H.; Mika, S.; Masako, O.; Kazushige, T. Subjective unpleasantness of malodors induces a stress response. *Psychoneuroendo Crinology* **2019**, *106*, 206–215.
6. Jugreet, B.S.; Fawzi, M.M.; Gokhan, Z.; Filippo, M. Essential Oils as Natural Sources of Fragrance Compounds for Cosmetics and Cosmeceuticals. *Molecules* **2021**, *26*, 666. [CrossRef]
7. Brain, K.R.; Green, D.M.; Jones, A.C.; Walters, K.A.; Api, A.M.; Selechnik, D.; Joshi, K. In vitro human skin absorption of linalool: Effects of vehicle composition, evaporation and occlusion on permeation and distribution. *Int. J. Pharm.* **2022**, *622*, 121826. [CrossRef]
8. Shinobu, N.; Mio, M.; Mitsuhiro, D. Effects of trans-2-nonenal and olfactory masking odorants on proliferation of human keratino cytes. *Biochem. Biophys. Res. Commun.* **2021**, *548*, 1–6.
9. Kenta, I.; Hidehisa, M.; Kenta, I.; Koji, T.; Takahiro, A.; Yasuhiko, I.; Kohji, M. Gas-Phase Biosensors (Bio-Sniffers) for Measurement of 2-Nonenal, the Causative Volatile Molecule of Human Aging-Related Body Odor. *Sensors* **2023**, *23*, 5857. [CrossRef]
10. Mathias, B.; Daniel, M.; David, F.D. Validity and Sensitivity of a Brief Psychomotor Vigilance Test (PVT-B) to Total and Partial Sleep Deprivation. *Acta Astronaut.* **2011**, *69*, 949–959.
11. Crosswell. Available online: https://crosswell.co.jp (accessed on 20 June 2024).
12. Shinya, T.; Ineko, T.; Koki, M.; Keiko, M. Study on Ventilation Issues Focused on Ventilation Behavior during the Inter-mediate Season of Nursery Facilities in Urban Area. *J. Environ. Eng.* **2023**, *88*, 288–299.
13. GMS. Available online: http://gms-jp.com/index.html (accessed on 29 August 2024).
14. Task Force of the European Society of Cardiology; the North American Society of Pacing and Electrophysiology. Heart rate variability: Standards of measurement, physiological interpretation and clinical use. *Circulation* **1996**, *93*, 1043–1065. [CrossRef]
15. Elghozi, J.L.; Laude, D.; Girard, A. Effects of respiration on blood pressure and heart rate variability in humans. *Clin. Exp. Pharmacol. Physiol.* **1991**, *18*, 735–742. [CrossRef]
16. Rozentryt, P.; Trzos, G.; Strłojewski, D.; Kozlowski, J.W.; Maciejewski, M. The effect of orthostatic provocation on the spectral pattern of heart rate variability in healthy subjects. *Przegl. Lek.* **1996**, *53*, 534–539. [PubMed]
17. Thorsten, S.; Bernhard, H.; Christian, W.; Jürgen, S.; Christian, J. Evaluation of techniques for estimating the power spectral density of RR-intervals under paced respiration conditions. *J. Clin. Monit. Comput.* **2014**, *28*, 481–486.

18. Yasuyuki, S.; Yoshinori, K.; Taketaro, S.; Koichiro, A.; Keitaro, A.; Sarasa, I.; Fumiaki, Y.; Kazutaka, M.; Takahiko, N.; Yuichi, T.; et al. Real-Time Analysis of the Heart Rate Variability during Incremental Exercise for the Detection of the Ventilatory Threshold. *J. Am. Heart Assoc.* **2018**, *7*, e006612.
19. Al-Baraa, A.A.; Ahmad, S.N.I.; Maged, S.A.; Noreen, K. Implementation of a psychomotor vigilance test to investigate the effects of driving fatigue on oil and gas truck drivers' performance. *Front. Public Health* **2023**, *11*, 1160317.
20. Thitaporn, C.; Emily, K.S.; Connie, L.T.; Margaux, E.B.; John, D.H.; Thomas, J.B.; Tracy, J.D. Quantifying the effects of sleep loss: Relative effect sizes of the psychomotor vigilance test, multiple sleep latency test, and maintenance of wakefulness test. *Sleep Adv.* **2022**, *3*, zpac034.
21. Dinges, D.F.; Powell, J.W. Microcomputer analysis of performance on a portable, simple visual RT task during sustained operations. *Behav. Res. Methods Instrum. Comput.* **1985**, *17*, 652–655. [CrossRef]
22. Yutaka, Y.; Emi, Y. Workout Detection by Wearable Device Data Using Machine Learning. *Appl. Sci.* **2023**, *13*, 4280. [CrossRef]
23. Sumitomo Riko. Available online: https://www.sumitomoriko.co.jp/product/health/SVZB4545L/ (accessed on 29 August 2024).
24. Mitsuhiro, A. Orthostatic Test. *Equilibrium Res.* **2021**, *80*, 159–166.
25. Bruno, E.; Ana, L.R.; Raúl, M.M.; Rube, F.; Fermín, G.; Katherine, B.; Sofía, M.B.; Guillermo, D.G.; Alejandro, F. From supine to standing: In vivo segregation of myogenic and baroreceptor vasoconstriction in humans. *Physiol. Rep.* **2016**, *4*, e13053.
26. Masahito, S. Evaluation of Heart Rate Variability and Application of Heart Rate Variability Biofeedback: Toward Further Research on Slow-Paced Abdominal Breathing in Zen Meditation. *Appl. Psychophysiol. Biofeedback* **2022**, *47*, 345–356.
27. Masahito, S.; Munehisa, K.; Leo, O.O. Efficacy of Paced Breathing at the Low-frequency Peak on Heart Rate Variability and Baroreflex Sensitivity. *Appl. Psychophysiol. Biofeedback* **2020**, *45*, 31–37.
28. Lin, H.; Lluis, C. Aromatherapy Improves Work Performance Through Balancing the Autonomic Nervous System. *J. Altern. Complement. Med.* **2017**, *23*, 214–221.
29. Eva, H.; Sandra, R.; Gerhard, B. Transdermal absorption of (−)-linalool induces autonomic deactivation but has no impact on ratings of well-being in humans. *Neuropsychopharmacology* **2004**, *29*, 1925–1932.
30. Kyoko, K.; Naohiko, I.; Yuriko, I.; Kikue, K.; Akio, S.; Takami, K.; Tohru, F. Sedative effects of the jasmine tea odor and (R)-(−)-linalool, one of its major odor components, on autonomic nerve activity and mood states. *Eur. J. Appl. Physiol.* **2005**, *95*, 107–114.
31. Croy, I.; Maboshe, W.; Hummel, T. Habituation effects of pleasant and unpleasant odors. *Int. J. Psychophysiol.* **2013**, *88*, 104–108. [CrossRef]
32. Iordanis, K.; Thomas, H.; Maria, L. Identification of unpleasant odors is independent of age. *Arch. Clin. Neuropsychol.* **2006**, *21*, 615–621.
33. Mateus, H.G.M.; Leandro, Y.M.; Janaina, P.S.; Gerson, A.P.J.; Alessandra, M. Emotional recognition for simulated clinical environment using unpleasant odors: Quasi-experimental study. *Rev. Lat. Am. Enfermagem.* **2020**, *28*, e3248.
34. Servant, D.; Logier, R.; Mouster, Y.; Goudemand, M. Heart rate variability. Applications in psychiatry. *Encephale* **2009**, *35*, 423–428. [CrossRef] [PubMed]
35. Willem, J.K.; Stephen, J.S.; Miranda, E.N.; Louis, A.S.; Shari, R.W.; Nathan, A.F. Autonomic nervous system reactivity to positive and negative mood induction: The role of acute psychological responses and frontal electrocortical activity. *Biol. Psychol.* **2011**, *86*, 230–238.

Disclaimer/Publisher's Note: The statements, opinions and data contained in all publications are solely those of the individual author(s) and contributor(s) and not of MDPI and/or the editor(s). MDPI and/or the editor(s) disclaim responsibility for any injury to people or property resulting from any ideas, methods, instructions or products referred to in the content.

Article

Artificial Intelligence Implementation in Internet of Things Embedded System for Real-Time Person Presence in Bed Detection and Sleep Behaviour Monitor

Minh Long Hoang *, Guido Matrella * and Paolo Ciampolini

Department of Engineering and Architecture, University of Parma, 43124 Parma, Italy; paolo.ciampolini@unipr.it
* Correspondence: minhlong.hoang@unipr.it (M.L.H.); guido.matrella@unipr.it (G.M.)

Abstract: This paper works on detecting a person in bed for sleep routine and sleep pattern monitoring based on the Micro-Electro-Mechanical Systems (MEMS) accelerometer and Internet of Things (IoT) embedded system board. This work provides sleep information, patient assessment, and elderly care for patients who live alone via tele-distance to doctors or family members. About 216,000 pieces of acceleration data were collected, including three classes: no person in bed, a static laying position, and a moving state for Artificial Intelligence (AI) application. Six well-known Machine-Learning (ML) algorithms were evaluated with precision, recall, F1-score, and accuracy in the workstation before implementing in the STM32-microcontroller for real-time state classification. The four best algorithms were selected to be programmed into the IoT board and applied for real-time testing. The results demonstrate the high accuracy of the ML performance, more than 99%, and the Classification and Regression Tree algorithm is among the best models with a light code size of 1583 bytes. The smart bed information is sent to the IoT dashboard of Node-RED via a Message Queuing Telemetry broker (MQTT).

Keywords: person on bed detection; sleep pattern; machine learning; artificial intelligence; accelerometer; smart bed

Citation: Hoang, M.L.; Matrella, G.; Ciampolini, P. Artificial Intelligence Implementation in Internet of Things Embedded System for Real-Time Person Presence in Bed Detection and Sleep Behaviour Monitor. *Electronics* **2024**, *13*, 2210. https://doi.org/10.3390/electronics13112210

Academic Editors: Ilaria Sergi and Teodoro Montanaro

Received: 30 April 2024
Revised: 30 May 2024
Accepted: 3 June 2024
Published: 6 June 2024

Copyright: © 2024 by the authors. Licensee MDPI, Basel, Switzerland. This article is an open access article distributed under the terms and conditions of the Creative Commons Attribution (CC BY) license (https://creativecommons.org/licenses/by/4.0/).

1. Introduction

The incorporation of cutting-edge technologies such as Micro-Electro-Mechanical Systems (MEMS) accelerometers [1–3], Internet of Things (IoT) frameworks [4–7], and Machine-Learning (ML) [8–10] algorithms has significantly transformed healthcare monitoring, specifically in the field of sleep pattern analysis. Sleeping on time and a deep sleep are key to health maintenance [11]. For restless sleep, like insomnia [12], examples of symptoms shown would be tossing and turning, and trying to get settled and comfortable [13]. The capacity to autonomously identify the existence of an individual on a bed and differentiate between their stationary rest and restless movements carries great importance in diverse healthcare settings. The significance of adequately classifying sleep conditions, such as stationary lying positions or frequent motion, cannot be underestimated. Detecting variations from typical sleep patterns can assist in the early identification of sleep disorders, assess the efficacy of therapics, and reduce potential health hazards linked to inadequate sleep quality. Moreover, for persons with persistent ailments or elderly individuals who are susceptible to falls or disruptions while sleeping, prompt intervention with live monitoring can significantly improve their quality of life and autonomy.

In the article [14], movement activity was extracted from the multichannel ballistocardiography measurements based on Emfit sensor foils placed in the bed mattress, which has a total accuracy of 83%. However, the BCG data's noise, artifacts, or signal distortions can complicate the signal processing algorithms and reduce their accuracy in detecting movement events. Maintaining and calibrating Emfit sensor foils regularly is necessary to ensure their optimal performance over time. Not properly maintaining or calibrating the sensors may result in sensor readings drifting or a decrease in measurement precision, which can affect the reliability of detecting movement activity. This paper discusses the crucial role of technological improvements in enabling patient assessment and aged care, particularly for persons who live alone. It focuses on using remote sleep pattern monitoring to provide valuable information and actionable insights for healthcare professionals and family members.

Another work of research with bed sensors [15] uses eight pressure sensor signals for movement on bed detection by calculating the respiration amplitude using the Hilbert transform, and then identifying events based on a 20% amplitude reduction from the baseline signal. On the other hand, pressure sensor signals can be susceptible to noise and artifacts from various sources, such as movement unrelated to respiration, environmental vibrations, or sensor malfunctions. These noise sources can affect the accuracy of respiration amplitude calculations and event detection, leading to false positives or false negatives in identifying respiration events.

Therefore, we use the MEMS accelerometer, which has a high sensitivity and accuracy in detecting even subtle movements, allowing for the precise monitoring of movements on the bed, including behaviours during sleep. In addition, the MEMS accelerometer is capable of measuring acceleration in multiple axes, providing comprehensive movement data that can capture movements in different directions and orientations on the bed. The ML implementation based on MEMS accelerometers with IoT systems provides a non-invasive and economical method of collecting uninterrupted sleep-related data in real time. The utilization of ML algorithms for classification tasks is crucial in this context because of their ability to identify complicated structures with a high precision.

Various papers apply ML into accelerations for sleep assessment [16]. In [17], a random forest algorithm is used to classify sleep using wrist-worn accelerometer data. Another article [18] uses ActiGraph wGT3X-BT accelerometers on the user's hip for sleep classification with ML. Work [19] creates a device that monitors the sleep stages with a pulse oximeter and accelerometer placed on the wrist, and then applies ML for sleep monitoring. Another work of research [20] develops deep learning for sleep–wake classification with three types of wearable sensors: Faros sensors, a motion watch, and a head watch. Although these approaches reach a certain accuracy, the wearable accelerometers still cause discomfort to the user during long usage.

The smartwatch is also a popular device for health monitoring. Article [21] states that it is safe to wear a smartwatch, but it needs to be removed for several hours to allow the skin to breathe and prevent the accumulation of bacteria beneath the watch. The illumination emanating from the watch or its strap can occasionally disrupt the natural rhythm of sleep. The smartwatch strap can cause skin irritation and inflammation for some people when tightly wrapped around the wrist or when exposed to residual water or sweat. The notifications from the smartwatch can also disturb sleep. It is difficult for many people, especially older people, to wear a device frequently due to annoyance.

Beside the ML algorithms, Deep-Learning (DL) [22] models also have a good command of classifying the signals, such as the Deep Neural Network (DNN) [23], Long Short-Term Memory (LSTM) [24], Bidirectional LSTM [25], etc. Nevertheless, ML has advantages with a simpler implementation, and ML algorithms typically require less computational resources compared to DL algorithms. This point is especially important in microcontroller applications where resources like memory and processing power are limited. In this case, the dataset is not extremely complicated and ML algorithms perform well with certain datasets. Additionally, pre-trained DL models require more time consumption due to their architecture. Thus, the ML approach is selected to minimize the complexity of the whole system.

This study aims to develop a nonwearable platform which is able to monitor the sleep state without physical contact with the users. In this way, comfort is guaranteed for the users, especially for old people who can forget to equip the wearable device frequently. Furthermore, this work identifies the most efficient models for real-time sleep state classification by evaluating various ML algorithms, including the Extra Tree Classifier (ET) [26–29], Logistic Regression (LR) [30–32], Linear Discriminant Analysis (LDA) [33,34], Classification and Regression Trees (CART) [35–40], Support Vector Machines (SVMs) [41,42], and Random Forest (RF) [43–45]. Afterward, the chosen algorithms are implemented in the STM32 embedded system [46] within the IoT framework, allowing a smooth integration into the current healthcare infrastructure for widespread adoption. This research adds to the advancement of sleep pattern monitoring and remote healthcare management by combining MEMS accelerometers, IoT frameworks, and ML algorithms with a microcontroller (MCU) platform. The impacts of our research's results spread throughout the field of sleep research, providing promising possibilities for individualized healthcare interventions and proactive wellness management.

The paper is organized as follows: First, the setup and devices will be depicted, together with the system working principle. In the next section, the ML algorithms will be described briefly; then, it will be their cross-validation and test part. The subsequent content is about the real-time test with the MCU operation and sleep state on the IoT dashboard demonstration. Finally, the conclusion and future work are at the end of the paper.

2. Materials and Methods

In this section, the system architecture and working principle will be shown, together with brief descriptions of the applied ML algorithms.

2.1. Setup and Devices

Figure 1 shows the data acquisition diagram from MCU and MEMS Accelerometer under the IoT bed to the workstation. The STM32 B-L475-IOT01A microcontroller board [47] from the IoT kit has acquired acceleration data using Serial Peripheral Interface (SPI) communication. The data collected by the accelerometer were sent to a workstation for immediate storage in text files. STM32 B-L475-IOT01A was made by STMicroelectronics company which is headquartered in Plan-les-Ouates, Switzerland.

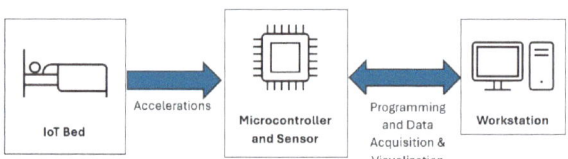

Figure 1. Data acquisition diagram.

For ML model evaluation, these files were trained using Python programming [48], with the packages Scikit-learn [49]. Then, the best models are chosen to implement into MCU via C programming language [50,51] to communicate with the IoT dashboard wirelessly as shown in Figure 2.

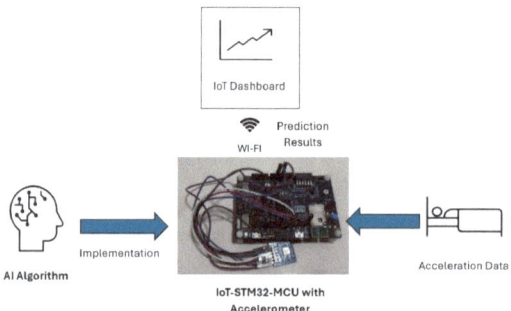

Figure 2. AI implementation in microcontroller (MCU) under IoT communication.

The MEMS accelerometer ADXL355 [52] is concealed within a protective enclosure and positioned accurately beneath the bed frame, as shown in Figure 3, and it is connected to the embedded system platform appropriately. The ADXL355 offers high-resolution measurement capabilities, allowing it to detect even subtle movements during sleep accurately. Its high sensitivity level can provide comprehensive insights into sleep quality and duration. Additionally, for applications like sleep monitoring where the device needs to operate continuously for extended periods, low power consumption is essential to prolong battery life and minimize the need for frequent recharging or replacement. The ADXL355's low power consumption ensures that it can monitor sleep patterns throughout the night without draining the device's battery quickly. ADXL355 was made by Analog Devices Company, which is headquartered in Wilmington, MA, USA.

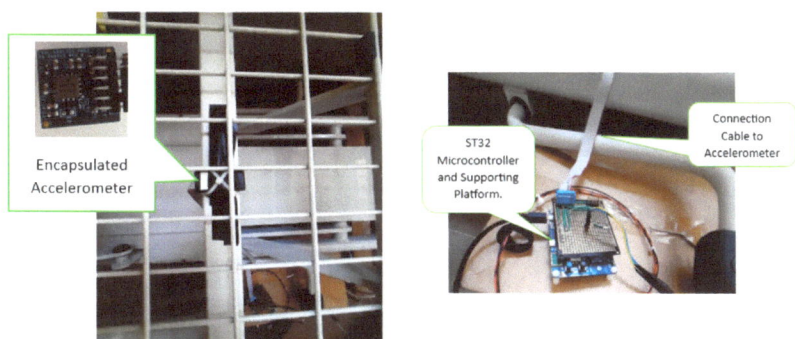

Figure 3. Encapsulated accelerometer and MCU platform under the bed frame.

All the devices were mounted under the bed as shown in Figure 4.

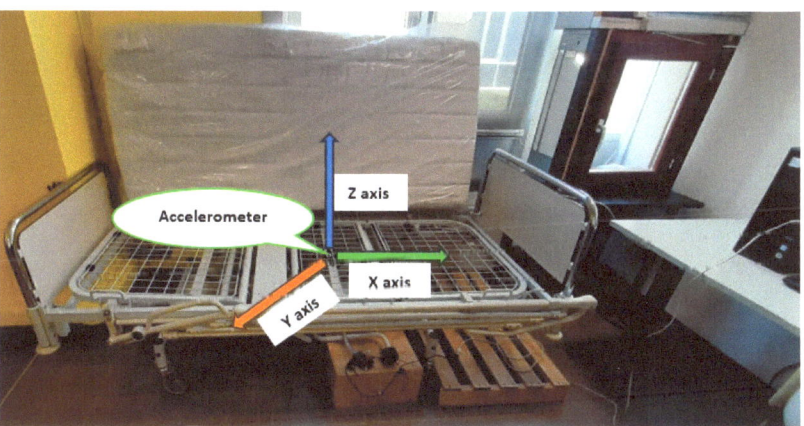

Figure 4. Smart bed under test.

2.2. Raw Data

During the experiment, the user lies on the bed in 4 stationary positions, prone, back, right side, and left side, to collect data for static state. In the dynamic state, the person moves and turns around. Finally, an empty state is carried out where no person is on the bed, and the sensor keeps acquiring the acceleration for data collection. The volunteer participant is more than 30 years old and has a sleeping issue.

Figure 5 shows the raw data in 3 concerned states on all axes: no person in bed; lying static positions (joined data from 4 lying positions), and dynamic motion in bed. It is complicated to detect a proper threshold to recognize and distinguish these states since the data conduct high variations, and their ranges are not so clearly different, especially in the case of no person in bed and lying in static positions. There are also influences from different sleep positions, which cause the data to be more intricate. Thus, it is necessary to use the ML approach to achieve high classification efficiency.

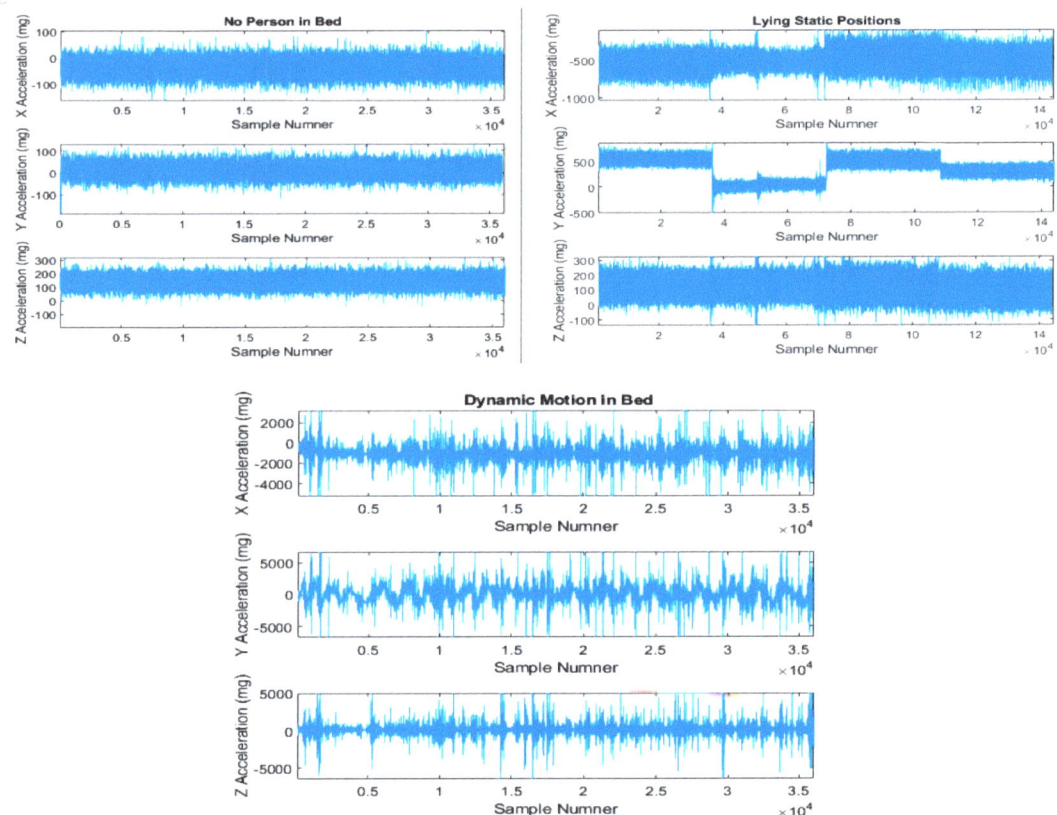

Figure 5. Raw data in 3 states.

2.3. Data Processing and ML features

The output data rate of the device is 200 Sa/s. The absolute difference between 2 consecutive accelerations (Δacc) on the X, Y, and Z axes are calculated as features. There are 216,000 data, containing 1080 windows of 200 samples. The sum of each window is calculated to form the final feature for each axis to classify 3 states: no person, static lying state, and moving state, as described in Table 1. 70% of data were used for training and validation; 30% of the rest is used for testing the ML models. For each second, the ML model will predict the presence of a person in bed and the lying state: static or dynamic state.

Table 1. ML feature and classification.

ML Input Features			Class
ΔXsum	ΔYsum	ΔZsum	• No Person • Static Lying State • Moving State

2.4. ML Algorithms

There are 6 powerful algorithms in consideration for ML classification:

LG is a statistical model that estimates the probability of an instance belonging to a specific class. LG does this by utilizing a logistic function, which is also referred to as the sigmoid function. This function maps any real-valued input to a value within the range of 0 to 1. This transformation is crucial as it enables LR to generate probabilities, which are subsequently utilized for binary classifications. During training, the logistic regression model learns the association between the input features and the target class by estimating coefficients for each feature. These coefficients indicate the individual impact of each attribute on the ultimate forecast. The model iteratively changes these coefficients to minimize the discrepancy between its predictions and the actual class labels in the training data. After being trained, LR utilizes the acquired coefficients to estimate the likelihood that a new instance is part of the positive class. The algorithm calculates a weighted total of the input features, multiplying each feature by its respective coefficient. The total is subsequently inputted into the logistic function to derive the likelihood. LR employs a threshold, usually set at 0.5, to determine the final binary classification based on the likelihood. If the estimated probability exceeds the specified threshold, the instance is categorized as belonging to the positive class; otherwise, it is categorized as belonging to the negative class. LR has a significant benefit in terms of interpretability. LR calculates coefficients for each feature, allowing us to understand the significance and direction of their impact on the projected probability, which assists in the comprehension of how various characteristics contribute to the determination of classification. Nevertheless, LR also possesses its constraints. It presupposes a linear correlation between the characteristics and the logarithm of the probability of the result, which may not consistently be accurate in some scenarios. LR is susceptible to the influence of outliers and multicollinearity among features, which can have a negative impact on the stability and dependability of its predictions.

LDA is a classification approach that identifies optimal linear combinations of characteristics to effectively distinguish between different classes in the data. LDA assumes that the features adhere to a normal (Gaussian) distribution and that the covariance of the features is uniform across all classes. The main objective of LDA is to identify a linear decision boundary that optimizes the distance between different classes and minimizes the variability within each class. In order to accomplish it, LDA initiates the process by creating a model that represents the distribution of features for each class. The algorithm calculates the average and covariance matrix for each class, assuming that the characteristics within each class adhere to a multivariate normal distribution. After modeling the class distributions, LDA computes the class priors, indicating the probability of meeting each class in the dataset. These prior probabilities are usually calculated by determining the relative frequencies of each class in the training data. LDA utilizes the class distributions and priors to create decision boundaries that define specific areas in the feature space for each class. The decision borders are established by optimizing a criterion to maximize the variance ratio across classes to variation within classes. When confronted with new data points, LDA employs the acquired decision boundaries to categorize them according on their feature values. The algorithm utilizes Bayes' theorem to compute the posterior probability of each class for a certain data point, considering both the class distribution and the class priors. The data point is allocated to the class with the greatest posterior probability afterward. LDA is able to handle high-dimensional data by lowering the number of dimensions while retaining most of the class-discriminating information. By mapping the data into a lower-dimensional subspace determined by the linear discriminants, LDA can effectively distinguish between classes, even when the original feature space has a high number of dimensions.

CART is a decision tree technique that iteratively divides the data space into areas according to the values of the features. The CART algorithm constructs a decision tree by dividing the feature space into subsets, each of which is assigned a particular class label.

This process is carried out iteratively and recursively. The CART algorithm commences by utilizing the complete dataset, taking into account all the features and cases. The objective is to identify the characteristic that most effectively divides the data into two groups while maximizing a measure such as Gini impurity or information gain. Gini impurity quantifies the likelihood of incorrectly classifying an instance if it were assigned a random label based on the class distribution within the subset. Information gain measures the decrease in entropy (uncertainty) when splitting is carried out using a specific feature. After selecting the initial feature, CART algorithm splits the dataset into two halves using a threshold value specific to that feature. The algorithm can generate a split for each category when dealing with categorical features. On the other hand, for numerical features, it can utilize a threshold to construct binary splits. The CART algorithm assesses all potential divisions and selects the one that optimizes the criterion, such as minimizing Gini impurity or maximizing information gain. This technique is iteratively applied to each subset, thus generating a tree structure. The process of recursion persists until a specified condition for termination is fulfilled. To ensure the model's generalization and prevent overfitting to the training data, it is important to control the depth of the tree and avoid splitting nodes with insufficient instances. In order to categorize a new instance, the decision tree must be followed from the starting point to the final point, taking into account the characteristics of the instance. At every node, it evaluates the feature value of the instance and compares it to the threshold for splitting. It then proceeds to the appropriate child node based on the comparison. This procedure iterates until it reaches a leaf node, when the projected class for the new instance is determined by selecting the majority class among the instances in that node. The main advantages of CART are its simplicity, interpretability, and capability to handle numerical and categorical data. The resulting decision tree may be readily visible and comprehended, rendering it a valuable instrument for elucidating the underlying decision-making process to stakeholders. Furthermore, CART is resistant to irrelevant characteristics and has the ability to automatically choose the most informative ones for splitting, hence minimizing the necessity for feature engineering.

ET differs from regular decision trees by incorporating an extra layer of randomization in selecting splits instead of evaluating all potential splits for each characteristic at every node. The core principle of ET revolves around the idea of employing randomization while selecting splits. When seeking the most favourable division to separate the samples of a node into two groups, ET generates random splits for each of the randomly chosen features. The randomization process is carried out separately for each feature and is iterated numerous times until a specified maximum number of splits is reached. ET enhances the decision-making process by introducing a greater level of variety and diversity by generating random splits for each characteristic. This point increased the level of randomness and helped mitigate the risk of overfitting by preventing the model from excessively depending on features or patterns in the data. Extra Trees employ a different approach than traditional methods of selecting the best split based on a predetermined criterion. Instead of relying on a single split, ET considers numerous random splits and selects the one that achieves the highest performance. ET mitigates overfitting by employing multiple random splits for each feature, resulting in decision boundaries that are less prone to overfitting the training data, which is especially advantageous when working with datasets that are noisy or have a high number of dimensions, as typical decision trees may have difficulty in properly generalizing. The increased level of unpredictability in the selection of splits enables ET to effectively capture a wider range of patterns and relationships in the data. Enhancing the model's capacity to extrapolate to unfamiliar data enhances its performance on test datasets. ET exhibits greater resilience to outliers and noisy features than conventional decision trees. The technique of randomization reduces the influence of particular data points or attributes that may significantly affect the decision-making process.

SVM is a highly adaptable supervised learning model extensively employed for classification and regression problems. The classification method employed here is distinctive as it focuses on finding the most suitable hyperplane that successfully distinguishes different classes in the feature space. The objective is to maximize the distance between the hyperplane and the nearest data points, referred to as support vectors. SVM in classification aims to identify the hyperplane that effectively separates the classes and optimizes the margin, which is the distance between the hyperplane and the nearest data points from each class. SVM seeks to obtain superior generalization performance and resilience to data noise by maximizing the margin. The data points located on the margin and closest to the hyperplane are known as support vectors. These support vectors are essential in determining the decision boundary. However, real-world data frequently lack linear separability, indicating that a solitary hyperplane cannot achieve perfect separation between the classes. In such situations, SVM employs kernel functions to transform the input data into a feature space with more dimensions. This transformation increases the probability of finding a hyperplane that can effectively separate the classes. The transformation enables SVM to effectively deal with non-linear decision boundaries by implicitly mapping the input into a higher-dimensional space where a linear separator may be applied. Kernel functions are crucial for SVM's capacity to handle non-linearities in the data. These functions calculate the inner product of data points in the input space, quantifying their similarity. SVM applies a kernel function to the input data, implicitly transforming the data into a feature space of greater dimensions. This transformation enables the possibility of achieving linear separation. In this application, Gaussian Kernel Radial Basis Function captures complex decision boundaries that conduct a non-linearity within the original space of features. SVM's adaptability allows it to capture variety of classification problems.

RF is a technique in ensemble learning that builds numerous decision trees during training and merges their predictions to enhance performance. RF is a fundamental technique in ensemble learning, known for its capacity to improve predictive accuracy by aggregating the outputs of many decision trees. RF addresses the problems of overfitting and high variance commonly associated with single decision trees. It achieves this by utilizing many trees, which introduces variety and helps to minimize these concerns, resulting in more reliable and accurate predictions. RF method functions by constructing several decision trees in the training phase. Every decision tree is trained using a bootstrap sample of the data, which involves training each tree on a randomly chosen subset of the original dataset with replacement. Bootstrap sampling creates variability among the trees, guaranteeing that each tree learns from a slightly distinct viewpoint of the data. In addition, RF offers further unpredictability at each node of every decision tree by examining only a subset of features for splitting. Instead of assessing all features to identify the best split, RF randomly chooses a subset of features and evaluates them to discover the most optimal split. This procedure introduces diversity into the model, preventing it from unnecessarily relying on any specific characteristic and encouraging the examination of other data elements. RF possesses good qualities due to the combination of bootstrapping and random feature selection. RF mitigates the risk of overfitting and enhances generalization performance by training each decision tree on a distinct subset of the data and restricting the number of features examined at each node. The RF guarantees that the combined predictions of the entire forest minimize the errors made by each individual tree. RF is particularly effective in situations where the dataset has a large number of dimensions. The method of randomly selecting features enables RF to prioritize the most informative ones and ignore unnecessary or redundant ones, making it particularly suitable for datasets with a high number of dimensions. RF has the ability to capture complex correlations between features that individual decision trees may overlook, which is achieved by integrating the predictions of numerous decision trees, each trained on a distinct subset of data and features. An ensemble approach allows the RF algorithm to effectively capture and represent complex interactions and non-linear relationships within the data, improving its ability to make accurate predictions.

2.5. Evaluation Metrics

In order to validate the described models, the ML factors of precision, recall, and F1-score were computed. These factors were based on the values of true positive (TPA), false positive (FPA), and false negative (FNA) for class A.

- TP_A refers to the count of predictions made by a classifier that accurately forecast class A;
- FP_A refers to the count of objects that are not part of class A, yet are incorrectly classified as class A;
- FN_A represents the count of objects belonging to class A that are anticipated to belong to a different class;
- Precision measures the proportion of positive class predictions that truly belong to the positive class. The calculation involves adding up the number of true positives for each class and dividing it by the sum of true positives and false positives for all classes:

$$\text{Precision} = \frac{TP_A}{TP_A + FP_A}$$

- Recall is a metric that measures the proportion of positive class predictions produced correctly out of all the positive examples in the dataset. Unlike precision, which only evaluates the accuracy of correctly predicted positive outcomes out of all positive predictions, recall measures the number of positive predictions that were missed. In the context of multiple categorizations, recall is calculated by adding up the number of true positives for each category and dividing it by the sum of true positives and false negatives across all categories:

$$\text{Recall} = \frac{TP_a}{TP_A + FN_A}$$

- F1-score is a unified metric that takes into account both precision and recall, providing a single score. The F-score provides a method to merge precision and recall into a single metric that encompasses both attributes. After obtaining the values for precision and recall in the multiclass classification issue, these two scores can be merged to calculate the F-Measure. Similar to precision and recall, an F-Measure score of 0.0 indicates poor performance, whereas a score of 1.0 represents the best or flawless performance:

$$\text{F1-score} = \frac{2 * \text{Precision} * \text{Recall}}{\text{Precision} + \text{Recall}}$$

- Accuracy is the ratio of correct predictions to the total number of predictions.

$$\text{Accuracy} = \frac{\text{Correct predictions}}{\text{Total predictions}}$$

3. Results and Discussion

This section shows the performances of ML models via cross-validation. The best models were programmed into the microcontroller for further analysis in real time and code size.

3.1. Model Comparison and Selection

K-fold cross-validation is a widely used technique in ML that validates the performance of a predictive model and mitigates the risk of overfitting. The process entails dividing the dataset into K subsets or folds, training, and evaluating the model K times. For each iteration, one specific fold is set aside as the test set, while the rest of the K-1 folds are used for training. The outcomes are calculated by averaging across K iterations, guaranteeing a more robust and reliable performance estimation. In this instance, the K-fold cross-validation was performed using a value of k equal to 10.

The AI models underwent training on the host computer, which was equipped with an NVIDIA Quadro P620 featuring a Pascal GPU boasting 512 CUDA cores (NVIDIA, Santa Clara, CA, USA). The system is equipped with 2 GB of GDDR5 memory, an Intel Core i7 vPro-10850H Processor operating at a speed of 2.70 GHz, and 32 GB of RAM. The machine is manufactured by Intel, located in Santa Clara, CA, USA.

As shown in Figure 6 and Table 2, ET, LR, CART, and RF have the highest accuracy among all the models. Among these four models, the LR and RF possess the lowest standard deviation (std), showing the small variance between all 10 results. LDA has a weaker prediction capability for this specific case with an accuracy of 0.8, and SVM has a poor accuracy of 0.6. It is essential to achieve more than 0.9 of accuracy for this sleep-monitoring task to handle the proper information, so the four models with an accuracy of 0.99 are selected for a further test procedure.

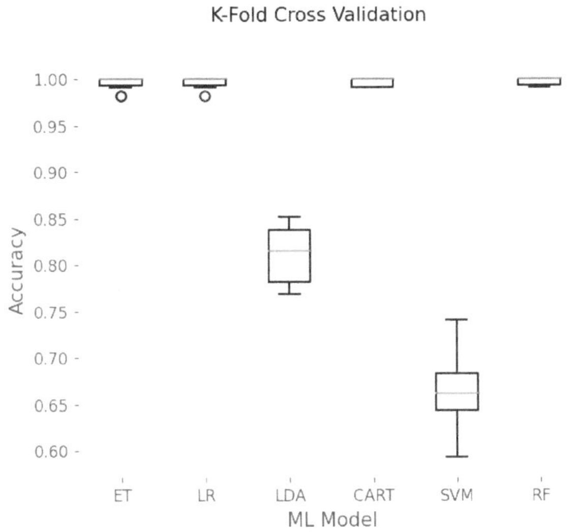

Figure 6. K-fold cross-validation for model evaluations.

Table 2. AI model comparison.

Models	Mean Accuracy	Std	10-Fold Cross Validation Time (s)
ET	0.997	0.007	0.029
LR	0.997	0.004	0.593
LDA	0.811	0.028	0.034
CART	0.997	0.005	0.029
SVM	0.666	0.045	1.307
RF	0.997	0.004	0.194

3.2. Test Process

In this test, 30% of the total data are used for testing the four selected models. Overall, all of them attain highly effective results. As reported in Table 3, all three tree algorithms have the same performance, with the precision, recall, and F1-score being similar. Their predictions are almost perfect, with a small misprediction between the moving state and static position. The moving state has a recall of 0.98, which means that the models correctly identified and classified 98% of the actual instances. Static position has a precision of 0.98, showing that, out of all instances predicted as a static position by the models, 98% are actually true static position instances.

Table 3. Test result on the selected models.

State	Precision				Recall				F1-Score			
	ET	LR	CART	RF	ET	LR	CART	RF	ET	LR	CART	RF
Moving State	1	1	1	1	0.98	0.96	0.98	0.98	0.99	0.98	0.99	0.99
No Person	1	0.98	1	1	1	0.99	1	1	1	0.99	1	1
Static Position	0.98	0.96	0.98	0.98	1	0.99	1	1	0.99	0.98	0.99	0.99

- Total Accuracy of ET, CART, and RF models: 99.34%
- Total Accuracy of LG model: 98.01%

Unlike the tree algorithms, LG has an inferior performance in the test process with the wrong predictions also in the case of no person, which leads to the precision, recall, and F1-score of the other classes not being as good as the ET, CART, and RF algorithms.

3.3. Real-Time Test with STM32-Microcontroller

In this stage, the trained models of the four selected algorithms are implemented in the IoT kit STM32 B-L475-IOT01A microcontroller board. The real-time test with the embedded system includes:

- No person is in bed with 720,000 data;
- A person statically lies on the bed with 1,440,000 data;
- A person moves on the bed with 180,000 data.

Table 4 reports the accuracy and the code size of the ML models. All the models demonstrate a good execution with an accuracy greater than 98%. The LR model has the advantage of the lightest code size, but a lower accuracy than the other models. Since the performance of the other three algorithms are almost the same, the CART model is the most suitable model for the MCU application, with the smallest code size among the tree models.

Table 4. Real-time test with microcontroller.

ML Model	Accuracy (%)	Code Size (Bytes)
ET	99.325	4346
LG	98.05	1480
CART	99.325	1583
RF	99.330	18,224

3.4. IoT Dashboard

With the MQTT [53–56] broker by HiveMQ [57], the Node Red [58–62] received the ML prediction about the monitoring state via Wi-Fi, which can be observed via tele-distance as a result of the IoT technology, as shown in Figure 7. Here, the numeric data means:

- 0: No person on bed;
- 1: Person stays in static position on the bed;
- 2: Person moves on bed.

The dashboard on Figure 7 shows a case where, in the first period, there is no person in bed (0), then the person goes to bed and turns himself to adjust the sleep position, causing a strong motion (2), then lays in a stationary position (1). In this way, the sleep routine of the concerned person will be monitored effectively from a far distance via Wi-Fi based on IoT communication.

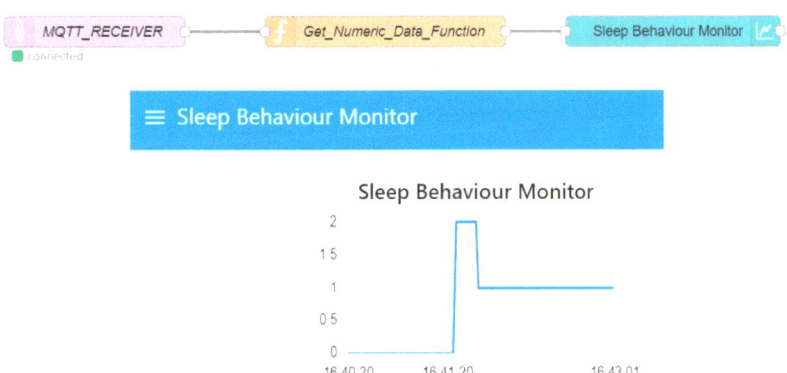

Figure 7. K-Node-RED block connection and IoT dashboard.

4. Discussion

This paper outlines the approaches and results of our study, which entailed gathering and examining more than 216,000 pieces of acceleration data of X, Y, and Z axes points. The difference of two consecutive samples are elaborated, and each of the 200 samples formed a window. These windows are the ML instances for the purpose of training and validating the ML algorithms. The results emphasize the outstanding performance of the chosen Machine-Learning models, reaching accuracy rates that surpass 99% in tests conducted on workstations. The CART technique stood out among the best models in terms of performance, showing both a high accuracy and the lightest code size that is suitable for effective deployment on a IoT microcontroller with limited memory. The monitoring process is carried out via the MQTT protocol and Node-RED development tool.

5. Conclusions

In conclusion, this study demonstrates the significant potential of integrating MEMS accelerometers, IoT frameworks, and Machine-Learning algorithms for automated sleep pattern analysis. By accurately detecting individuals in a bed and classifying their sleep states in real time, this approach offers promising avenues for enhancing patient outcomes, particularly in remote monitoring and elderly care scenarios. The findings underscore the transformative impact of technology-driven healthcare solutions and highlight the importance of continued innovation in this field to realize its full potential in improving healthcare delivery and patient well-being.

Three algorithms, ET, CART, and RF, accomplish the best performances. LG also has a high efficiency with a light code size, although its accuracy is still lower than that of the tree models. This work shows the potential of the automated sleep pattern analysis of a real-time ML model implementation. By remotely monitoring sleep patterns, healthcare professionals can tailor interventions and treatment plans based on individualized data insights, enhancing patient outcomes and fortifying elderly care. Furthermore, the scalability and accessibility afforded by IoT devices promise to democratize access to sleep-monitoring services, ensuring equitable healthcare provision across diverse populations.

As we navigate towards this future, it is imperative to harness the full potential of these technologies to realize their transformative impact on healthcare delivery and improve the lives of individuals worldwide. In future work, more algorithms with more tests will be carried out for the developed platform. Other types of beds and more patients will be tested with the developed system.

Author Contributions: Methodology, M.L.H.; software, M.L.H.; validation, G.M.; formal analysis, M.L.H.; investigation, P.C.; resources, G.M.; writing—original draft, M.L.H.; writing—review and editing, G.M.; supervision, P.C.; project administration, P.C. All authors have read and agreed to the published version of the manuscript.

Funding: This study has been realized with the co-financing of the Ministry of University and Research in the framework of PNC "DARE—Digital lifelong prevention project" (PNC0000002—CUP B53C22006450001). The views and opinions expressed are solely those of the authors and do not necessarily reflect those of the European Union, nor can the European Union be held responsible for them.

Data Availability Statement: The data are contained within the article.

Acknowledgments: The authors would like to thank the University of Parma for supporting this project.

Conflicts of Interest: The authors declare no conflicts of interest.

Notations and Abbreviations

CART	Classification and Regression Trees
ET	Extra Tree Classifier
IoT	Internet of Things
LR	Logistic Regression
LDA	Linear Discriminant Analysis
MCU	Microcontroller
ML	Machine Learning
MQTT	Message Queuing Telemetry broker
RF	Random Forest
SVM	Support Vector Machines

References

1. Hoang, M.L.; Carratu, M.; Ugwiri, M.A.; Paciello, V.; Pietrosanto, A. A New Technique for Optimization of Linear Displacement Measurement Based on MEMS Accelerometer. In Proceedings of the 2020 International Semiconductor Conference (CAS), Sinaia, Romania, 7–9 October 2020. [CrossRef]
2. Hoang, M.L.; Pietrosanto, A. New Artificial Intelligence Approach to Inclination Measurement Based on MEMS Accelerometer. *IEEE Trans. Artif. Intell.* **2021**, *3*, 67–77. [CrossRef]
3. Hoang, M.L.; Pietrosanto, A. An Effective Method on Vibration Immunity for Inclinometer Based on MEMS Accelerometer. In Proceedings of the 2020 International Semiconductor Conference (CAS), Sinaia, Romania, 7–9 October 2020. [CrossRef]
4. Alqahtani, A.; Alsubai, S.; Bhatia, M. IoT-Edge–Cloud-Assisted Intelligent Framework for Controlling Dengue. *IEEE Internet Things J.* **2023**, *11*, 15682–15689. [CrossRef]
5. AbdelHafeez, M.; AbdelRaheem, M. AssIUT IOT: A Remotely Accessible Testbed for Internet of Things. In Proceedings of the IEEE Global Conference on Internet of Things (GCIoT), Alexandria, Egypt, 5–7 December 2018. [CrossRef]
6. Chataut, R.; Phoummalayvane, A.; Akl, R. Unleashing the Power of IoT: A Comprehensive Review of IoT Applications and Future Prospects in Healthcare, Agriculture, Smart Homes, Smart Cities, and Industry 4.0. *Sensors* **2023**, *23*, 7194. [CrossRef] [PubMed]
7. Ullah, I.; Ullah, A.; Sajjad, M. Towards a Hybrid Deep Learning Model for Anomalous Activities Detection in Internet of Things Networks. *IoT* **2021**, *2*, 428–448. [CrossRef]
8. Hosseini, M.-P.; Hosseini, A.; Ahi, K. A Review on Machine Learning for EEG Signal Processing in Bioengineering. *IEEE Rev. Biomed. Eng.* **2021**, *14*, 204–218. [CrossRef] [PubMed]
9. Hoang, M.L.; Nkembi, A.A.; Pham, P.L. Real-Time Risk Assessment Detection for Weak People by Parallel Training Logical Execution of a Supervised Learning System Based on an IoT Wearable MEMS Accelerometer. *Sensors* **2023**, *23*, 1516. [CrossRef] [PubMed]
10. Hoang, M.L.; Delmonte, N. K-Centroid Convergence Clustering Identification in One-Label per Type for Disease Prediction. *IAES Int. J. Artif. Intell.* **2024**, *13*, 1149–1159. [CrossRef]
11. Jara-Díaz, S.R.; Rosales-Salas, J. Time Use: The Role of Sleep. *Transp. Res. Part A Policy Pract.* **2020**, *136*, 1–20. [CrossRef]
12. National Institute on Aging a Good Night's Sleep. Available online: https://www.nia.nih.gov/health/sleep/good-nights-sleep/ (accessed on 25 January 2024).
13. Suni, E.; Wright, H. What Causes Restless Sleep? Available online: https://www.sleepfoundation.org/how-sleep-works/what-causes-restless-sleep (accessed on 25 January 2024).

14. Mendez, M.O.; Matteucci, M.; Cerutti, S.; Bianchi, A.M.; Kortelainen, J.M. Automatic Detection of Sleep Macrostructure Based on Bed Sensors. In Proceedings of the 2009 Annual International Conference of the IEEE Engineering in Medicine and Biology Society, Minneapolis, MN, USA, 3–6 September 2009. [CrossRef]
15. Guerrero, G.; Kortelainen, J.M.; Palacios, E.; Bianchi, A.M.; Tachino, G.; Tenhunen, M.; Mendez, M.O.; van Gils, M. Detection of Sleep-Disordered Breating with Pressure Bed Sensor. In Proceedings of the 2013 35th Annual International Conference of the IEEE Engineering in Medicine and Biology Society (EMBC), Osaka, Japan, 3–7 July 2013. [CrossRef]
16. Intongkum, C.; Sasiwat, Y.; Sengchuai, K.; Booranawong, A.; Phukpattaranont, P. Monitoring and Classification of Human Sleep Postures, Seizures, and Falls from Bed Using Three-Axis Acceleration Signals and Machine Learning. *SN Comput. Sci.* **2023**, *5*, 104. [CrossRef]
17. Sundararajan, K.; Georgievska, S.; te Lindert, B.H.W.; Gehrman, P.R.; Ramautar, J.; Mazzotti, D.R.; Sabia, S.; Weedon, M.N.; van Someren, E.J.W.; Ridder, L.; et al. Sleep Classification from Wrist-Worn Accelerometer Data Using Random Forests. *Sci. Rep.* **2021**, *11*, 24. [CrossRef]
18. Kuzik, N.; Spence, J.C.; Carson, V. Machine Learning Sleep Duration Classification in Preschoolers Using Waist-Worn ActiGraphs. *Sleep Med.* **2021**, *78*, 141–148. [CrossRef]
19. Navarro, M.; Nicdao, A.I.; Dela, J.C. Machine Learning Based Sleep Phase Monitoring Using Pulse Oximeter and Accelerometer. In Proceedings of the 5th International Conference on Electrical, Telecommunication and Computer Engineering (ELTICOM), Medan, Indonesia, 15–16 September 2021. [CrossRef]
20. Chen, Z.; Wu, M.; Wu, J.; Ding, J.; Zeng, Z.; Surmacz, K.; Li, X. A Deep Learning Approach for Sleep-Wake Detection from HRV and Accelerometer Data. In Proceedings of the IEEE EMBS International Conference on Biomedical & Health Informatics (BHII), Chicago, IL, USA, 19–22 May 2019. [CrossRef]
21. INTEX Sleep Tracking in Smartwatches—Everything You Need to Know! Available online: https://www.intex.in/blogs/blogs/sleep-tracking-in-smartwatches-everything-you-need-to-know (accessed on 10 December 2023).
22. Miotto, R.; Wang, F.; Wang, S.; Jiang, X.; Dudley, J.T. Deep Learning for Healthcare: Review, Opportunities and Challenges. *Brief. Bioinform.* **2018**, *19*, 1236–1246. [CrossRef] [PubMed]
23. Shamshirband, S.; Fathi, M.; Dehzangi, A.; Chronopoulos, A.T.; Alinejad-Rokny, H. A Review on Deep Learning Approaches in Healthcare Systems: Taxonomies, Challenges, and Open Issues. *J. Biomed. Inform.* **2020**, *113*, 103627. [CrossRef] [PubMed]
24. Shung, D.; Huang, J.; Castro, E.; Tay, J.K.; Simonov, M.; Laine, L.; Batra, R.; Krishnaswamy, S. Neural Network Predicts Need for Red Blood Cell Transfusion for Patients with Acute Gastrointestinal Bleeding Admitted to the Intensive Care Unit. *Sci. Rep.* **2021**, *11*, 8827. [CrossRef] [PubMed]
25. Shi, J.; Ye, M.; Chen, H.; Lu, Y.; Tan, Z.; Fan, Z.; Zhao, J. Enhancing Efficiency and Capacity of Telehealth Services with Intelligent Triage: A Bidirectional LSTM Neural Network Model Employing Character Embedding. *BMC Med. Inform. Decis. Mak.* **2023**, *23*, 269. [CrossRef] [PubMed]
26. Dhananjay, B.; Venkatesh, N.P.; Bhardwaj, A.; Sivaraman, J. Cardiac Signals Classification Based on Extra Trees Model. In Proceedings of the 8th International Conference on Signal Processing and Integrated Networks (SPIN), Greater Noida, India, 26–27 August 2021. [CrossRef]
27. Upadhyay, R.; Tanwar, P.S.; Degadwala, S. Fracture Type Identification Using Extra Tree Classifier. In Proceedings of the 2021 Fifth International Conference on I-SMAC (IoT in Social, Mobile, Analytics and Cloud) (I-SMAC), Palladam, India, 11–13 November 2021. [CrossRef]
28. Wahid, N.; Zaidi, A.; Dhiman, G.; Manwal, M.; Soni, D.; Maaliw, R.R. Identification of Coronary Artery Disease Using Extra Tree Classification. Available online: https://ieeexplore.ieee.org/abstract/document/10134338/ (accessed on 13 June 2023).
29. Majumder, A.B.; Gupta, S.; Singh, D.; Acharya, B.; Gerogiannis, V.C.; Kanavos, A.; Pintelas, P. Heart Disease Prediction Using Concatenated Hybrid Ensemble Classifiers. *Algorithms* **2023**, *16*, 538. [CrossRef]
30. Choi, Y.; Boo, Y. Comparing Logistic Regression Models with Alternative Machine Learning Methods to Predict the Risk of Drug Intoxication Mortality. *Int. J. Environ. Res. Public Health* **2020**, *17*, 897. [CrossRef] [PubMed]
31. Prakhar, J.; Haider, M.T.U. Automated Detection of Biases within the Healthcare System Using Clustering and Logistic Re-gression. In Proceedings of the 2023 15th International Conference on Computer and Automation Engineering (ICCAE), Sydney, Australia, 3–5 March 2023.
32. Adil, S.H.; Ebrahim, M.; Raza, K.; Azhar Ali, S.S.; Ahmed Hashmani, M. Liver Patient Classification Using Logistic Regression. Available online: https://ieeexplore.ieee.org/abstract/document/8510581 (accessed on 17 February 2023).
33. Adebiyi, M.O.; Arowolo, M.O.; Mshelia, M.D.; Olugbara, O.O. A Linear Discriminant Analysis and Classification Model for Breast Cancer Diagnosis. *Appl. Sci.* **2022**, *12*, 11455. [CrossRef]
34. Gaudenzi, P.; Nardi, D.; Chiappetta, I.; Atek, S.; Lampani, L.; Pasquali, M.; Sarasini, F.; Tirilló, J.; Valente, T. Sparse sensing detection of impact-induced delaminations in composite laminates. *Compos. Struct.* **2015**, *133*, 1209–1219. [CrossRef]
35. Pathak, S.; Mishra, I.; Swetapadma, A. An Assessment of Decision Tree Based Classification and Regression Algorithms. In Proceedings of the 2018 3rd International Conference on Inventive Computation Technologies (ICICT), Coimbatore, India, 15–16 November 2018. [CrossRef]
36. Pereira, S.; Karia, D. Prediction of Sudden Cardiac Death Using Classification and Regression Tree Model with Coalesced Based ECG and Clinical Data. In Proceedings of the 2018 3rd International Conference on Communication and Electronics Systems (ICCES), Coimbatore, India, 15–16 November 2018.

37. Lemon, S.C.; Roy, J.; Clark, M.A.; Friedmann, P.D.; Rakowski, W. Classification and Regression Tree Analysis in Public Health: Methodological Review and Comparison with Logistic Regression. *Ann. Behav. Med.* **2003**, *26*, 172–181. [CrossRef]
38. Ozcan, M.; Peker, S. A Classification and Regression Tree Algorithm for Heart Disease Modeling and Prediction. *Healthc. Anal.* **2023**, *3*, 100130. [CrossRef]
39. Kuhn, L.; Page, K.; Ward, J.; Worrall-Carter, L. The Process and Utility of Classification and Regression Tree Methodology in Nursing Research. *J. Adv. Nurs.* **2013**, *70*, 1276–1286. [CrossRef]
40. Speybroeck, N. Classification and Regression Trees. *Int. J. Public Health* **2011**, *57*, 243–246. [CrossRef]
41. Scikit-Learn. Support Vector Machine. Available online: https://scikit-learn.org/stable/modules/svm.html (accessed on 24 August 2023).
42. Martinez-Alanis, M.; Bojorges-Valdez, E.; Wessel, N.; Lerma, C. Prediction of Sudden Cardiac Death Risk with a Support Vector Machine Based on Heart Rate Variability and Heartprint Indices. *Sensors* **2020**, *20*, 5483. [CrossRef]
43. Ye, Y.; He, W.; Cheng, Y.; Huang, W.; Zhang, Z. A Robust Random Forest-Based Approach for Heart Rate Monitoring Using Photoplethysmography Signal Contaminated by Intense Motion Artifacts. *Sensors* **2017**, *17*, 385. [CrossRef]
44. Scikit-Learn. Sklearn. Ensemble. RandomForestClassifier. Available online: https://scikit-learn.org/stable/modules/generated/sklearn.ensemble.RandomForestClassifier.html (accessed on 24 August 2023).
45. Mbonyinshuti, F.; Nkurunziza, J.; Niyobuhungiro, J.; Kayitare, E. Application of Random Forest Model to Predict the Demand of Essential Medicines for Noncommunicable Diseases Management in Public Health Facilities. *Pan Afr. Med. J.* **2022**, *42*, 89. [CrossRef]
46. ST STM32 32-Bit Arm Cortex MCUs—STMicroelectronics. Available online: https://www.st.com/en/microcontrollers-microprocessors/stm32-32-bit-arm-cortex-mcus.html (accessed on 25 January 2024).
47. ST B-L475E-IOT01A—STMicroelectronics. Available online: https://www.st.com/en/evaluation-tools/b-l475e-iot01a.html (accessed on 22 September 2023).
48. Python. Available online: https://www.python.org/ (accessed on 21 September 2023).
49. Scikit-Learn: Machine Learning in Python. Available online: https://scikit-learn.org/stable/ (accessed on 1 November 2023).
50. Ritchie Dennis, M.; Kernighan, B.W. *The C Programming Language*; Prentice Hall: Hoboken, NJ, USA, 1988.
51. Ryan, R.R.; Spiller, H. The c Programming Language and a c Compiler. *IBM Syst. J.* **1985**, *24*, 37–48. [CrossRef]
52. ANALOG DEVICES ADXL355 Datasheet and Product Info | Analog Devices. Available online: https://www.analog.com/en/products/adxl355.html#product-documentation (accessed on 5 October 2023).
53. MQTT—The Standard for IoT Messaging. Available online: https://mqtt.org/ (accessed on 20 January 2024).
54. Manowska, A.; Wycisk, A.; Nowrot, A.; Pielot, J. The Use of the MQTT Protocol in Measurement, Monitoring and Control Systems as Part of the Implementation of Energy Management Systems. *Electronics* **2023**, *12*, 17. [CrossRef]
55. D'Ortona, C.; Tarchi, D.; Raffaelli, C. Open-Source MQTT-Based End-to-End IoT System for Smart City Scenarios. *Future Internet* **2022**, *14*, 57. [CrossRef]
56. Shahri, F.; Pedreiras, P.; Almeida, L. Extending MQTT with Real-Time Communication Services Based on SDN. *Sensors* **2022**, *22*, 3162. [CrossRef]
57. HiveMQ MQTT Essentials—All Core Concepts Explained. Available online: https://www.hivemq.com/mqtt/ (accessed on 25 January 2024).
58. OpenJS Foundation Node-RED. Available online: https://nodered.org/ (accessed on 24 September 2023).
59. Torres, D.; Dias, J.P.; Restivo, A.; Ferreira, H.S. Real-Time Feedback in Node-RED for IoT Development: An Empirical Study. Available online: https://ieeexplore.ieee.org/abstract/document/9213544 (accessed on 15 January 2024).
60. Lekic, M.; Gardasevic, G. IoT Sensor Integration to Node-RED Platform. In Proceedings of the 2018 17th International Symposium INFOTEH-JAHORINA (INFOTEH), East Sarajevo, Bosnia and Herzegovina, 21–23 March 2018. [CrossRef]
61. Thomas, L.; Mv, M.K.; Sl, S.D.; Bs, P. Towards Comprehensive Home Automation: Leveraging the IoT, Node-RED, and Wireless Sensor Networks for Enhanced Control and Connectivity. *Eng. Proc.* **2023**, *59*, 173. [CrossRef]
62. Medina-Pérez, A.; Sánchez-Rodríguez, D.; Alonso-González, I. An Internet of Thing Architecture Based on Message Queuing Telemetry Transport Protocol and Node-RED: A Case Study for Monitoring Radon Gas. *Smart Cities* **2021**, *4*, 803–818. [CrossRef]

Disclaimer/Publisher's Note: The statements, opinions and data contained in all publications are solely those of the individual author(s) and contributor(s) and not of MDPI and/or the editor(s). MDPI and/or the editor(s) disclaim responsibility for any injury to people or property resulting from any ideas, methods, instructions or products referred to in the content.

Article

Evaluation of Fatigue in Older Drivers Using a Multimodal Medical Sensor and Driving Simulator

Yutaka Yoshida [1], Kohei Kowata [2], Ryotaro Abe [2] and Emi Yuda [1,*]

1. Graduate School of Information Sciences, Tohoku University, 6-3-09 Aoba, Aramaki-aza Aoba-ku, Sendai 980-8579, Japan; yutaka.yoshida.e3@tohoku.ac.jp
2. TS TECH Co., Ltd., 118-1, Ota Takanezawa-machi, Shioya-gun, Tochigi 329-1217, Japan; kohei.kowata@tstech.com (K.K.); ryotaro.abe@tstech.com (R.A.)
* Correspondence: emi.a.yuda@tohoku.ac.jp

Abstract: In recent years, the spread of wearable medical sensors has made it possible to easily measure biological signals such as pulse rate and body acceleration (BA), and from these biological signals, it is possible to evaluate the degree of biological stress and autonomic nervous activity in daily life. Accumulated fatigue due to all-day work and lack of sleep is thought to be a contributing factor to distracted driving, and technology to estimate fatigue from biological signals during driving is desired. In this study, we investigated fatigue evaluation during a driving simulator (DS) using biological information on seven older subjects. A DS experiment was performed in the morning and afternoon, and no significant differences were observed in the change over time of heart rate variability and skin temperature. On the other hand, in the afternoon DS, changes in arousal and body movements were observed based on BA calculated from the three-axis acceleration sensor and fingertip reaction time in a psychomotor vigilance test. It is suggested that by combining biological information, it may be possible to evaluate the degree of fatigue from the presence or absence of arousal and changes in body movements while driving.

Keywords: driving simulator (DS); fatigue evaluation; biological information; medical sensor

Citation: Yoshida, Y.; Kowata, K.; Abe, R.; Yuda, E. Evaluation of Fatigue in Older Drivers Using a Multimodal Medical Sensor and Driving Simulator. *Electronics* **2024**, *13*, 1126. https://doi.org/10.3390/electronics13061126

Academic Editor: Jichai Jeong

Received: 8 February 2024
Revised: 12 March 2024
Accepted: 14 March 2024
Published: 20 March 2024

Copyright: © 2024 by the authors. Licensee MDPI, Basel, Switzerland. This article is an open access article distributed under the terms and conditions of the Creative Commons Attribution (CC BY) license (https://creativecommons.org/licenses/by/4.0/).

1. Introduction

Older drivers may be at increased risk for traffic accidents, and one of the main factors is fatigue. Older adults generally sleep less well and are more prone to daytime drowsiness and fatigue. Driving under these conditions can lead to reduced driving ability and reaction time, posing a serious risk to road safety [1,2].

The objective of this study is to develop an effective method for detecting fatigue in older drivers. Specifically, we will examine which indicators have prognostic power by using a combination of conventional biometric autonomic estimation, the analysis of bio-accelerations, sitting pressure, subjective evaluation, and arousal level testing.

Previous studies have proposed many methods for detecting driver fatigue. Some studies have attempted to identify fatigue states by measuring physiological parameters (heart rate (HR), nystagmus, electromyography, etc.). Others use sensors and cameras in a vehicle to collect information about the driver's behavior patterns and vehicle controls to help identify fatigue. However, the application of physiological parameters has significant noise processing problems, and facial image analysis of cameras in the vehicle cabin has human privacy issues and lighting environment limitations [3–18].

This study explores a simple index for detecting fatigue in the older through multimodal signal processing, including wearable sensors. This will contribute to human-centered design in the age of automated driving. Our aim is to evaluate the degree of fatigue during driving by the multimodal technology that combines multiple types of biological information using inexpensive and highly versatile medical sensors that can easily measure biological information. In this paper, in addition to HR and pulse wave measurement, we investigated fatigue evaluation for seven older subjects using a three-axis acceleration sensor, skin temperature (ST), seat pressure, reaction time of fingertips, and so on, during a driving simulator (DS).

This paper is organized as follows. Section 2 (Methods) describes the experimental methodology and data collection techniques. Section 3 (Results) reports the experimental and analytical results. Finally, we provide a discussion and conclusions.

2. Methods

2.1. Participants

In order to avoid bias in the subject group, the selection criteria for the subjects were that in addition to the absence of medication and chronic diseases, the subjects must be healthy older adults with driving experience and no traffic accidents or serious violations in the past year. In addition, the following 6 exclusion criteria were used to select subjects:

i.   Cataracts that require treatment (excluding those after treatment).
ii. Color blindness.
iii. Persistent atrial fibrillation and frequent premature contractions.
iv. Hospitalization history within 3 months.
v.   Diabetes requiring insulin treatment.
vi. Debilitating diseases and acute diseases.

An announcement was made to recruit subjects, 7 older subjects applied, and all older subjects were accepted. A screening process was conducted for eligible subjects. This included medical evaluations, driving history checks, and schedule adjustments. 7 healthy older subjects (4 males) participated in this study. The mean age of the participants was 70 ± 3 y.o., and their mean driving history was 35 years. All subjects received an explanation from the experimenter in advance, and after being fully satisfied with the content, agreed to participate in the experiment.

2.2. Measurement Techniques

2.2.1. Measurement of Physiological Parameters

To assess the fatigue status of the participants, electrocardiogram (ECG), ST, and physical activity (body movement) were measured. ECG was measured by an ECG sensor attached to the chest, and ST activity was obtained from a skin conductivity sensor attached to the wrist during driving. Figure 1 shows the sensors used in the experiment and the situation during the DS.

ECG was measured using the Holter ECG with a built-in 3-axis accelerometer (Cardy303 Pico, Suzuken, Japan, Figure 1a). It has dimensions of 28 mm (W) × 42 mm (D) × 9 mm (H), a weight of 13 g, and a recording time of 24 h and uses a button-type lithium battery. The sampling frequency is 125 Hz, the sampling frequency of the acceleration is 31.25 Hz, and the 3-axis acceleration of −4.5 to 4.5 G can be measured. From the ECG signal, all R waves (sharp deflections corresponding to the ventricular electrical excitation) were detected, and R-R interval time series were obtained. If there was an arrhythmia, the R-R interval was deleted and resampled at 2 Hz using the step function. Time domain indices and frequency domain indices of heart rate variability (HRV) were calculated from the R-R interval time series. The mean HR [bpm] was calculated as an index of the time domain. As indices in the frequency domain, LFP (power of low-frequency component; 0.04~0.15 Hz, [ln, ms^2]), HFP (power of high-frequency component; 0.15~0.45 Hz, [ln, ms^2]), LFP/HFP (LFP to HFP ratio), and HFF (peak frequency of the HF component, Hz) were calculated. Indices in the frequency domain were calculated by FFT (fast Fourier transform). LFP reflects both sympathetic and parasympathetic activity and baroreceptor reflex sensitivity, and HFP reflects para-sympathetic activity. LFP/HFP reflects sympathetic nerve activity, and HFF reflects respiratory frequency [19,20].

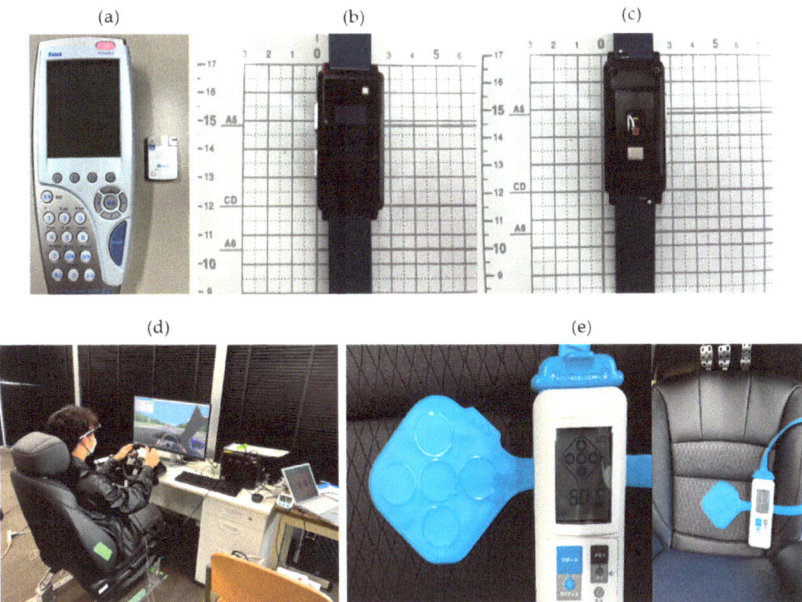

Figure 1. The sensors used in the experiment and the situation during the DS. (**a**) Holter ECG with built-in 3-axis accelerometer and handy controller. (**b**,**c**) Wristwatch-type wearable (sensor Silmme22). (**b**) Display; (**c**) Sensor part. (**d**) Scenery during the experiment. (**e**) Measurement of seating pressure by Palm Q.

Body acceleration (BA) was calculated from the 3-axis acceleration. The x-axis is recorded in the right-hand direction, the y-axis in the vertical upward direction, and the z-axis in the forward direction. The 3-axis acceleration was resampled to 10 Hz, and the square root of the sum of the squares of each axis was calculated to obtain the resultant acceleration. Furthermore, a high-pass filter was used to extract fluctuating components, and the sum of absolute value for the fluctuating components was defined as BA [G].

ST was measured with a wristwatch-type wearable sensor (Silmme22, TDK, Tokyo, Japan, Figure 1b,c) [21]. The sensor size is approximately 52 mm × 24.5 mm × 13.5 mm, and the weight is approximately 26 g. The following four types of sensors are inside the device: a pulse sensor, an acceleration sensor, a UV sensor, and a temperature sensor. In this experiment, it was used for the purpose of measuring ST. The temperature sensor uses a digital semiconductor temperature sensor to measure the ST of the wrist in the range of −10 °C to 45 °C. Measured values are output every minute.

2.2.2. DS Software

The DS software used was CarSim (Mechanical Simulation, Version 2022.0, Ann Arbor, MI, USA). The cockpit consisted of a car seat, steering wheel controller games for games, and an accelerator pedal. The course was designed as a public road, assuming a commuting route. The backgrounds were set in the morning and in the evening, assuming commuting time and return time. It was designed to follow the vehicle in front at a speed of 50 km/h or less. The driving time was 60 min. Figure 1d shows the situation during the experiment.

2.2.3. Measurement of Seating Pressure

The pressure and positioning of the sheet during the experiment were measured using a portable contact pressure measuring device Palm Q (CAPE CO., LTD., Kanagawa, Japan, Figure 1e) [22]. The body size of Palm Q is 65 mm (W) × 175 mm (L) × 35 mm (H), its weight is 160 g, and its power source is a 9 V square alkaline battery. The sensor pad size is

130 mm (W) × 130 mm (L), the pressure tube is about 75 cm long and weighs 50 g, and the materials are urethane, ABS resin, and polyacetal resin. The pressure measurement range is 0 mmHg–200 mmHg, and the measurement accuracy is ±3 mmHg. The sensor pad is placed at four points on the circumference at equal angles around one point, allowing you to check the position of the highest pressure.

2.2.4. Measurement of Fatigue Stress

The subjects' fatigue stress before and after the experiment was evaluated using an Autonomic fatigue measurement device (MF100, Murata, Kyoto, Japan) [23]. The body size of MF100 is 100 mm (W) × 152 mm (L) × 67 mm (H), its weight is 110 g, and its power source is 2 AA alkaline batteries. MF100 uses optical and electrical measurement methods to measure the thumb pulse rate for approximately 90–120 s. Low-frequency components (0.04–0.15 Hz) and high-frequency components (0.15–0.40 Hz) are calculated from the pulse wave interval time series by frequency spectrum analysis. The area of the LF component is evaluated as sympathetic nerve activity, the area of the HF component as parasympathetic nerve activity, and the sum of the LF area and HF area as the overall autonomic nerve activity. Autonomic balance (ANB), deviation value (DV), total pulse rate (TPR, [beats]), and arrhythmia rate (AR, [beats]) is calculated from autonomic nerve activity. The higher the ANB value, the more dominant sympathetic nerve activity. The DV value indicates the degree of fatigue, and the standard value is 42. If the value is lower than 42, the degree of fatigue increases. The vital data measured by the MF100 is analyzed on a cloud server connected to the Internet, and the results are displayed on the iOS/Android app on a mobile device.

The psychomotor vigilance test (PVT) is widely used to measure sleepiness and arousal based on finger reactivity [24]. The PVT was conducted to examine arousal before and after driving, fingertip reaction time (RT, [ms]), and the number of times RT was 500 ms or more (ML: minor lap frequency). The subject clicked the mouse at the moment the elapsed time was suddenly displayed on the screen, and the elapsed time became the reaction time of the fingertip. The PVT used a 15.6-inch laptop (Panasonic, Windows11, Let's note SV8). The distance from the subject's eyes to the screen was approximately 70 cm, and the PVT font was 72 pt.

After the DS, as a subjective evaluation using a questionnaire, the participants answered the sickness questionnaire (SSQ) to estimate their degree of sickness. SSQ is the most commonly used subjective evaluation of motion sickness. This is a result of a factor analysis of 1119 pairs of Motion Sickness Questionnaire (MSQ) data measured before and after the simulator experience, from which 16 subjective items were extracted (e.g., eyestrain, blurred vision, dizziness, nausea, burping) that are more effective in evaluating simulator sickness [25]. These 16 items can be quantified into the following 4 items: nausea, oculomotor, disorientations, and total scores.

2.3. Experimental Protocol

The participants participated in an experiment in a DS where they drove a specific route. The experiment took place in the morning and in the afternoon, with each session lasting one hour. No specific task was given to the participants during the driving session, and they drove for one hour on a plain, flat road.

The experiment was performed at Tohoku University between 2 February 2023 and 12 February 2023. The subjects were prohibited from drinking alcohol starting the evening before the experiment. DS driving was performed for 1 h each in the morning and afternoon for each subject. Table 1 shows the experimental protocol. The morning experiment started between 7:30 and 8:00. First, the subjects performed the PVT and measurement of fatigue stress (MF100) before DS driving and then wore the measurement equipment. ECG, BA, ST, and seating pressure were measured during DS driving. Seating pressure (Palm Q, Cape Inc., Yokosuka, Japan) was measured once before and after starting DS driving. After DS driving, SSQ, PVT, and MF100 were measured, and the morning experiment ended.

Afterward, the subjects were allowed some free time before performing the experiment in the afternoon. The afternoon experiment started between 16:30 and 17:00. The experimental protocol for the afternoon was similar to the morning. The morning DS background was the morning background, and the afternoon DS background was the evening background. The mean illuminance in the laboratory during DS driving was 601 lux in the morning and 21 lux in the afternoon.

Table 1. Experimental protocol.

Events	MF100	PVT	DS	SSQ	MF100	PVT
Time [min]	2	5	60	2	2	5

The same experiment was performed in the morning and afternoon.

2.4. Statistical Analysis

Statistical analysis was performed to determine if significant changes in biological information were observed between the morning and afternoon DS driving. The mean values of HRV indices during DS driving were compared between the morning and afternoon using a paired t-test. In addition, to examine the significance of changes in the HRV indices, ST, and BA over time, the mean values for each 10-minute period were analyzed using one-way ANOVA. Post hoc tests used Bonferroni multiple comparisons; PVT, Palm Q, and MF100 were compared before and after the DS driving operation and between the morning and afternoon using paired t-tests; and SSQ was compared between the morning and afternoon using paired t-tests. These statistical analyzes were performed for the older subjects (7 subjects). The statistical software used was IBM SPSS Statistics (version 28.0.1.0, Armonk, NY, USA). The significance level was set at 5%, $p < 0.05$ for significance, and $p < 0.1$ for trend.

3. Results

The SSQ, PVT, and standard fatigue detection test for the assessment of autonomic function were used to evaluate driver fatigue detection, and the results showed that drivers had higher finger reactivity and arousal in the afternoon than in the morning (Table 2). In addition, physiological indices such as ECG and bio-acceleration were analyzed in this experiment, and the results are shown in the table below (Figures 2–4).

Table 2. Comparison of Palm Q, MF100, PVT, and SSQ.

Indices		Morning		Afternoon		p-Value			
		Before	After	Before	After	AM (Before vs. After)	PM (Before vs. After)	Before (AM vs. PM)	After (AM vs. PM)
Palm Q	Seat pressure [mmHg]	79.3 ± 6.4	57.4 ± 8.2	92.7 ± 16.4	73.4 ± 10.1	0.067	0.444	0.390	0.147
MF100	ANB	0.99 ± 0.27	0.75 ± 0.15	0.90 ± 0.24	0.99 ± 0.16	0.399	0.760	0.794	0.294
	DV	46.7 ± 8.5	49.6 ± 15.9	43.6 ± 7.2	36.9 ± 3.0	0.738	0.230	0.498	0.364
	TPR [beats]	125 ± 7	117 ± 4	124 ± 6	119 ± 5	0.136	0.562	0.630	0.729
	AR [beats]	8 ± 7	5 ± 3	6 ± 6	2 ± 2	0.408	0.411	0.105	0.243
PVT	RT [ms]	283 ± 8	286 ± 5	274 ± 10	280 ± 4	0.804	0.539	0.052	0.241
	ML [frequency]	2.1 ± 0.6	0.9 ± 0.3	0.9 ± 0.5	0.6 ± 0.3	0.122	0.654	0.049	0.604
SSQ	Nausea	—	19.1 ± 8.8	—	17.7 ± 10.5				0.846
	Oculomotor		40.1 ± 11.4		31.4 ± 12.8				0.311
	Disorientation		31.8 ± 16.8		31.8 ± 19.4				1
	Total scores		26.2 ± 9.5		23.0 ± 11.4				0.482

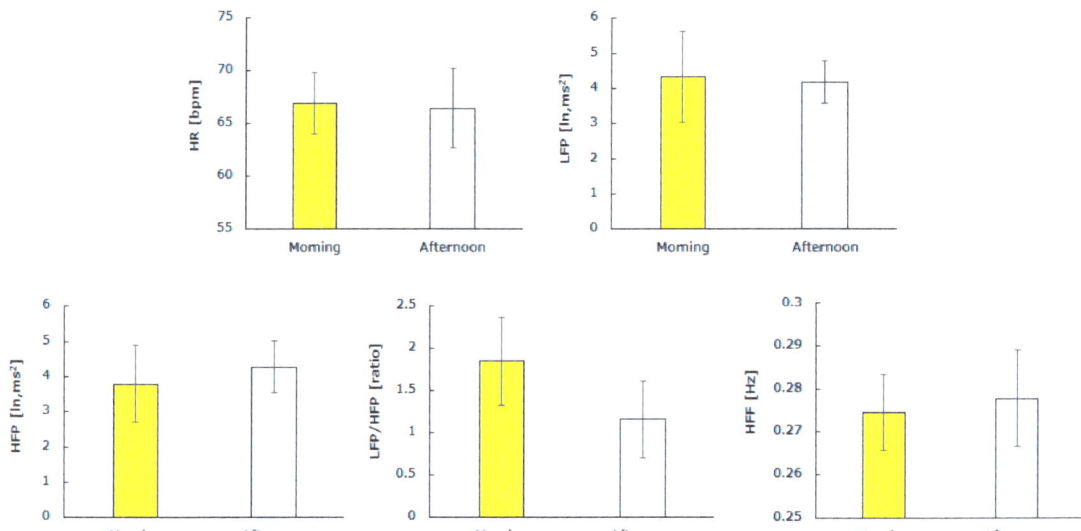

Figure 2. Mean and standard error of HRV indices during morning and afternoon DS driving. The figure shows the mean value and standard error.

The evaluation of the effectiveness of the detection model showed that changes in BA could be detected during afternoon DS driving when arousal is high. Additionally, changes in seat pressure were observed before and after morning DS driving. The position of seat pressure varied depending on the subject, and some subjects' body movements transitioned while others did not.

Figure 2 shows the mean and standard error of the HRV indices during morning and afternoon DS driving. There was no significant difference in HRV indices. Figure 3 shows the change in HRV indices over time during morning and afternoon DS driving. Figure 4 shows the change in ST and BA over time during morning and afternoon DS driving. No significant changes were observed in SK for either morning or afternoon DS driving. BA from 50 to 60 min was significantly increased compared with 30 to 40 min during afternoon DS driving ($p = 0.036$) based on Bonferroni multiple comparisons. Table 2 shows the mean values and standard errors of Palm Q, MF100, PVT, and SSQ. There was a tendency for seat pressure to decrease after DS driving in the morning compared with before DS driving in the morning ($p = 0.067$). In the PVT, RT tended to decrease ($p = 0.052$) and ML decreased significantly ($p = 0.049$) before the start of DS driving in the afternoon compared with before the start of DS driving in the morning. There were no significant differences in the MF100 and SSQ indicators before and after DS driving or between the morning and afternoon. Table 3 shows the change in the position of the highest seat pressure before and after DS driving. Regardless of whether it was the morning or afternoon, there were subjects whose positions changed (five cases) and subjects whose positions did not change (nine cases). Among the subjects whose posture changed, four cases showed a tendency to sit on the left side after DS driving.

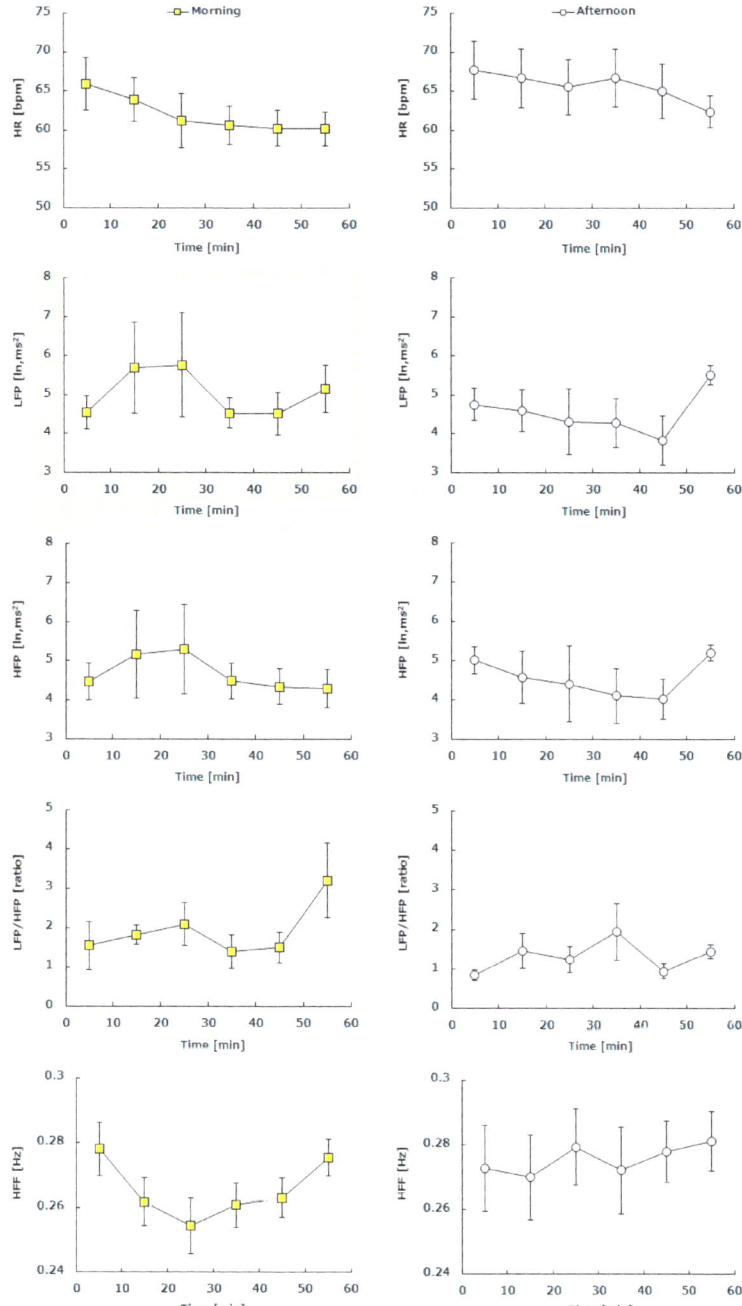

Figure 3. Change in HRV indices over time during morning and afternoon DS driving.

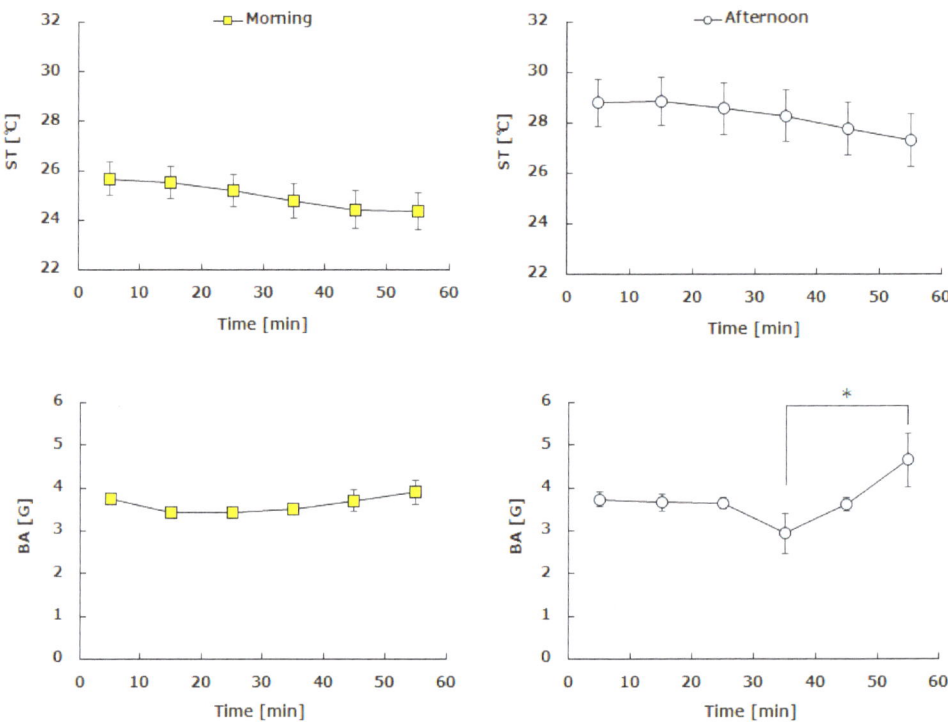

Figure 4. Changes in ST and BA over time during morning and afternoon DS driving. BA from 50 to 60 min was significantly increased compared with 30 to 40 min during afternoon DS driving. (* p = 0.036). Upper: ST, Lower: BA.

Table 3. Change in position of the highest seat pressure before and after DS driving.

Subjects	Sex	Morning		Afternoon	
		Before	After	Before	After
1	male	right	front	right	right
2	male	front	left	front	left
3	male	back	back	left	left
4	male	left	left	front	front
5	female	right	right	front	left
6	female	front	left	front	front
7	female	left	left	left	left

4. Discussion

This paper presents a novel approach to fatigue detection in older drivers based on a subjective evaluation and multimodal analysis of biological signals. The novelty of this research lies in the fact that it focuses on characteristics unique to older drivers that have been overlooked by conventional fatigue detection systems. Because older people are generally prone to arrhythmias, conventional physiological assessment of autonomic nervous system analysis using biometric signal analysis had limitations [26–28]. In this study, we demonstrated the possibility of detecting fatigue continuously from transitions in seat pressure and BA by taking into account the onset of fatigue during long drives, which is unique to older people. This has the potential to significantly reduce the risk of traffic accidents for older drivers. Such fatigue technology could be incorporated into vehicle systems and smartphones. In particular, the possibility of connecting to smartwatches, smart bands, and other wearable devices was considered. Not only would this facilitate more convenient monitoring of fatigue conditions for drivers, but it would also provide a means of continuous monitoring without compromising data quality.

The monitoring of seat pressure is non-invasive, and the measurement of BA also places a low measurement burden on the subject. Further exploration of the integration of these research findings with everyday technology could benefit from more integrated real-life applications. Revisiting the possibilities of connecting to smart devices could increase the applicability of our solution to a wider audience and facilitate its integration into everyday life.

However, this study has a number of limitations. Focusing only on older participants and the relatively small sample size are notable limitations. Future studies should seek to address these limitations by conducting larger studies that include a broader range of participants and test the applicability of the study results across different age groups and categories of drivers.

In this experiment, which evaluated fatigue during DS driving in the morning and afternoon, no significant difference was observed in HRV analyzed from ECG between the morning and afternoon, and no significant difference was observed in the changes over time during DS driving. Furthermore, no significant difference was observed in ST over time, but ST was clearly higher in the afternoon than in the morning. This may be due to the regulation of body temperature by human circadian rhythms [29]; the interrelationship between HRV and circadian rhythms is not clear due to individual differences, and HRV increases or decreases depending on lifestyle and activity status [30]. Furthermore, HRV decreases with age [31], so HRV in an older adult is unlikely to change under the burden of DS driving. In this experiment, SSQ was investigated to determine if simulator sickness occurred in addition to fatigue caused by DS driving. The results showed no significant difference between the morning and afternoon. However, interpretation of the score values is difficult [32]. Regarding fatigue indices, there were no significant differences before and after DS in the morning and afternoon. The fatigue index measured by MF100 uses pulse wave variability to observe the balance of autonomic nerve activity and the rate of arrhythmia. Pulse wave variability is affected by HRV and aging, so it is possible that no significant changes were observed before and after DS. However, just because there are no significant changes in HRV or pulse wave variability in older people does not mean that they are not fatigued. It is also thought that a significant difference is difficult to find due to the decrease in HRV associated with aging. Furthermore, the incidence of arrhythmia changes depending on the time of day, so it cannot be determined whether this is because of the effects of DS [33]. Comparing RT and ML with the PVT before DS driving, reactivity and arousal improved more in the afternoon than in the morning. Thus, it is suggested that in the older group, the experiment was conducted in the afternoon when finger reactivity and arousal were higher.

BA (body activity) during DS driving changed significantly in the afternoon; DS driving time was 60 min, and a gradual increase in body activity was observed, especially in the second half of the driving time. This phenomenon is thought to be due to unconscious body movement to prevent loss of concentration after 30-60 min of driving, and the increase in body movement during the latter half of the DS in the older group is thought to have increased their arousal level.

Regarding seat pressure, in the morning, it was lower after DS driving than before DS driving. In the afternoon, no significant difference was observed before and after DS driving. In the morning and afternoon, considering the position of the measured seat pressure, there were five cases in which the seat position changed during DS driving, and four of these cases tilted to the left after DS driving. Among the nine cases in which the seat pressure position did not change, there were four cases in which the seat pressure tilted to the left after DS driving, and a total of eight cases, or approximately 57% of all cases, tilted to the left after DS driving. Due to experimental constraints, these seat pressure measurements were taken once before the start of DS driving and once after the end of DS driving, so changes in seat pressure during DS driving are unknown. However, based on these results, seat pressure is thought to be related to individual differences in sitting style and daily driving habits, as well as the effects of fatigue and arousal, so a more detailed study is required.

Studies on seating pressure during driving have investigated factors such as driver comfort, seating pressure, seat shape, and cushioning material during long-distance driving. Pascaline L et al. (2021) evaluated the effects of driver seating behavior during long-distance driving by measuring seat pressure in three different seats and found that an increase in general discomfort with driving time was similarly observed in the three seats [34]; Mathieu L et al. (2020) used surface electromyography to assess neuromuscular fatigue and discomfort during long-distance driving [35]. Soft and hard seats have been shown to exhibit different neuromuscular fatigue profiles, with soft seats inducing greater activation of lumbar back muscles and hard seats increasing lumbar back support. Sooho C et al. (2021) reported that self-shaping cushions improve sitting comfort. They reported that by adjusting the shape of the cushion to the driver's body shape, the pressure distribution becomes more uniform, reducing pressure concentrated on the sitting bones and improving sitting comfort and safety [36].

Based on the above, older subjects in this DS driving experiment had higher arousal in the afternoon than in the morning, and their BA increased in the latter half of DS driving. No significant differences were observed overall in HRV or ST over time during DS driving, and no significant differences were observed in fatigue indicators based on pulse wave fluctuations. It is difficult to estimate driver fatigue with these indices. The seat pressure measured in this study was not in a time series, so it was not possible to confirm changes in seat pressure or seat pressure position over time. Previous research has revealed the possibility of fatigue evaluation using seat pressure. It has been suggested that by combining BA and PVT in addition to a detailed analysis of sitting pressure, a detailed fatigue evaluation based on the balance of arousal may be possible.

No significant differences were found in HRV or ST changes calculated from ECG over time, but the results suggest that sitting pressure and body movement have some power to detect fatigue even in such cases. Body motion and BA, in particular, have already been recognized for their usefulness in biometric measurements in various fields. Seat pressure sensors and body motion sensors play an important role in health management and lifestyle monitoring, as well as in the field of care for the older and disabled.

Sitting pressure and body movement sensors monitor sitting and movement patterns in daily life, which can be useful for health management and lifestyle improvement. This makes it possible to identify health risks, such as a lack of exercise and prolonged sitting habits, and to take preventive measures. We look forward to the upcoming possibilities in conventional medical diagnosis and treatment support as well, as it will be useful in diagnosing specific diseases and disorders and monitoring the effects of treatment.

5. Conclusions

In conclusion, this study investigated the feasibility and effectiveness of a system to detect fatigue in older drivers through multimodal analysis. By focusing on characteristics specific to this population, such as BA and seat pressure, as well as driving behavior, we were able to identify indicators that can detect to some extent the state of driving fatigue in older drivers, which has been difficult in the past, such as in subjects with frequent irregular heartbeats. Our findings underscore the importance of considering age-specific factors. As the population ages and the number of older drivers increases, addressing the specific needs of this population will be essential to ensure road safety.

Author Contributions: E.Y. designed the main conceptual ideas and supervised the project. E.Y. collected the data. Y.Y. analyzed the data and wrote this manuscript. K.K. and R.A. supported the design of the experiment design and interpreted the results. All authors have read and agreed to the published version of the manuscript.

Funding: This work was supported by the New Energy and Industrial Technology Development Organization (NEDO), Intensive Support Program for Young Promising Researchers.

Institutional Review Board Statement: The studies involving human participants were reviewed and approved by the Center for Data-driven Science and Artificial Intelligence Tohoku University Institutional Review Board (No. 2022-11, approved 30 January 2023).

Informed Consent Statement: Informed consent was obtained from all subjects involved in this study.

Data Availability Statement: Data are contained within the article.

Conflicts of Interest: Part of this research was funded by a grant from the New Energy and Industrial Technology Development Organization (NEDO). K.K. and R.A. receive compensation from the TS TECH Co., Ltd., to which they belong.

References

1. Staplin, L.; Lococo, K.H.; Mastromatto, T.; Sifrit, K.J.; Trazzera, K.M. CE: Can Your Older Patients Drive Safely? *Am. J. Nurs.* **2017**, *117*, 34–43. [CrossRef]
2. Lukas, A. Elderly Drivers: Danger or Person at Risk? *Dtsch. Med. Wochenschr.* **2018**, *143*, 778–782. [PubMed]
3. Lu, K.; Dahlman, A.S.; Karlsson, J.; Candefjord, S. Detecting driver fatigue using heart rate variability: A systematic review. *Accid. Anal. Prev.* **2022**, *178*, 106830. [CrossRef]
4. Buendia, R.; Forcolin, F.; Karlsson, J.; Arne Sjöqvist, B.; Anund, A.; Candefjord, S. Deriving heart rate variability indices from cardiac monitoring-An indicator of driver sleepiness. *Traffic Inj. Prev.* **2019**, *20*, 249–254. [CrossRef]
5. Persson, A.; Jonasson, H.; Fredriksson, I.; Wiklund, U.; Ahlstrom, C. Heart Rate Variability for Driver Sleepiness Classification in Real Road Driving Conditions. *Annu. Int. Conf. IEEE Eng. Med. Biol. Soc.* **2019**, *2019*, 6537–6540. [PubMed]
6. Badgujar, P.; Selmokar, P. Driver gaze tracking and eyes off the road detection. *Mater. Today Proc.* **2023**, *72*, 1863–1868. [CrossRef]
7. Zhu, T.; Zhang, C.; Wu, T.; Ouyang, Z.; Li, H.; Na, X.; Liang, J.; Li, W. Research on a Real-Time Driver Fatigue Detection Algorithm Based on Facial Video Sequences. *Appl. Sci.* **2022**, *12*, 2224. [CrossRef]
8. Ashiqur, R.; Mamun, B.; Harun, H.; Riasat, K. Computer vision-based approach to detect fatigue driving and face mask for edge computing device. *Heliyon* **2022**, *8*, e11204.
9. Ren, Z.; Li, R.; Chen, B.; Zhang, H.; Ma, Y.; Wang, C.; Lin, Y.; Zhang, Y. EEG-Based Driving Fatigue Detection Using a Two-Level Learning Hierarchy Radial Basis Function. *Front. Neurorobot.* **2021**, *15*, 618408. [CrossRef]
10. Zeng, C.; Mu, Z.; Wang, Q. Classifying Driving Fatigue by Using EEG Signals. *Comput. Intell. Neurosci.* **2022**, *2022*, 1885677. [CrossRef]
11. Liu, Y.; Ji, Y.; Gao, Y.; Ping, Z.; Kuang, L.; Li, T.; Xu, W. A Novel Fatigue Driving State Recognition and Warning Method Based on EEG and EOG Signals. *J. Healthc. Eng.* **2021**, *2021*, 7799793. [CrossRef] [PubMed]
12. Zheng, Y.; Ma, Y.; Cammon, J.; Zhang, S.; Zhang, J.; Zhang, Y. A new feature selection approach for driving fatigue EEG detection with a modified machine learning algorithm. *Comput. Biol. Med.* **2022**, *147*, 105718. [CrossRef] [PubMed]
13. Hu, J. Automated Detection of Driver Fatigue Based on AdaBoost Classifier with EEG Signals. *Front. Comput. Neurosci.* **2017**, *11*, 72. [CrossRef] [PubMed]
14. Wang, H.; Dragomir, A.; Abbasi, N.I.; Li, J.; Thakor, N.V.; Bezerianos, A. A novel real-time driving fatigue detection system based on wireless dry EEG. *Cogn. Neurodyn.* **2018**, *12*, 365–376. [CrossRef] [PubMed]
15. Du, H.; Zhao, X.; Zhang, X.; Zhang, Y.; Rong, J. Effects of fatigue on driving performance under different roadway geometries: A simulator study. *Traffic Inj. Prev.* **2015**, *16*, 468–473. [CrossRef]
16. Oron-Gilad, T.; Ronen, A. Road characteristics and driver fatigue: A simulator study. *Traffic Inj. Prev.* **2007**, *8*, 281–289. [CrossRef]
17. Desmond, P.A.; Matthews, G. Implications of task-induced fatigue effects for in-vehicle countermeasures to driver fatigue. *Accid. Anal. Prev.* **1997**, *29*, 515–523. [CrossRef]
18. Zhang, Q.; Wu, C.; Zhang, H. Driving Fatigue Prediction Model considering Schedule and Circadian Rhythm. *J. Adv. Trans.* **2020**, *2020*, 9496259. [CrossRef]
19. Task Force of the European Society of Cardiology and the North American Society of Pacing and Electrophysiology. Heart rate variability: Standards of measurement, physiological interpretation and clinical use. *Circulation* **1996**, *93*, 1043–1065. [CrossRef]
20. Elghozi, J.L.; Laude, D.; Girard, A. Effects of respiration on blood pressure and heart rate variability in humans. *Clin. Exp. Pharmacol. Physiol.* **1991**, *18*, 735–742. [CrossRef]
21. TDK, Silmee W22. Available online: https://product.tdk.com/ja/products/biosensor/biosensor/silmee_w22/index.html (accessed on 1 February 2024).
22. CAPE. Available online: https://www.cape.co.jp/products/pdt017 (accessed on 1 February 2024).
23. Murata Manufacturing, MF100. Available online: https://medical.murata.com/ja-jp/products/fatigue (accessed on 1 February 2024).
24. Dinges, D.F.; Powell, J.W. Microcomputer analysis of performance on a portable, simple visual RT task during sustained operations. *Behavior Research Methods. Instrum. Comput.* **1985**, *17*, 652–655. [CrossRef]

25. Kennedy, R.; Lane, N.; Berbaum, K.; Lilienthal, M. A simulator sickness questionnaire(SSQ):A new method for quantifying simuiator sickness. *Int. J. Aviat. Psychol.* **1993**, *3*, 203–220. [CrossRef]
26. Koh, D.W.; Lee, S.G. An Evaluation Method of Safe Driving for Senior Adults Using ECG Signals. *Sensors* **2019**, *19*, 2828. [CrossRef] [PubMed]
27. Luis Alberto Lasses y, O. Heart arrhythmia in the elderly. *Arch. Cardiol. Mex.* **2002**, *72* (Suppl. 1), S106–S110.
28. Levy, S. Atrial fibrillation, the arrhythmia of the elderly, causes and associated conditions. *Anadolu Kardiyol. Derg.* **2002**, *2*, 55–60.
29. Kim, D.W.; Mayer, C.; Lee, M.P.; Choi, S.W.; Tewari, M.; Forger, D.B. Efficient assessment of real-world dynamics of circadian rhythms in heart rate and body temperature from wearable data. *J. R. Soc. Interface* **2023**, *20*, 20230030. [CrossRef]
30. Yoshida, Y.; Yuda, Y.; Yokoyama, K.; Hayano, J. Evaluation of nocturnal heart rate variability for strenuous exercise day using wearable photoelectric pulse wave sensor. *J. Exerc. Rehabil.* **2018**, *14*, 633–637. [CrossRef]
31. Leopoldo, G.; Damián, G.; Magdalena, M.D.; Julieta, T.M.; Isabel, M.I. The effect of age on the heart rate variability of healthy subjects. *PLoS ONE* **2021**, *16*, e0255894.
32. Yoshida, Y.; Kaneko, I.; Hayano, J.; Yokoyama, K.; Yuda, E. Evaluation of Tympanic Temperature, Heart Rate Variability and Finger-Foot Reaction Using VR in the Elderly. *J. Adv. Comput. Intell. Intell. Inform.* **2022**, *26*, 309–314. [CrossRef]
33. Portaluppi, F.; Tiseo, R.; Smolensky, M.H.; Hermida, R.C.; Ayala, D.E.; Fabbian, F. Circadian rhythms and cardiovascular health. *Sleep. Med. Rev.* **2012**, *16*, 151–166. [CrossRef]
34. Pascaline, L.; Mathieu, L.; Clément, B.; Erick, D.; Tanguy, M.; Christophe, B.; Jean-Marc, A.; Laurent, B.; Serge, M. Car seat impact on driver's sitting behavior and perceived discomfort during prolonged real driving on varied road types. *PLoS ONE* **2021**, *16*, e0259934.
35. Lecocq, M.; Lantoine, P.; Bougard, C.; Allègre, J.M.; Bauvineau, L.; Bourdin, C.; Marqueste, T.; Dousset, E. Neuromuscular fatigue profiles depends on seat feature during long duration driving on a static simulator. *Appl. Ergon.* **2020**, *87*, 103118. [CrossRef] [PubMed]
36. Choi, S.; Kim, H.; Kim, H.; Yang, W. A Development of the Self Shape Adjustment Cushion Mechanism for Improving Sitting Comfort. *Sensors* **2021**, *21*, 7959. [CrossRef] [PubMed]

Disclaimer/Publisher's Note: The statements, opinions and data contained in all publications are solely those of the individual author(s) and contributor(s) and not of MDPI and/or the editor(s). MDPI and/or the editor(s) disclaim responsibility for any injury to people or property resulting from any ideas, methods, instructions or products referred to in the content.

Article
Gait Pattern Identification Using Gait Features

Min-Jung Kim, Ji-Hun Han, Woo-Chul Shin ⬚ and Youn-Sik Hong *

Department of Computer Science and Engineering, Incheon National University, Incheon 22012, Republic of Korea; alswjdsla47@inu.ac.kr (M.-J.K.); jin4884@inu.ac.kr (J.-H.H.); crepas2@inu.ac.kr (W.-C.S.)
* Correspondence: yshong@inu.ac.kr

Abstract: Gait analysis plays important roles in various applications such as exercise therapy, biometrics, and robot control. It can also be used to prevent and improve movement disorders and monitor health conditions. We implemented a wearable module equipped with an MPU-9250 IMU sensor, and Bluetooth modules were implemented on an Arduino Uno R3 board for gait analysis. Gait cycles were identified based on roll values measured by the accelerometer embedded in the IMU sensor. By superimposing the gait cycles that occurred during the walking period, they could be analyzed using statistical methods. We found that the subjects could be identified using the gait feature points extracted through the statistical modeling process. To validate the feasibility of feature-based gait pattern identification, we constructed various machine learning models and compared the accuracy of their gait pattern identification. Based on this, we also investigated whether there was a significant difference between the gait patterns of people who used cell phones while walking and those who did not.

Keywords: IMU (Inertial Measurement Unit); gait analysis; healthcare; internet of things; gait pattern recognition

Citation: Kim, M.-J.; Han, J.-H.; Shin, W.-C.; Hong, Y.-S. Gait Pattern Identification Using Gait Features. *Electronics* **2024**, *13*, 1956. https://doi.org/10.3390/electronics13101956

Academic Editors: Ilaria Sergi and Teodoro Montanaro

Received: 19 April 2024
Revised: 12 May 2024
Accepted: 14 May 2024
Published: 16 May 2024

Copyright: © 2024 by the authors. Licensee MDPI, Basel, Switzerland. This article is an open access article distributed under the terms and conditions of the Creative Commons Attribution (CC BY) license (https://creativecommons.org/licenses/by/4.0/).

1. Introduction

Walking is the most common health activity in daily life and the first activity to be affected by physical disabilities. Gait analysis is the systematic study of human walking using detailed observations and measurements of bodily movements, mechanics, and muscle activity. The purpose of gait analysis is to identify any abnormalities in the way a person walks, evaluate walking efficiency, and assess the overall biomechanical health of the individual. Gait analysis can help improve pedestrian safety and security in public spaces, transportation systems, commercial facilities, and more. Motion detection technology such as CCTV can be used to identify dangerous situations, and pedestrian identification can be used in secure systems to prevent unauthorized access. Gait analysis also has applications in business, such as providing customized products and services by identifying customer preferences and behaviors through their movements. Currently, it is being commercialized in the healthcare sector, such as using treadmills to detect gait and provide exercise therapy.

Identifying walking patterns has important applications in many aspects of health, security, and business. Some studies have suggested a link between walking and brain health, highlighting that walking can support brain function and improve cognition [1]. Other studies are investigating the interaction between walking and cognition in patients with geriatric diseases such as Alzheimer's [2–4]. These studies are expected to help us understand the impact of walking patterns on cognition and brain health and to aid in the early detection and management of these conditions. They also show the potential for innovative uses of walking pattern identification in health and medicine, providing useful information to monitor and treat patient conditions [5].

Recent research related to gait analysis includes the use of multiple infrared cameras [6–8] and markers [9] to analyze the movement of markers in an indoor area and the use of foot pressure sensors [10] and treadmills to analyze plantar pressure distribution [11]. The infrared camera method has limitations in terms of location, the inconvenience of wearing the equipment, and cost, while the pressure sensor method requires the equipment to be customized to the size of a person's foot. Treadmills are less useful for the elderly and patients who have difficulty walking.

Lin, C.-L. et al. [12] implemented deep learning neural network models using pedestrian color image sequences as an input and found them to be effective for pedestrian detection and recognition. They extracted moving silhouette figures from the walking image sequences and used the correlation between the original and new silhouettes as a primitive feature of human walking.

Lee et al.'s work [13] describes a sensor compensation algorithm that transforms an unstable sensor coordinate system into a stable anatomical coordinate system and enhances the distinction between individual gait patterns through the introduction of 2D cyclogram features.

Recently, many effective research methods using inertial sensors have been proposed. T. Gujarathi et al. [14] compared joint angles measured using an inertial sensor and a 3D motion capture system and presented results indicating that the deviation was not significant. H. Kim et al. [15] showed that the joint movement patterns of the hip and knee joints during walking can be recognized using an MPU-9150 IMU (Inertial Measurement Unit). Methods using inertial sensors offer the convenience of wearing equipment, have no space restrictions, and can be implemented at a low cost. IMUs with built-in inertial sensors are small, easy to attach to the body, and relatively inexpensive (USD 150 to USD 200). Furthermore, IMU sensor-based gait analysis does not require additional equipment to be installed to configure the experimental environment.

An IMU consists of a gyroscope, an accelerometer, and a geomagnetic sensor. An accelerometer is a sensor that measures the acceleration of an object, while a gyroscope measures the rotational speed and angular velocity (rad/s) of an object. A magnetometer is a sensor that detects the magnetic field of an object. In the previous studies using IMUs, about 70% of the experiments were conducted by attaching them to the shanks or ankles of the subjects [16–21]. These studies mainly focused on extracting gait parameters such as gait speed, gait cycle, cadence, stance time, and swing time.

In this study, a wearable module with an IMU [14,15,22] was used for gait analysis on flat ground. Unlike treadmill walking, people walk at different speeds and move their feet at different angles on flat ground. A person's gait parameters are variable depending on their physical condition, gender, and age. By superimposing gait cycles over a period of walking, it may be possible to extract significant gait parameters using statistical methods. If statistically significant discrete gait features can be extracted from continuous gait data, it will be possible to identify gait patterns using these gait features.

Our proposed method to eliminate the uncertainty brought by highly variable gait data involves superimposing gait cycles. The advantage of superimposing gait cycles is that it can eliminate outliers and identify statistically significant features.

The three feature points extracted in our proposed method varied depending on the collected data. However, the superimposed gait cycles were not expected to have large statistical deviations, and we confirmed through experiments that the gait cycles converged to a constant value after preprocessing. This means that the gait cycles stabilized as walking continued. This was also the purpose behind our attempt at superimposing gait cycles.

This paper is organized as follows. Section 2 describes a wearable module with an embedded IMU sensor and a method of gait cycle recognition used in this study. Section 3 discusses the relationship between left and right foot walking. Section 4 proposes a method of gait pattern identification using gait features. Section 5 applies the proposed method to a real application model. Section 6 concludes this work.

2. Gait Cycle Recognition Using IMU Sensors

On a flat surface, a person's gait pattern (walking speed, steps per minute, etc.) is not constant, but they repeat a regular gait cycle. The gait cycle consists of eight gait phases from Heel Strike to Terminal Swing. In this study, we built a wearable module using the MPU9250 IMU sensor (by InvenSense Inc., San Hose, CA, USA) for the experiment. Although the IMU sensor consisted of nine-axis sensors, the gait parameters (roll, pitch, and yaw) extracted from the three-axis acceleration sensor were mainly utilized for gait parameter analysis. For this paper, we focused on the roll value, which could track changes in leg movement. By repeatedly superimposing roll data with the periodicity in the gait cycle for a certain walking time, statistically significant gait parameters could be extracted. We extracted three statistically significant features from the superimposed graphs and used them for statistical modeling.

2.1. Gait Cycle

The gait cycle is divided into a stance phase and a swing phase, as shown in Figure 1 [23]. The stance phase, which accounts for 60% of the total gait, is when the sole of the foot is in contact with the ground and supports the body's weight. The swing phase, which accounts for the remaining 40% of the gait, is when the foot is in the air. The gait cycle can be further broken down into eight patterned gait phases. The stance phase can be divided into five phases, from Heel Strike (HS) to Pre-Swing (PS), and the swing phase can be divided into three phases, from Toe-Off (TO) to Terminal Swing (TS). The main characteristics of each part of the gait cycle are as follows:

- Heel Strike (HS): Gait begins in the Heel Strike phase, which is the moment when the heel touches the ground. At this point, the foot is placed on the ground and the leg movement begins.
- Loading Response: In this phase, weight is placed on the legs and the body is lifted upward. This process propels the pedestrian's body further forward.
- Mid-Stance: In this phase, the body weight is fully supported on one foot and the legs are straight. The body stabilizes in the Mid-Stance phase.
- Terminal Stance: In this phase, the legs are responsible for moving the body forward. The knees should be kept pinned and the weight should be shifted forward.
- Pre-Swing (PS): In this phase, the sole of the foot begins to push off the ground. This acts as a springboard for the next gait cycle.
- Toe-Off (TO): This is the moment when the sole of the foot leaves the ground, preparing for the next gait cycle.
- Mid-Swing (MS): The Mid-Swing phase is entered with the legs crossed in midair. This is when knee extension is maximized to prepare for the next phase, the Heel Strike.
- Terminal Swing (TS): In this phase, the gait cycle is completed as the legs prepare to return to the ground from the air.

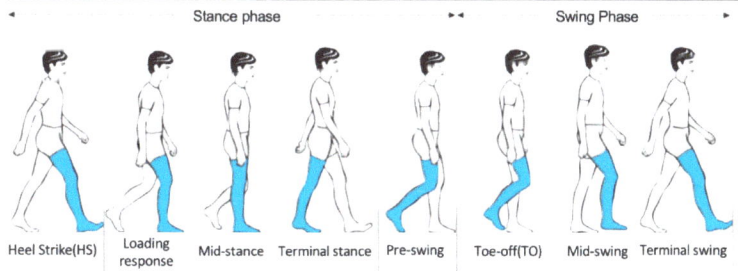

Figure 1. Gait phases and detailed gait steps in a gait cycle [23].

2.2. IMU Sensor

IMU sensors are used to simplify gait analysis without any restrictions on the configuration of the experimental environment. An IMU sensor basically consists of a three-axis gyroscope, a three-axis accelerometer, and a three-axis magnetic sensor. An accelerometer is a sensor that measures the acceleration of an object on the x-, y-, and z-axes. It is used to measure the acceleration of an object or to detect shocks, tilt, etc. A gyroscope measures the rotational speed and angular velocity (rad/s) of an object along the x-, y-, and z-axes. The values measured by a gyroscope are used to calculate the pitch value. A magnetometer is a sensor that measures the azimuth angle and magnetic field of an object on the x-, y-, and z-axes. IMU sensors are categorized into six-axis and nine-axis sensors depending on whether they have a magnetometer, with six-axis IMU sensors being more common. It is also possible to use two IMU sensors instead of one.

The locations where IMU sensors are mounted on the body are mainly concentrated on the lower body, such as the top of the foot, the back of the foot, the thigh, and the shank. This representative study of gait analysis using IMU sensors attempted to distinguish the Heel Strike (HS) point and the Toe-Off (TO) point in the gait cycle by attaching six-axis IMU sensors (accelerometers and gyroscopes) to both shanks. Using the raw data acquired from the IMU sensors, the research objective was to distinguish the stance phase from the swing phase in the gait cycle.

The MPU 9250 IMU sensor is a nine-axis IMU sensor. It consists of three accelerometer axes, three gyroscope axes, three magnetometer axes, and one temperature axis. The coordinate system of a three-axis sensor is shown in Figure 2.

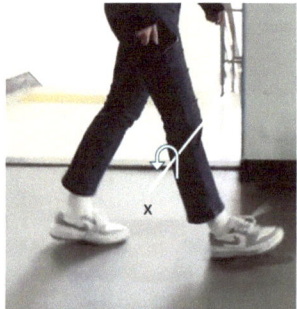
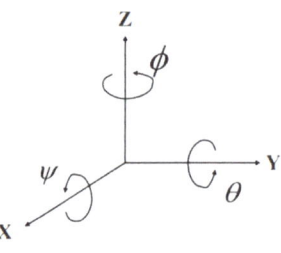

Figure 2. The x-axis (**left**) and MPU9250 coordinate system (**right**) when the module is attached to the right shank.

Roll, pitch, and yaw can be calculated from the raw data measured by the MPU-9250's built-in sensors. The radius of rotation indicated by roll, pitch, and yaw when the sensor is attached to the ankle is shown in Figure 2. The yaw value can be calculated from the raw data measured by the magnetic sensor. The rotation speeds in the x, y, and z axis directions are used to determine the rotation of an object. The pitch and yaw values are used to determine movement, such as the direction of rotation of the ankle during walking. However, since the object of analysis in this paper was straight walking on a flat surface, the pitch and yaw values were not processed.

The roll value is the angle of the knee, and it can be used to determine how much the knee extends and flexes. The roll value was obtained using data measured by the accelerometer. The acceleration of the accelerometer in the x, y, and z axis directions was related to the tilt of the object and could be calculated based on that. The roll value was found using Equation (1). Notice that A_x, A_y, and A_z represent the acceleration values of the x-axis, y-axis, and z-axis, respectively.

$$\psi = atan\left(\frac{A_Y}{\sqrt{A_X^2 + A_Z^2}}\right) \qquad (1)$$

2.3. Configuration of a Wearable Module

Since an IMU sensor is worn on the body to collect data, we chose the MPU-9250 for its small size. The Arduino Uno R3 model was used as an embedded board for a wearable module. Although the Arduino Nano model has an advantage in terms of size and ease of mounting on the body, we chose the Uno R3 model to utilize the HC-05 and HC-06 Bluetooth modules instead of the Nano's built-in Bluetooth module. The HC-05 and HC-06 modules are devices that transmit and receive data via Bluetooth wireless communication and are mainly used in embedded systems such as Arduino or Raspberry Pi boards. By adding ankle pads to the embedded board, we built a wearable module that could be attached to the body.

The wearable module implemented for use in gait experiments is shown in Figure 3. The MPU-9250 was mounted on the Uno R3 board and connected to the HC-05. The board was bonded to the ankle pads. HC-05 operated in master mode, whereas HC-06 operated in slave mode. The raw data measured by the MPU-9250 sensor were received by the HC-05, which transmitted them to the HC-06. The HC-06 transmitted the data to the server via Bluetooth.

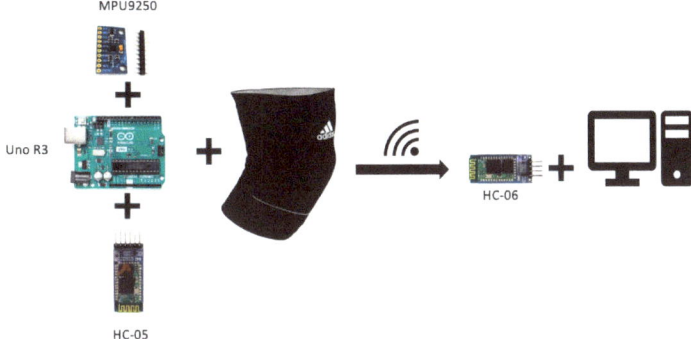

Figure 3. Data transmission process using the wearable module.

2.4. Roll Data-Based Gait Cycle Recognition

The raw data measured by the accelerometer were converted into analyzable roll data through preprocessing and data refinement such as outlier removal and filtering. Figure 4a shows the preprocessing of raw data with a Kalman filter, and Figure 4b shows the results after removing outliers. Figure 4b shows a graph of gait cycles that were extracted and continuously superimposed, with the red lines being the outlier gait cycles.

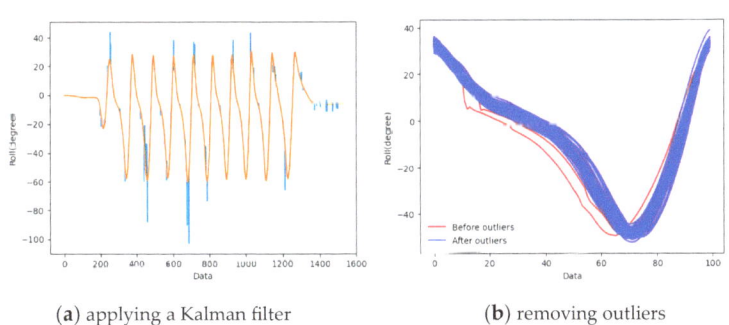

(**a**) applying a Kalman filter (**b**) removing outliers

Figure 4. Preprocessing applied to raw data.

The beginning stage of the gait cycle, "Foot-Flat", is the state when the foot is flat on the ground while the person is standing. However, this cannot be used as a starting point because each subject has a different Foot-Flat state point. In order to classify the gait cycle with certainty, we identified the gait cycle as the Toe-Off (TS) point (marked with a blue dot), corresponding to the minimum roll value, and the Heel Strike (HS) point (marked with a red dot), corresponding to the maximum roll value, as shown on the left side of Figure 5. The TS point and HS point correspond to the beginning and end of the gait cycle, respectively. The gait cycle can be identified based on these two points, and thus gait parameters can be extracted based on the gait cycle.

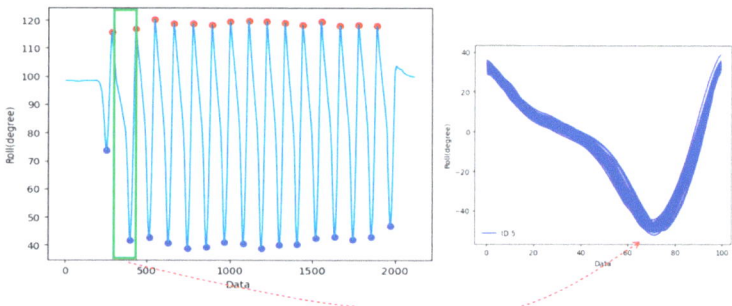

Figure 5. (**left**) TS points (marked with blue dots) and HS points (marked with red dots) and (**right**) the superimposed gait cycles for the subject (ID 5).

We split the roll data into sub-graphs for each gait cycle and then overlaid each sub-graph by aligning it with the beginning of the gait cycle. The right side of Figure 5 shows the superimposed graph for subject 5. The graph generated by overlaying gait cycles describes the gait characteristics of subject 5. By overlaying gait cycles, we can identify the statistical characteristics of the gait cycles.

2.5. Experimental Conditions and Subject Information

The subjects' natural walking was measured in a 15-meter-long flat area. To induce normal walking, the subjects went through two practice walks before starting the gait measurement. Fourteen volunteers (six men and eight women) with no physical disabilities participated in this experiment. The average age of the participants was 24 years (23 to 29 years), and the average height was 167 cm (156 cm to 190 cm). They were fully informed of the purpose and procedures of this experiment and gave their consent to participate in it.

3. Relationship between Left and Right Foot Walking Based on Gait Parameters

Although the left and right feet perform similar functions in walking, their use, efficiency, and roles in movement can vary due to a wide range of factors. In a healthy and typical gait, there is an expectation of symmetry between the left and right feet in terms of timing, force distribution, and range of motion. Symmetry is often an indicator of efficiency and normal gait patterns. The fundamental biomechanical processes that govern walking apply to both feet, which go through similar gait phases, such as the stance and swing phases, regardless of being the left or right foot.

Although perfect symmetry is rare, a functionally symmetric gait is often the goal of rehabilitation. Small differences are normal, but significant asymmetries may indicate underlying issues. Through biomechanical and kinematic analysis, we can quantitatively evaluate the similarities and differences between left and right foot walking. For this, gait parameters such as stride length, cadence, and the stance/swing time ratio are compared. In this study, we analyzed the differences between left and right foot walking using TO and HS.

The subjects wore the wearable modules attached to the knee protector pads on both shanks. The first step was to start with the left foot. Each subject was asked to walk a total of 10 times. As shown in Table 1, the average values of the gait time (unit: 1/100 s) of the right foot stabilized as the experiment was repeated. Therefore, the number of footsteps after preprocessing also converged to a certain value. However, the standard deviation (SD) of the gait time of the right foot was larger than that of the left foot.

Table 1. Comparison of left and right foot gait characteristics after preprocessing.

Trial	Left Foot			Right Foot		
	Mean (1/100 s)	SD (1/100 s)	Gait Numbers	Mean (1/100 s)	SD (1/100 s)	Gait Numbers
1st	54.39	8.71	23	51.35	17.37	20
2nd	54.91	11.46	23	56.94	19.95	26
3rd	53.96	9.73	23	54.68	20.86	22
4th	54.48	16.13	23	54.09	16.77	22
5th	53.77	13.95	22	54.23	22.05	22
6th	54.39	17.29	23	60.94	14.27	16
7th	51.91	18.22	23	53.86	24.11	22
8th	54.57	21.04	23	53.54	14.78	24
9th	52.83	11.16	23	52.75	16.53	20
10th	54.35	19.58	23	53.04	15.57	23
Avg.	53.96	14.73	22.9	54.54	18.23	21.7

As shown in Table 1, the gait numbers of the left and right feet did not match, which caused a discrepancy in the gait cycles of the left and right feet. Thus, a direct comparison of the gait cycles based on the gait number was not feasible due to the lack of matching gait cycles between the two feet. Without overlapping gait numbers, we could not directly compare the same gait events across the left and right feet. Therefore, we performed separate analyses for each foot regarding HS and TO to understand the gait characteristics of each foot.

The visualizations shown in Figure 6 provide insights into the distributions of the HS and TO values and the relationships between them for both the left and right feet. The HS distribution indicates that both feet showed a range of HS values, and the distributions indicate variability in Heel Strike positions and intensities across different gait cycles. Similarly, the TO values for both feet display variability, reflecting differences in the Toe-Off phase of the gait cycle. The scatter plots in Figure 6 reveal the relationships between the HS and TO values for each foot, highlighting how these two parameters vary together across different gait cycles.

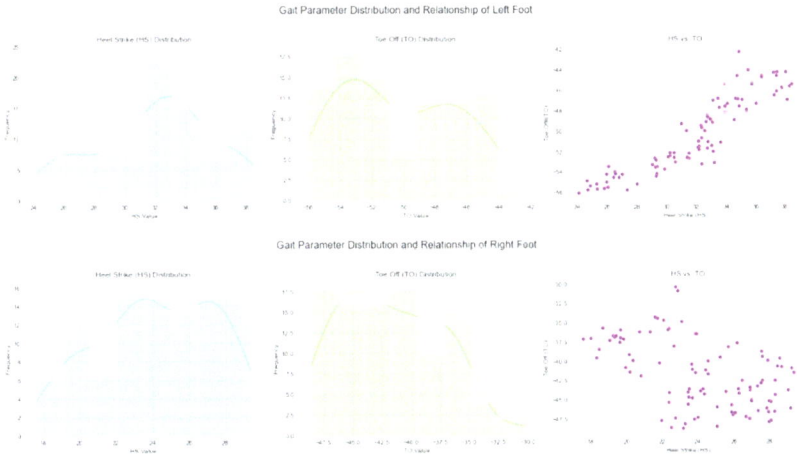

Figure 6. Gait parameter distribution. The graph (**above**) is for the left foot, and the graph (**below**) is for the right foot.

These visual comparisons allow us to observe that while there may be similarities in the distribution of gait parameters between the left and right feet, each foot exhibits unique characteristics. Figure 7 shows boxplots to compare the ranges and central tendencies of the HS and TO values. Figure 7 provides insights into the ranges, medians, and variability of these gait parameters for both feet. The boxplot of the HS values helps clarify how the Heel Strike phase might differ between the two feet in terms of intensity or position. Similarly, the boxplot of the TO values compares the distributions between the left and right feet, highlighting differences in the Toe-Off phase's timing and intensity.

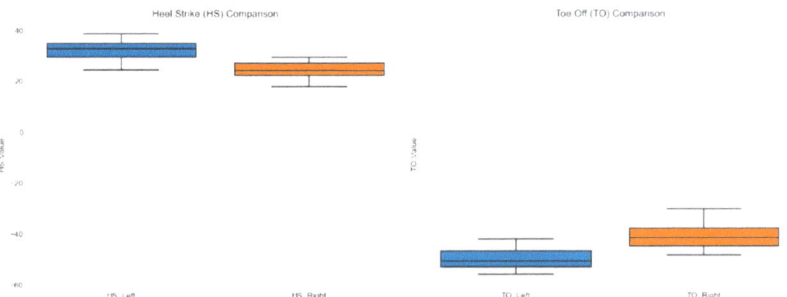

Figure 7. Comparison of gait parameters across left and right feet. The (**left**) graph is for HS, while the (**right**) graph is for TO.

4. Gait Pattern Recognition Based on Gait Feature Points

We proposed a method for identifying individuals by analyzing walking patterns using gait feature points. First, we examined whether there were significant differences in the gait parameters extracted from the subjects. Then, the gait cycles were superimposed into a single graph to identify the statistical characteristics of the gait parameters. Three feature points that can identify walking patterns were extracted. We checked whether individuals could be identified using these gait features. Finally, we analyzed the accuracy of individual identification by building several machine learning models with these feature points as a dataset.

4.1. Extraction of Gait Parameters

Gait parameters were extracted from the data obtained from the subjects, and they are summarized in Table 2. The extracted gait parameters include the stance time, swing time, gait time, and cadence. The unit of all gait parameters except cadence is seconds. In Table 2, all gait parameter values except cadence are average values. The gait cycle is a duration, as it is the time between taking a left footstep (or right footstep) and taking the next left footstep (or right footstep). The gait cycle is the sum of the stance time and swing time.

Table 2. Summary of the gait parameters extracted from the subjects.

ID	Sex	Age	Height (cm)	Stance Time/Swing Time Ratio	Gait Time (s)	Cadence
1	F	23	163	1.46	9.99	128
2	F	24	159	2.33	14.74	112
3	F	23	158	2.18	10.06	127
4	F	23	159	1.83	10.93	109
5	F	23	162	2.51	11.48	114
6	F	23	157	2.3	11.4	130
7.	F	23	156	1.97	9.84	129
8.	F	23	159	1.73	10.21	130
		Avg. (female)		2.04	11.08	122.38

Table 2. Cont.

ID	Sex	Age	Height (cm)	Stance Time/Swing Time Ratio	Gait Time (s)	Cadence
9	M	25	173	2.36	10.97	106
10	M	26	173	2.43	9.59	112
11	M	23	179	2.22	8.84	115
12	M	23	190	2.29	9.6	114
13	M	25	172	2.3	11.4	130
14	M	29	182	2.28	11.46	101
Avg. (male)				2.31	10.31	113
Overall Avg.				2.16	10.75	118.36

As can be seen in Table 2, the average gait time of the male subjects was shorter than that of the female subjects. We expected that the difference in the gait cycles between the men and women would also affect the cadence values. We also predicted that there would be differences in gait time, even within the same gender or age group. There were clear differences in the gait parameters among the subjects, and based on this, we proposed a method for extracting feature points that can distinguish individual gait characteristics from the gait cycle.

4.2. Extraction of Gait Features from Superimposed Gait Cycles

The proportion of the stance phase in the gait cycle was measured to be 70%. In addition, the swing phase, which corresponded to 30% of the gait cycle, showed little variation compared to the other gait-related parameters, with the largest standard deviation being only 0.17 in each gait cycle. Therefore, we focused on the inflection point of the gait cycle curve in the section corresponding to the stance phase.

As shown in Figure 8, we can extract two points (GP1 and GP3) with the maximum and minimum values in the stance phase interval. In addition, we can identify the inflection point (GP2) in the interval (GP1, GP3). Gait feature points GP1, GP2, and GP3 can be associated with the points where Heel Strike, Mid-Stance, and Toe-Off occur in the gait segment. GP1 (Heel Strike) and GP3 (Toe-Off) are the points where the knee angle (roll value) shows its maximum and minimum values, respectively. The closed interval (GP1, GP3) corresponds to the start and end of the stance phase. Gait feature point GP2 is the point where inflection occurs and corresponds to Mid-Stance in the gait cycle. GP2 is also the point with the greatest variation between subjects. Table 3 shows the gait features extracted from the subjects.

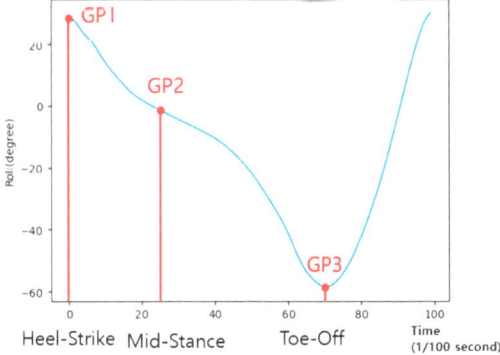

Figure 8. Extraction of feature points from the stance phase.

Table 3. The gait feature points of the subjects.

ID	Left Foot			Right Foot		
	GP1	GP2	GP3	GP1	GP2	GP3
1	23.69	−2.43	−56.27	19.17	−3.98	−48.7
2	22.14	−11.07	−48.61	19.41	−13.17	−50.88
3	18.37	−8.88	−46.8	12.84	−9.19	−40.05
4	20.13	−10.34	−56.40	16.59	−14.77	−37.35
5	24.95	−4.73	−45.01	23.25	−6.23	−49.10
6	25.42	−2.97	−51.07	25.59	−6.15	−48.93
7	28.14	−5.84	−43.90	26.60	−3.31	−61.64
8	22.41	−4.30	−54.15	18.30	−7.07	−55.38
Avg. (female)	23.16	−6.32	−50.28	20.22	−7.98	−49.0
9	27.94	−2.88	−58.91	25.50	−4.86	−56.16
10	32.51	0.72	−44.11	35.24	2.47	−51.70
11	37.60	−1.90	−44.17	30.60	−3.81	−49.51
12	26.11	−5.04	−43.08	25.50	−4.86	−56.16
13	31.85	−4.39	−50.24	25.65	−7.40	−41.92
14	31.85	−2.43	−56.27	28.17	−1.60	−43.67
Avg. (male)	31.31	−1.84	−49.46	27.08	−3.34	−49.85
Avg	26.65	−4.75	−49.93	23.74	−6.00	−49.34

4.3. Identification of Individual Gait Patterns Based on Feature Points

Figure 9 presents a 3D scatter plot showing the relationship between the values across GP1, GP2, and GP3 for each individual. In this visualization, the x, y, and z axes represent the GP1, GP2, and GP3 values, respectively, with the color intensity reflecting the normalized GP3 values.

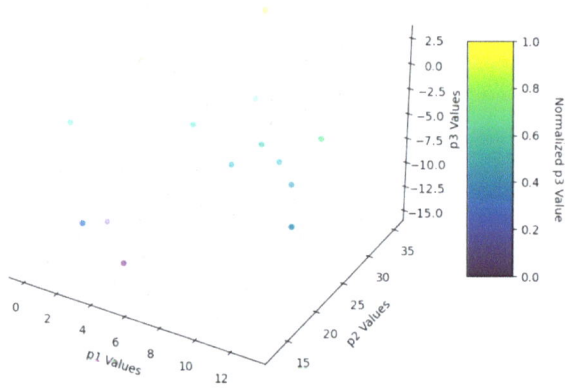

Figure 9. A 3D scatter plot showing the relationship between the values across GP1, GP2, and GP3.

This 3D perspective provides a comprehensive view of how these three dimensions correlate for each person. With only these three feature points, it is possible to distinguish each subject's walking pattern.

4.4. MLP Model for Gait Pattern Identification

We showed that the gait features extracted through statistical modeling can be used to identify the walking patterns of the subjects. We built several machine learning models using the gait-related data as a training dataset and analyzed their classification performance.

As summarized in Table 2, the gait intervals varied from subject to subject. Since datasets for training a machine learning model must be the same size, we needed to unify the gait cycles of the different intervals. To make the different lengths of the gait cycles equal, we normalized them based on the gait cycle with the maximum period. Although the gait cycles varied between the subjects, their differences were relatively small. Thus, it was necessary to reduce the variation by minimizing the standard deviation of the gait cycles. In these experiments, we obtained an average of 10 ± 2 gait cycles. Therefore, to reduce the variation in the gait cycles (average) for each subject, we collected 100 ± 20 data by running the experiment 10 times.

The classification accuracy of each of the four machine learning models is summarized in Table 4. The classification accuracy of most models ranged from 95 to 97%. The evaluation using eXtreme gradient boosting showed a strong performance with an accuracy of 0.97, a precision of 0.97, a recall of 0.97, and an F1-Score of 0.97. This demonstrated that the gait feature-based model can be used to identify individuals.

Table 4. Classification accuracy of each model.

Model	Accuracy	Precision	Recall	F1-Score
Multi-Layer Perceptron (MLP)	0.95	0.95	0.95	0.95
Random Forest	0.95	0.95	0.95	0.95
Support Vector Machine (SVM)	0.95	0.95	0.94	0.94
eXtreme Gradient Boosting	0.97	0.97	0.97	0.97

5. Determining Whether to Use a Mobile Phone Based on Walking Pattern

To demonstrate the usability of the gait pattern identification using gait features, we applied it to a real application. We conducted an experiment to determine whether there was a significant difference between the walking patterns of those who used a mobile phone while walking and those who did not. There were a total of seven subjects (16 years old—four persons (three males and one female), 23 years old—one person (female), 26 years old—one person (male), and 29 years old—one person (male)). They walked a total of 15 m in a straight line while using their mobile phones, then walked on the same line again without using their phones. The subjects were asked to walk as normal as possible. This experiment was repeated five times.

Walking begins at the heel strike (HS) stage, the moment the heel touches the ground. At this time, the foot is placed on the ground and the leg starts to move. The toe-off (TO) stage is the moment when the sole of the foot is lifted off the ground, preparing for the next gait cycle. Among the subject's gait parameters, the HS and the TO values were visualized as a scatter plot in Figure 10. In Figure 10, the HS and the TO values when a mobile phone was not used and when used are indicated by red and blue circles, respectively. The TO average was higher in the case of not using a mobile phone than in the case of using a mobile phone. There is a clear difference in the scatter plot, enough to distinguish whether or not a mobile phone was used for most of the subjects (5 out of 7).

Figure 10. Heel Strike (HS) and Toe-Off (TO) distributions of subjects.

In Figure 11, shows the averages of 10 footsteps using a bar graph. The right and left bars for each subject represent the number of steps (average) when a mobile phone was or was not used, respectively. It can be seen that the number of steps taken when using a mobile phone was higher than the number of steps taken when not using a mobile phone.

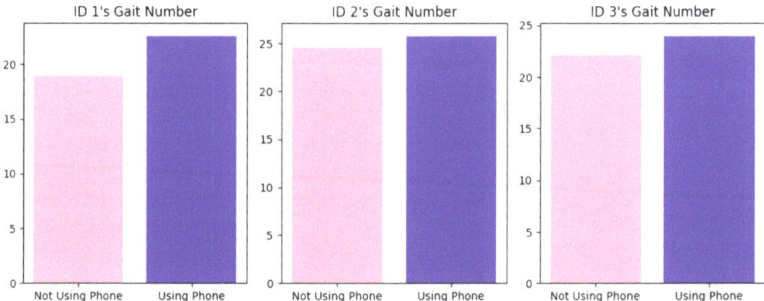

Figure 11. Gait numbers that occurred when a mobile phone was or was not used by the subjects.

Through the analysis of gait parameters, it was confirmed that mobile phone usage had a significant impact on walking patterns. The classification performance was evaluated using machine learning modeling (logistic regression and random forest) using six gait parameters (HS, TO, PTP (peak-to-peak), gait cycle, gait number, and gait time) as a dataset. Note that HS and TO corresponded to the feature points GP1 and GP3, respectively. Even though the dataset was not large enough, the classification accuracy for both methods on the test set was 86%. The precision, recall, and F1-Score of the logistic regression model were 0.92, 0.85, and 0.88, respectively, while the precision, recall, and F1-Score of the random forest model were 1.00, 0.75, and 0.86, respectively.

6. Conclusions

In this study, we built a wearable module with an MPU-9250 IMU sensor for gait analysis. The gait cycle could be determined using roll data measured by the accelerometer built into the IMU sensor. By superimposing the gait cycles determined during the walking period, gait-related parameters could be extracted using statistical techniques. We proposed a method for identifying individuals by analyzing their walking patterns using gait feature points. We extracted two points, GP1 and GP3, with the maximum and minimum values in the stance phase interval. In addition, we could identify the point GP2, where the inflection point occurred in the interval (GP1, GP3). GP1, GP2, and GP3 could be associated with the points where Heel Strike, Mid-Stance, and Toe-Off occurred in the gait segment. Three feature points that could identify walking patterns were extracted.

To verify the feasibility of feature-based gait pattern recognition, we analyzed the accuracy of individual identification by building several machine learning models using these feature points as a dataset. The classification accuracy of most models ranged from 95 to 97%. To demonstrate the usability of the gait pattern identification using gait features, we conducted an experiment to determine whether there was a significant difference between the walking patterns of those who used a mobile phone while walking and those who did not. The classification performance was evaluated using two machine learning models and a dataset that included two gait features (HS and TO). Although the number of subjects was limited to seven, the classification accuracy of the machine learning models reached 92–100%.

Author Contributions: Conceptualization, Y.-S.H.; methodology, Y.-S.H. and W.-C.S.; software, M.-J.K. and J.-H.H.; validation, Y.-S.H., M.-J.K., and J.-H.H.; formal analysis, Y.-S.H. and W.-C.S.; investigation, M.-J.K. and J.-H.H.; resources, M.-J.K. and J.-H.H.; data curation, M.-J.K. and J.-H.H.; writing—original draft preparation, M.-J.K. and J.-H.H.; writing—review and editing, Y.-S.H.; visualization, M.-J.K. and J.-H.H.; supervision, Y.-S.H.; project administration, Y.-S.H.; funding acquisition, Y.-S.H. All authors have read and agreed to the published version of the manuscript.

Funding: This research was partially funded by Incheon National University (grant number 2023-0144).

Institutional Review Board Statement: This study was conducted in accordance with the Declaration of Helsinki and was approved by the Institutional Review Board of Incheon National University (7007971-202303-004, 18 May 2023).

Informed Consent Statement: Not applicable.

Data Availability Statement: All data used in this paper were dependent on the sensors used and the measurement environments. The measurement values of each sensor used in our experiments will be provided upon request by e-mail.

Conflicts of Interest: The authors declare no conflicts of interest.

References

1. Montero-Odasso, M.; Verghese, J.; Beauchet, O.; Hausdorff, J.M. Gait and Cognition: A complementary approach to understanding brain function and the risk of falling. *J. Am. Geriatr. Soc.* **2012**, *60*, 2127–2136. [CrossRef] [PubMed]
2. Beauchet, O.; Allali, G.; Berrut, G.; Hommet, C.; Dubost, V.; Assal, F. Gait analysis in demented subjects: Interests and perspectives. *Neuropsychiatr. Dis. Treat.* **2008**, *4*, 155–160. [CrossRef] [PubMed] [PubMed Central]
3. Allali, G.; Kressig, R.W.; Assal, F.; Herrmann, F.R.; Dubost, V.; Beauchet, O. Changes in gait while backward counting in demented older adults with frontal lobe dysfunction. *Gait Posture* **2007**, *26*, 572–576. [CrossRef] [PubMed]
4. Lee, N.G.; Kang, T.W.; Park, H.J. Relationship Between Balance, Gait, and Activities of Daily Living in Older Adults with Dementia. *Geriatr. Orthop. Surg. Rehabil.* **2020**, *11*, 2151459320929578. [CrossRef] [PubMed]

5. Vu, H.T.T.; Dong, D.; Cao, H.L.; Verstraten, T.; Lefeber, D.; Vanderborght, B.; Geerooms, J. A Review of Gait Phase Detection Algorithms for Lower Limb Prostheses. *Sensors* **2020**, *20*, 3972. [CrossRef] [PubMed] [PubMed Central]
6. Kanwar, A.; Upadhyay, P. An appearance-based approach for gait identification using infrared imaging. In Proceedings of the 2014 International Conference on Issues and Challenges in Intelligent Computing Techniques (ICICT), Ghaziabad, India, 7–8 February 2014; pp. 719–724. [CrossRef]
7. Prakash, C.; Gupta, K.; Mittal, A.; Kumar, R.; Laxmi, V. Passive Marker Based Optical System for Gait Kinematics for Lower Extremity. *Procedia Comput. Sci.* **2015**, *45*, 176–185. [CrossRef]
8. Kwolek, B.; Michalczuk, A.; Krzeszowski, T.; Switonski, A.; Josinski, H.; Wojciechowski, K. Calibrated and synchronized multi-view video and motion capture dataset for evaluation of gait recognition. *Multimed. Tools Appl.* **2019**, *78*, 32437–32465. [CrossRef]
9. Carse, B.; Meadows, B.; Bowers, R.; Rowe, P. Affordable clinical gait analysis: An assessment of the marker tracking accuracy of a new low-cost optical 3D motion analysis system. *Physiotherapy* **2013**, *99*, 347–351. [CrossRef] [PubMed]
10. Aqueveque, P.; Germany, E.; Osorio, R.; Pastene, F. Gait Segmentation Method Using a Plantar Pressure Measurement System with Custom-Made Capacitive Sensors. *Sensors* **2020**, *20*, 656. [CrossRef] [PubMed] [PubMed Central]
11. Kim, H.; Kang, Y.; Valencia, D.R.; Kim, D. An Integrated System for Gait Analysis Using FSRs and an IMU. In Proceedings of the 2018 Second IEEE International Conference on Robotic Computing (IRC), Laguna Hills, CA, USA, 31 January–2 February 2018; pp. 347–351. [CrossRef]
12. Lin, C.-L.; Fan, K.-C.; Lai, C.-R.; Cheng, H.-Y.; Chen, T.-P.; Hung, C.-M. Applying a Deep Learning Neural Network to Gait-Based Pedestrian Automatic Detection and Recognition. *Appl. Sci.* **2022**, *12*, 4726. [CrossRef]
13. Lee, S.-B.; Lee, S.-J.; Park, E.; Lee, J.; Kim, I. Gait-based continuous authentication using a novel sensor compensation algorithm and geometric features extracted from wearable sensors. *IEEE Access* **2022**, *10*, 120122–120135. [CrossRef]
14. Seel, T.; Raisch, J.; Schauer, T. IMU-Based Joint Angle Measurement for Gait Analysis. *Sensors* **2014**, *14*, 6891–6909. [CrossRef] [PubMed]
15. Moon, K.S.; Lee, S.Q.; Ozturk, Y.; Gaidhani, A.; Cox, J.A. Identification of Gait Motion Patterns Using Wearable Inertial Sensor Network. *Sensors* **2019**, *19*, 5024. [CrossRef] [PubMed]
16. Lee, T.; Kim, I.; Lee, S.-H. Estimation of the Continuous Walking Angle of Knee and Ankle (Talocrural Joint, Subtalar Joint) of a Lower-Limb Exoskeleton Robot Using a Neural Network. *Sensors* **2021**, *21*, 2807. [CrossRef] [PubMed]
17. Shin, D.; Lee, S.; Hwang, S. Locomotion Mode Recognition Algorithm Based on Gaussian Mixture Model Using IMU Sensors. *Sensors* **2021**, *21*, 2785. [CrossRef]
18. Gujarathi, T.; Bhole, K. Gait Analysis Using IMU Sensor. In Proceedings of the 2019 10th International Conference on Computing, Communication and Networking Technologies (ICCCNT), Kanpur, India, 6–8 July 2019; pp. 1–5. [CrossRef]
19. Park, S.; Yoon, S. Validity Evaluation of an Inertial Measurement Unit (IMU) in Gait Analysis Using Statistical Parametric Mapping (SPM). *Sensors* **2021**, *21*, 3667. [CrossRef] [PubMed] [PubMed Central]
20. Hacker, S.; Kalkbrenner, C.; Algorri, M.-E.; Blechschmidt, R. Gait Analysis with IMU. Gaining New Orientation Information of the Lower Leg. In Proceedings of the International Joint Conference on Biomedical Engineering Systems and Technologies (BIOSTEC 2014), Angers, Loire Valley, France, 3–6 March 2014. [CrossRef]
21. Prasanth, H.; Caban, M.; Keller, U.; Courtine, G.; Ijspeert, A.; Vallery, H.; Von Zitzewitz, J. Wearable Sensor-Based Real-Time Gait Detection: A Systematic Review. *Sensors* **2021**, *21*, 2727. [CrossRef] [PubMed]
22. Han, Y.C.; Wong, K.I.; Murray, I. Gait Phase Detection for Normal and Abnormal Gaits Using IMU. *IEEE Sens. J.* **2019**, *19*, 3439–3448. [CrossRef]
23. Pirker, W.; Katzenschlager, R. Gait disorders in adults and the elderly: A clinical guide. *Wien. Klin. Wochenschr.* **2016**, *129*, 81–95. [CrossRef] [PubMed]

Disclaimer/Publisher's Note: The statements, opinions and data contained in all publications are solely those of the individual author(s) and contributor(s) and not of MDPI and/or the editor(s). MDPI and/or the editor(s) disclaim responsibility for any injury to people or property resulting from any ideas, methods, instructions or products referred to in the content.

Analysis of Magnetotherapy Device-Induced Fields Using Cylindrical Human Body Model

Mario Cvetković *,† and Bruno Sučić †

Faculty of Electrical Engineering, Mechanical Engineering and Naval Architecture, University of Split, 21000 Split, Croatia; bruno.sucic.00@fesb.hr
* Correspondence: mcvetkov@fesb.hr
† These authors contributed equally to this work.

Abstract: This paper deals with the analysis of induced current density and the induced electric field in the body of a human exposed to the magnetic field of a magnetotherapy device. As the displacement currents at extremely low frequencies can be neglected, the biological tissues can thus be considered a weakly conducting medium, facilitating the use of a quasi-static eddy current approximation. The formulation is based on the surface integral equation for the unknown surface charges, whose numerical solution is obtained using the method of moments technique. A simplified model of the human body is utilized to examine various scenarios during the magnetotherapy procedure. The numerical results for the induced current density and the induced electric field are obtained using the proposed model. The analyses of various stimulating coil parameters, human body model parameters, and a displacement of the magnetotherapy coil were carried out to assess their effects on the induced current density. The results suggest that selection of the stimulating coil should be matched based on the size of the human body, but also that the position and orientation of the coil with respect to the body surface will result in different distributions of the induced fields. The results of this study could be useful for medical professionals by showing the importance of various magnetotherapy coil parameters for preparation of various treatment scenarios.

Keywords: magnetotherapy; integral equation formulation; induced current density; induced electric field; biomedical application

1. Introduction

Magnetotherapy is a non-invasive form of medical treatment used to relieve joint or muscular pain and decrease stress. It represents a complementary approach utilized in physiotherapy and rehabilitation of locomotive organs in humans, as well as in veterinary medicine. The technique, in its most frequently used form, is based on the use of extremely low-frequency (ELF) magnetic fields generated by solenoidal coils of various sizes administered over a patient's extremities, neck, or back.

The beginning of modern magnetotherapy is associated with the 1950s, initially starting in Japan and later moving to Europe and the former Soviet Union [1]. Later, during the 1970s, it became a new modality in treating delayed bone fractures [2], subsequently resulting in US Food and Drug Administration approval. Initially, a very specific ELF biphasic signal was used, while a decade later an approach based on the use of a pulsed electromagnetic field (pulsed EMF or PEMF) with a high-frequency was approved for the treatment of superficial soft tissue pain and edema. Compared to time varying EMFs such as those used in PEMF it should be emphasized that the use of static magnets in both reducing pain and altering physiological responses is associated with questionable therapeutic benefits as research studies do not provide conclusive support [3,4].

The historical review of the therapeutic use of static electric and magnetic fields and their current acceptance as alternative and complementary therapies can be found in [5].

Despite of the persisting interest in these medical modalities, the medical establishment is still unconvinced due to the lack of unambiguous proof. The use of a static magnetic field as a form of therapy has been considered in treatments including, but not limited to, chronic pelvic pain [6], carpal tunnel syndrome pain [7], and inflammation due to rheumatoid arthritis [8]. There are many available magnetic devices including bracelets, bands, insoles, braces, pillows, and mattresses that are often marketed as having medical benefits; however, there are no consistent studies showing their therapeutic benefits [9].

Another form of magnetotherapy is PEMF, which has many possible applications. For example, the study in [10] assessed the efficacy of low-frequency PEMF therapy in patients with knee osteoarthritis, concluding that a statistically significant benefit in terms of pain reduction was demonstrated. On the other hand, the sono-electro-magnetic treatment of chronic pelvic pain syndrome did not find a significant improvement compared to the placebo-controlled group, as shown in [11]. Another study [12] examined the effectiveness of magnetotherapy for decreasing chronic low back pain and did not find a statistically significant improvement when compared to control subjects exposed to a non-functioning placebo device. One recent review [13] analyzed the use of PEMF even in non-invasive cancer treatment and concluded that further studies are necessary to establish the efficiency in a clinical environment. Finally, a meta analysis in [14] considered the efficacy of the magnetotherapy approach in the rehabilitation field and concluded that electromagnetic field therapy could alleviate pain and improve function in patients with various forms of musculoskeletal pain.

The applied fields used in ELF magnetotherapy are generally of a sinusoidal waveform with frequencies ranging between 1 Hz and 300 Hz, with a typical frequency of 100 Hz, but there are also high-frequency pain treatment modalities such as non-invasive transcranial magnetic stimulation (TMS) [15] or invasive spinal cord stimulation (SCS) [16], which operate at 10 kHz. The maximum magnetic flux density achieved using a typical magnetotherapy coil is generally between 1 mT and 10 mT.

The exposure of humans to ELF magnetic fields generated by magnetotherapy devices has been analyzed in a number of papers including [17–21]. The study in [17] is based on the analytical approach featuring the disk model of the human body, while most often the numerical approach is based on the use of the finite-difference time-domain method [18,19]. In many numerical analyses, the main focus when calculating the induced eddy current distribution is restricted to a particular body part, such as a knee joint [18,19,21] or a forearm [22]. The full human body model exposure during the magnetotherapy procedure is used to a lesser extent, as evidenced from the available literature [17].

This paper is on the analysis of magnetotherapy device-induced fields in a simplified human body model based on the surface integral equation approach featuring the method of moments technique. This work is an extension of our previous conference paper [23] where our simplified body model was introduced. Compared to [23], additional calculations were carried out to determine the effects of different model parameters on the induced current density distribution. Also, we have extended the analysis to assess the effects of the coil positioning on the induced current density.

This paper is organized as follows: After the current Section 1, Section 2 will provide an overview of the mathematical background, including the formulation based on the quasi-static eddy current approximation for a biological body and its derivation using the boundary conditions for the induced current density. Then, the surface integral equation for the unknown surface charges solved by numerical approach are also discussed. In Section 3, the simplified human body model is introduced, whose validation is carried out by comparing the numerical results with the analytical approach. Section 4 discusses the numerical results for the induced current density and the induced electric field, due to a magnetotherapy procedure, obtained via our proposed model. The analysis of stimulating coil parameters, human body model parameters, and the position of magnetotherapy coil are also discussed in this section. Section 5 provides the concluding remarks. The analytical expression for the induced current density is derived in Appendix A.

2. Mathematical Details

2.1. Problem Formulation

The human body tissues can be considered as weakly conducting, facilitating the use of a quasi-static eddy current approximation. Consider a biological body, represented by the region of electrical conductivity σ_1, enclosed with the boundary surface S, as depicted in Figure 1.

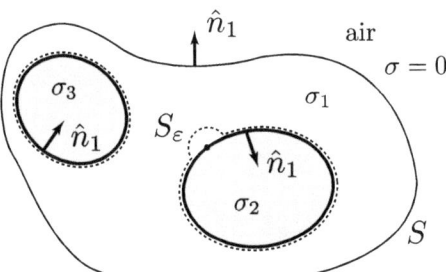

Figure 1. Weakly conducting biological media with conductivity σ_1.

The body is surrounded by an air medium ($\sigma = 0$), but it can also be in contact with regions with different values of conductivity, e.g. σ_2 and σ_3.

The differential form of Ohm's law can be used to relate the induced eddy current density with the induced electric field in biological tissue:

$$\vec{J} = \sigma \vec{E} \tag{1}$$

where σ represents the electrical conductivity of tissue.

The normal component of $\vec{J}$ is continuous across interfaces between regions with different parameters. The boundary conditions on the surface S can thus be written as:

$$\sigma_{int}\hat{n}_1 \cdot \vec{E}_{int}(\vec{r}) = \sigma_{ext}\hat{n}_1 \cdot \vec{E}_{ext}(\vec{r}) \tag{2}$$

where $\sigma_{int} = \sigma_1$ is the conductivity of biological media, and σ_{ext} is the conductivity of external medium, σ_2, σ_3, or $\sigma_{air} = 0$. $\vec{E}_{int} = \vec{E}_1$ denotes the electric field in biological media, while $\vec{E}_{ext}$ is the electric field in external regions. The boundary condition on the interface between body and air is thus:

$$\sigma_1\hat{n}_1 \cdot \vec{E}_1(\vec{r}) = 0 \tag{3}$$

with $\hat{n}_1$ unit as the normal vector.

For time harmonic fields, the electric field can be expressed as follows:

$$\vec{E}(\vec{r}) = -j\omega \vec{A}(\vec{r}) - \nabla \varphi(\vec{r}) \tag{4}$$

where $\vec{A}$ is the magnetic vector potential and φ is the electric scalar potential, while f is the operating frequency where $\omega = 2\pi f$.

The first term in (4) is due to current flowing in the magnetotherapy device (coil), while the second one is due to accumulated free surface charges, represented by charge density ρ_s on the boundary S between regions with different material properties.

The electric scalar potential is governed by the Laplace equation

$$\Delta \varphi = 0 \tag{5}$$

everywhere except at the interfaces. The solution of (5) is integral of the following form:

$$\varphi(\vec{r}) = \int_S \frac{\rho_s(\vec{r}')}{4\pi\varepsilon_0} \frac{dS'}{R} \tag{6}$$

where $R = |\vec{r} - \vec{r}'|$ is the distance between the observation point $\vec{r}$ and the source point $\vec{r}'$. Inserting (6) into (4), we obtain:

$$\vec{E}(\vec{r}) = -j\omega \vec{A}(\vec{r}) - \int_S \frac{\rho_s(\vec{r}')}{4\pi\varepsilon_0} \nabla \frac{1}{R} dS' \qquad (7)$$

where ε_0 is the free space permittivity.

In case of singularity, where $R \to 0$, it is necessary to find the limiting values of the integral from (7), once when $\vec{r} \to \vec{r}'$ from the inside and the other time from the outside. In this limiting case, a small hemispherical region of radius ε needs to be excluded around the point on surface S. This region is denoted as S_ε, as depicted in Figure 2.

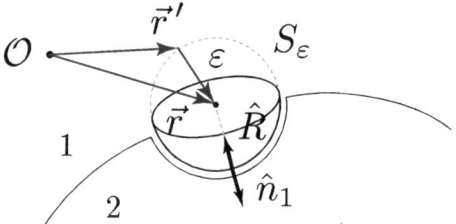

Figure 2. Treatment of singularity on the surface S [24].

The value of the surface integral (7) in the limiting case can be easily found [24]:

$$\lim_{R \to 0} \int_{S_\varepsilon} \frac{\rho_s(\vec{r}')}{4\pi\varepsilon_0} \nabla \frac{1}{R} dS' = \lim_{R \to 0} \frac{\rho_s(\vec{r}')}{4\pi\varepsilon_0} \int_{\theta=0}^{\pi/2} \int_{\varphi=0}^{2\pi} \left(-\frac{\vec{R}}{R^3}\right) \varepsilon^2 \sin\theta \, d\theta \, d\varphi = -\frac{\rho_s(\vec{r}')}{2\varepsilon_0}(\hat{R}) \qquad (8)$$

where $\hat{R} = -\hat{n}_1$ in region 1 and $\hat{R} = \hat{n}_1$ in surrounding region 2.

Using (8) and (7), the following expressions for the electric field are obtained in the vicinity of surface S, from the interior and the exterior side, respectively:

$$\vec{E}_{int}(\vec{r}) = -j\omega \vec{A}(\vec{r}) - \int_S \frac{\rho_s(\vec{r}')}{4\pi\varepsilon_0} \nabla \frac{1}{R} dS' - \hat{n}_1 \frac{\rho_s(\vec{r}')}{2\varepsilon_0} \qquad (9)$$

$$\vec{E}_{ext}(\vec{r}) = -j\omega \vec{A}(\vec{r}) - \int_S \frac{\rho_s(\vec{r}')}{4\pi\varepsilon_0} \nabla \frac{1}{R} dS' + \hat{n}_1 \frac{\rho_s(\vec{r}')}{2\varepsilon_0} \qquad (10)$$

By inserting (9) and (10) into boundary condition (2), followed by some additional steps, the following integral equation formulation can be obtained [25]:

$$\frac{\rho_s(\vec{r}')}{2\varepsilon_0} + \frac{\sigma_{int} - \sigma_{ext}}{\sigma_{int} + \sigma_{ext}} \int_S \frac{\rho_s(\vec{r}')}{4\pi\varepsilon_0} \nabla \frac{1}{R} dS' = \frac{\sigma_{ext} - \sigma_{int}}{\sigma_{int} + \sigma_{ext}} j\omega \vec{A}(\vec{r}) \cdot \hat{n}_1; \quad \vec{r} \in S \qquad (11)$$

The surface integral Equation (11) is written in terms of the unknown free surface charge density ρ_s on the surface S, hence it is sometimes called ρ-formulation. σ_{ext} in (11) denotes the known value of electrical conductivity σ_2, σ_3 or $\sigma_{air} = 0$, depending on the boundary.

After the surface charges ρ_s are determined, the eddy current density can be found using:

$$\vec{J}(\vec{r}) = \sigma_n \left[-j\omega \vec{A}(\vec{r}) - \nabla \varphi(\vec{r}) \right] \qquad (12)$$

where σ_n is the conductivity of the medium.

2.2. Excitation by Magnetotherapy Coil

Assuming a uniform current density I over a coil cross-section, the magnetic vector potential at observation point $\vec{r}$ can be determined from the integral [26]:

$$\vec{A}(\vec{r}) = \frac{\mu_0 M I}{4\pi} \oint_l \frac{\vec{dl}}{|\vec{r} - \vec{r}'|} \quad (13)$$

where μ_0 is the free space permeability, M is the number of coil windings, and $\vec{r}'$ is the position of the source point along the coil. The orientation of differential element $\vec{dl}$ along the coil is the same as the direction of coil current I. The magnetic vector potential (13) due to circular stimulating coil can be calculated easily if the coil is approximated by the N-sided polygon as follows:

$$\vec{A}(\vec{r}) = \frac{\mu_0 M I}{4\pi} \sum_{i=1}^{N} \frac{\Delta l_i}{R} \quad (14)$$

where Δl_i is the length of the polygon line segment, and R is the distance from observation to source point on the coil. The resultant magnetic vector potential at an arbitrary point in space can be determined by assembling the contributions from all linear segments.

The electric field due to stimulating coil can be found using:

$$\vec{E}(\vec{r}) = -j\omega \vec{A}(\vec{r}) \quad (15)$$

where ω is the angular frequency.

An illustrative example of the normalized electric field distribution in the plane below the circular coil and the so-called figure-of-eight coil can be seen in Figure 3.

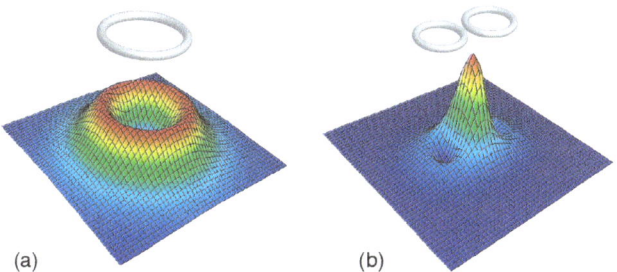

(a)　　　　　　　　　(b)

Figure 3. Normalized electric field above the circular coil (**a**) and the figure-of-eight coil (**b**). Adapted from [27].

As evidenced from Figure 3, in case of the circular coil, which is used traditionally in magnetotherapy, the maximum value of the electric field will be in the vicinity of coil windings, whereas in case of the figure-of-eight coil, this place is directly below the coil geometric center.

2.3. Numerical Solution

The numerical solution to integral Equation (11) was carried out via moments method (MoM). The boundary surface S of the human body is first discretized with triangular elements. The expansion of unknown surface charge density ρ_s is carried out using known basis function f_n:

$$\rho_s(\vec{r}) = \sum_{n=1}^{N} a_n f_n(\vec{r}) \quad (16)$$

with N denoting the number of triangles used to discretize the surface S and a_n the unknown coefficients to be solved for, respectively. The pulse basis functions, equal to one for triangle T_n and zero elsewhere, have been utilized in the expansion, as depicted in Figure 4:

$$f_n(\vec{r}) = \begin{cases} 1 &, \vec{r} \in T_n \\ 0 &, \vec{r} \notin T_n \end{cases} \quad (17)$$

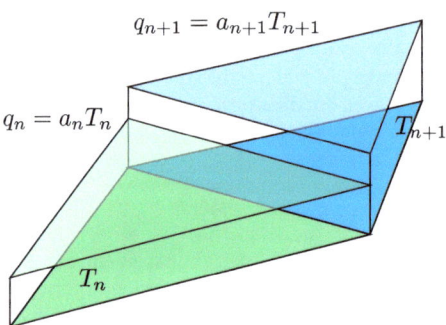

Figure 4. Illustration of piecewise-constant pulse basis function on triangles T_n and T_{n+1}. Electric charge on each triangle can be determined from charge density multiplied by triangle surface, denoted by T_n and T_{n+1}, respectively.

Inserting (17) into (16), the unknown surface charge density can be approximated. Multiplying Equation (11) with test functions $t_m(\vec{r})$, where $t_m(\vec{r}) = f_n(\vec{r})$, followed by integration over S, leads to the following system of N integral equations:

$$\sum_{n=1}^{N} a_n \int_S t_m(\vec{r}) \frac{\rho_s(\vec{r}')}{2\varepsilon_0} dS + \frac{\sigma_{int} - \sigma_{ext}}{\sigma_{int} + \sigma_{ext}} \sum_{n=1}^{N} a_n \int_S t_m(\vec{r}) \int_{S'} \frac{\rho_s(\vec{r}')}{4\pi\varepsilon_0} \nabla \frac{1}{R} dS' dS =$$

$$= \frac{\sigma_{ext} - \sigma_{int}}{\sigma_{int} + \sigma_{ext}} \sum_{n=1}^{N} a_n \int_S t_m(\vec{r}) j\omega \vec{A}(\vec{r}) \cdot \hat{n}_1 dS; \quad \vec{r} \in S \quad (18)$$

which can be recast in the following compact matrix form:

$$[\mathbf{Z}] \cdot \{\mathbf{I}\} = \{\mathbf{V}\} \quad (19)$$

The elements of the impedance matrix $\mathbf{Z}$ can be determined using:

$$Z_{mn} = \delta_{mn} \frac{T_m}{2\varepsilon_0} + \frac{\sigma_{int} - \sigma_{ext}}{\sigma_{int} + \sigma_{ext}} \int_{T_m} \int_{T_n} \frac{\hat{n}(\vec{r})}{4\pi\varepsilon_0} \nabla \frac{1}{R} dS' dS \quad (20)$$

while elements of the source vector $\mathbf{V}$ can be determined using the following:

$$V_m = \frac{\sigma_{ext} - \sigma_{int}}{\sigma_{int} + \sigma_{ext}} \int_{T_m} \hat{n}(\vec{r}) \cdot j\omega \vec{A}(\vec{r}) dS \quad (21)$$

In (20), T_m and T_n denote the surfaces of observation and source triangles, respectively, while δ_{mn} represents the Kronecker delta (equal to 1 for $m = n$ and 0 otherwise).

The solution to the matrix Equation (19) is a a column vector $\mathbf{I}$ containing the unknown coefficients a_n. From these coefficients, the unknown surface charges can be found using (16), while the electric field can be found using expression (4).

Numerical solution to integrals (20) and (21) can be found elsewhere, e.g., in [28,29].

3. Human Body Model
3.1. Cylindrical Model

The typical position of the human body during the magnetotherapy procedure is depicted in Figure 5a.

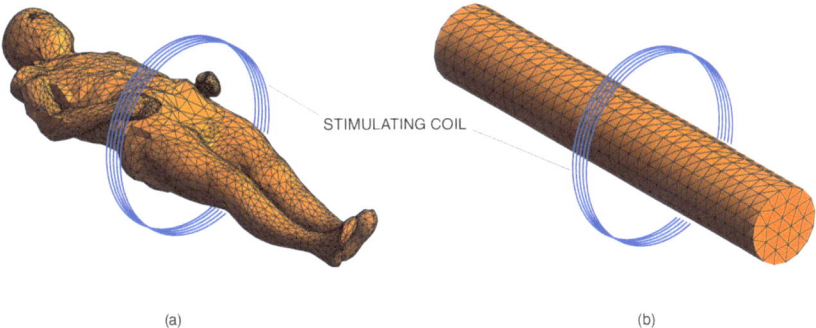

Figure 5. (**a**) Illustration of supine position during a magnetotherapy procedure. (**b**) Simple cylindrical human body model exposed to magnetic field of magnetotherapy device coil. The height of human body is 1.75 m, while diameter of cylindrical model is 0.3 m. Human body is modeled as having homogeneous conductivity $\sigma = 0.5$ S/m.

As a first approximation, the human body can be represented using a canonical geometry such as a parallelepiped [30,31] or a cylinder [31,32], as shown in Figure 5b.

The dimensions of the simplified cylindrical human body model are as follows: diameter $D = 30$ cm and height $h = 1.75$ m. Furthermore, the human body can be considered as having homogeneous properties, represented by the uniform value of electrical conductivity $\sigma = 0.5$ S/m.

It should be emphasized that the human body is of a geometrically complicated form whose composition is rather complex, consisting of various tissues with parameters that are often difficult to find. In addition to this, the electrical properties of tissues are dependent on the frequency, as depicted in Figure 6.

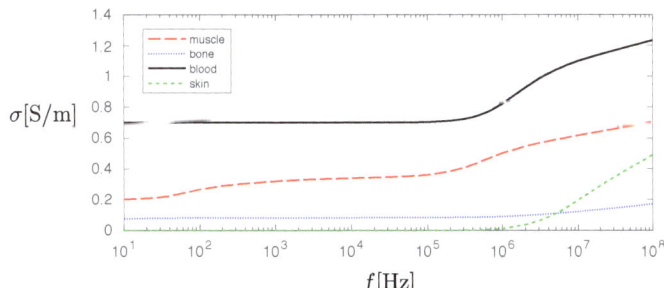

Figure 6. Frequency dependent electrical conductivity of several human body tissues and blood. Data from [33].

It should be noted that the numerical approach to magnetotherapy analysis presented in this work could be easily extended to include the anatomically realistic model of the human body, such as the one depicted in Figure 5a. The results presented in the following sections are obtained using a simplified cylindrical model.

3.2. Model Validation

The validation of the numerical model is carried out first. The results obtained using an approach based on integral equation Formulation (11), solved by MoM, is compared with the analytical approach. To this end, the disk model of human body [34] has been utilized. The human body exposed to ELF fields due to magnetotherapy device based on the analytical approach has been previously carried out in [17].

Assuming the exposure of human body to uniform magnetic flux density directed perpendicular to the human body, $(B = B_z)$, the induced current density J_ϕ, circulating around the body axis, can be obtained using the following [17]:

$$|J_\phi| = \sigma \pi a f B_z \tag{22}$$

where homogeneous body with radius $a = 0.14$ m and height a is assumed, while body conductivity is $\sigma = 0.5$ S/m. Derivation of the analytical expression (22) can be found in Appendix A.

The analytical results for the induced current density obtained at several frequencies (f) of interest are given in Table 1.

Table 1. Comparison of induced current density due to magnetic field exposure at frequencies: f = 50, 75, and 100 Hz. Analytical results from [17], and numerical results obtained using proposed approach. Numerical results obtained at two points: 13.95 cm and 10 cm from the model axis.

	Analytical [17]			Numerical, Point (13.95 cm)			Numerical, Point (10 cm)		
	J [mA/m²]			J [mA/m²]			J [mA/m²]		
B μT	f = 50 Hz	f = 75 Hz	f = 100 Hz	f = 50 Hz	f = 75 Hz	f = 100 Hz	f = 50 Hz	f = 75 Hz	f = 100 Hz
100	1.10	1.65	1.10	1.10	1.60	2.20	0.78	1.20	1.60
200	2.20	3.30	4.40	2.20	3.30	4.40	1.60	2.40	3.10
300	3.30	4.95	6.60	3.30	4.90	6.60	2.40	3.50	4.70
400	4.40	6.60	8.80	4.40	6.60	8.80	3.10	4.70	6.30
500	5.50	8.25	11.00	5.50	8.20	11.00	3.90	5.90	7.90

The results obtained using our numerical approach are also presented in Table 1. It is evident from Table 1 that excellent agreement between numerical and analytical approach is obtained at all three frequencies, thus validating the numerical approach. The only discrepancy found between the two approaches is in the scenario with $B = 100$ μT and $f = 100$ Hz, which can be attributed to a typographical error in [17].

The induced current density obtained obtained using our numerical approach is depicted in Figure 7.

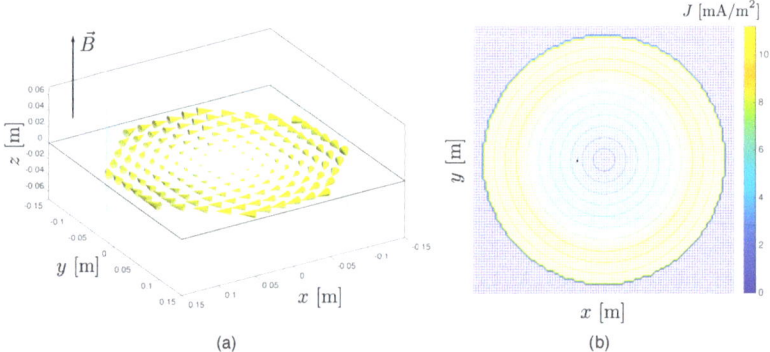

Figure 7. (a) Direction of the induced eddy current (yellow arrows) on the cross-section ($z = 0$) of homogeneous cylindrical model due to z-directed magnetic field B. (b) The induced eddy current values. The height of model is 0.14 m, while diameter of cylindrical model is 0.28 m. The conductivity $\sigma = 0.5$ S/m. $f = 100$ Hz and $B = 500$ μT.

The numerical results in Figure 7 are calculated in the x-y plane, i.e., in the transversal cross-section of homogeneous cylindrical model, at height $z = 0$. Note that the uniform magnetic field oriented in z direction will induce the circular current loops in the x-y plane. The value of the induced current density increases linearly as the axial distance increases, as shown in Figure 7b and Table 1, for two points ($r = 10$ cm and $r \approx 14$ cm).

4. Numerical Results and Discussion

The following sections presents some illustrative results of the magnetotherapy coil induced current density and the induced electric field obtained using the proposed numerical approach. The simplified human body model is utilized. The analyses of several magnetotherapy coil parameters as well as body conductivity are carried out to determine their effect on the induced current density and the induced electric field.

4.1. Parameter Analysis of Stimulating Coil

The first set of results are related to the magnetotherapy coil parameter analysis, such as the number of windings N, the coil diameter r, and the coil length L, as illustrated in Figure 8.

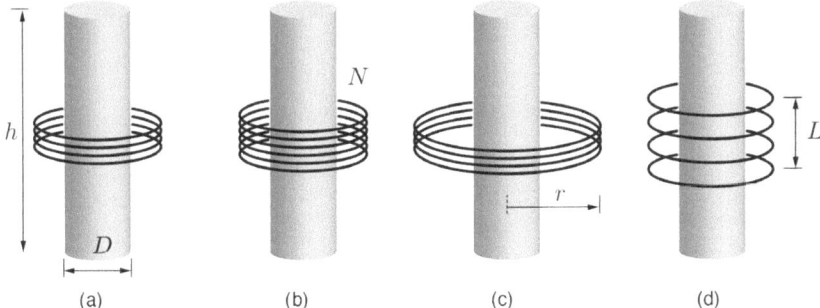

Figure 8. Analysis of coil parameters: (**a**) default configuration, (**b**) effect of coil windings N, (**c**) effect of coil radius r, and (**d**) effect of coil length L.

The numerical results are reported in Figure 9 and Tables 2 and 3.

4.1.1. Number of Coil Windings

The first set of results are related to varying number of coil windings. The default coil parameters are as follows: coil radius $r = 0.3$ m, coil length $L = 0.4$ m, coil current $I = 1$ A, and frequency $f = 10$ kHz. The coil is positioned coaxially with respect to human body, as depicted in Figure 8b. The geometrical center of the body ($z - 0$) corresponds to the center of the coil.

Magnetic coils of varying number of turns $N = [3, 4, 5, 6]$ have been considered, with the results presented in Table 2.

Table 2. The effect of number of coil windings N.

Coil Windings N	J [mA/m^2]	E [V/m]
3	10.1	0.0202
4	14.2	0.0284
5	18.2	0.0364
6	22.3	0.0446

Due to symmetry of the problem (the coil is concentric with regard to the body), the results given in Table 2 were obtained 1 cm from the model surface directly under the coil windings. Table 2 shows the linear dependence of both induced current density and induced electric field on the number of magnetotherapy coil windings. Doubling the coil windings (from 3 to 6), the values of both induced current density and induced electric field will roughly double. However, more importantly, for each coil turn the induced current density will increase by additional 4.1 mA/m^2.

4.1.2. Magnetotherapy Coil Radius

The following results are obtained using the coil of length L = 0.1 m, with N = 4 turns, f = 10 kHz, with varying coil radii, r = [0.175, 0.2, 0.25, 0.3] m. The axial distribution of the induced current density (depth 1 cm from the surface) is depicted in Figure 9.

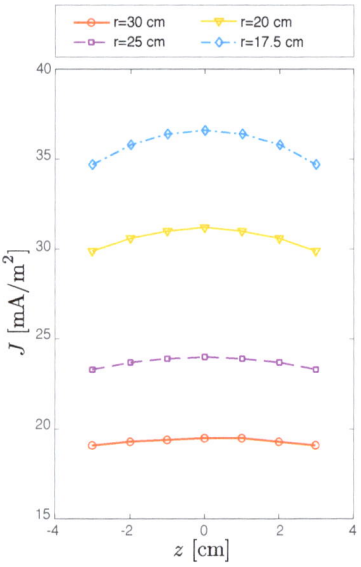

Figure 9. Axial distribution of induced current density directly under coil geometric center. Current density J [mA/m^2] calculated at points 1 cm under the cylinder surface. Coil radii: r = [17.5, 20, 25, 30] cm.

As seen from Figure 9, an approximate shape of a parabola is obtained. In all cases, the highest values of induced current density are at the point directly under the coil center (z = 0). The highest values of induced current density are achieved with smallest diameter coil as the coil is located closer to the body.

The results show that the gradient of the induced current density with decreasing coil radius will be more pronounced directly under the coil center. For example, when decreasing coil radius from 30 cm to 25 cm, the induced current will increase by 4.5 mA/m^2 at z = 0 compared to 4.2 mA/m^2 at the location 3 cm along the axial direction (z = 3 cm).

4.1.3. Coil Length

The next results are obtained for magnetotherapy coils of various lengths L, ranging from 10 cm to 40 cm, while other parameters were similar to previous calculations. The results for the induced fields are given in Table 3.

The results from Table 3 show approximately linear dependence. The shorter the length of the coil L, the higher the values of induced current density J and induced electric field E.

Table 3. The effect of coil length L.

Coil Length L [cm]	J [mA/m²]	E [V/m]
10	19.5	0.039
20	17.9	0.0358
30	16.0	0.032
40	14.2	0.0284

4.2. Human Body Model Parameter Analysis

The second set of results are related to the parameter analysis of the utilized simple human body model, i.e., the cylinder height h, the diameter D, and the electrical conductivity σ, as illustrated in Figure 10.

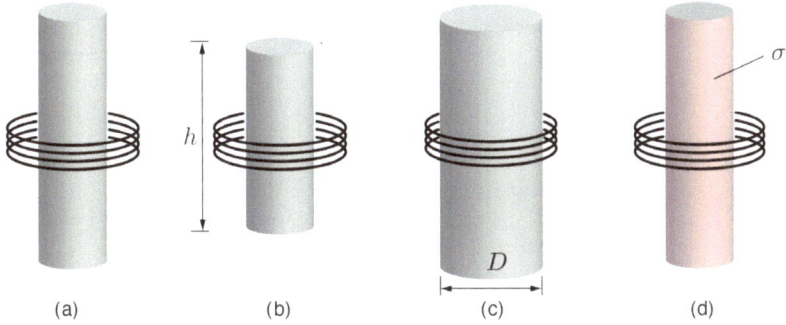

Figure 10. Analysis of model parameters: (**a**) default configuration, (**b**) effect of model height h, (**c**) effect of model diameter D, and (**d**) effect of body conductivity σ.

4.2.1. Effect of Model Height

The height h of the human model is varied first. The results obtained using the following values of $h = [1.55, 1.65, 1.75, 1.85, 1.95]$ m, are depicted in Figure 11.

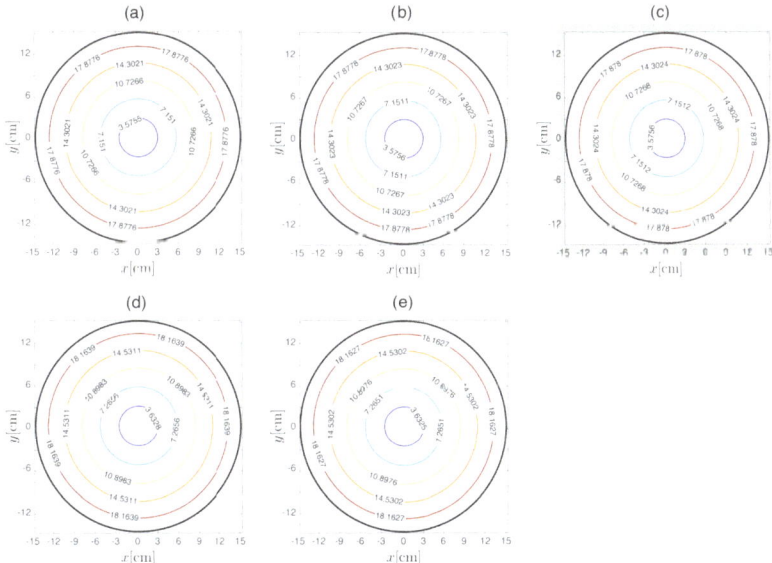

Figure 11. The effect of model height h: (**a**) 1.55 m, (**b**) 1.65 m, (**c**) 1.75 m, (**d**) 1.85 m, and (**e**) 1.95 m. Iso-contours of the induced current density in the x-y cross-section at $z = 0$. Boxed results denote the default model height.

The selected values of body height are related to the standing height percentiles for male and female Caucasian adult persons from nine countries studied in [35].

The results for the induced current density depicted in Figure 11 are obtained at the transversal cross-section ($x - y$ plane) with $z = 0$. The initial coil settings were utilized, with concentric position of the stimulating coil, as depicted in Figure 10b.

As seen from Figure 11, very similar distribution of the induced current density is obtained in all models. In two higher models (h = 1.85 m and h = 1.95 m), around a 2% higher value is obtained compared to the default model (h = 1.75 m), which can be attributed to the induced surface charges on the top and bottom base moved further from the coil central position. However, if this was the only reason, then the values of the induced current density in two smaller models h = 1.55 m and h = 1.65 m should have been lower than the default model, which was not the case. Another possible explanation for the different values could be attributed to the number of triangular elements used to discretize the model surface. Further analysis should be carried out to determine whether this is the possible reason; however, this is outside the scope of this work.

4.2.2. Effect of Model Thickness

The following results are obtained using body models of varying thickness. We considered different values of body diameter $D = [25, 30, 35, 40, 45]$ cm. The default magnetotherapy coil, positioned centrally to the model, was considered. The results are depicted in Figure 12.

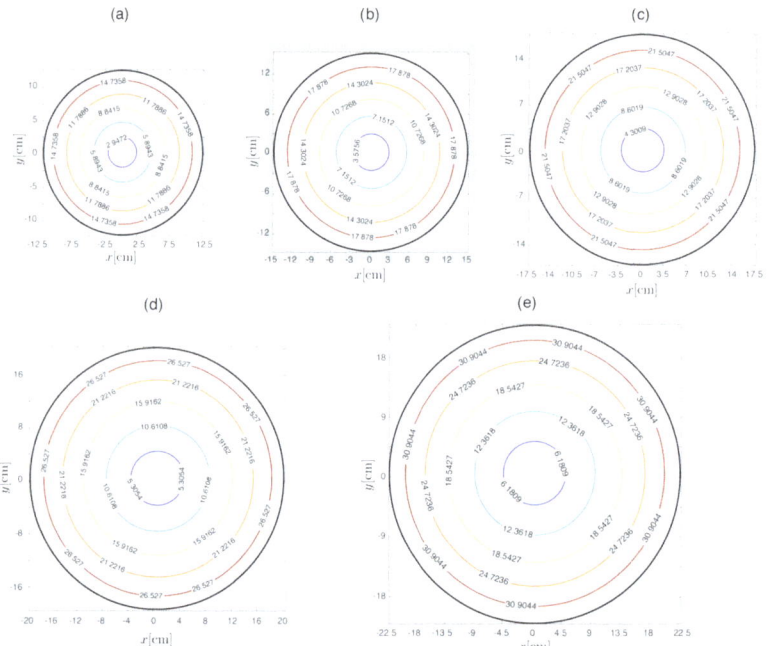

Figure 12. The effect of model diameter h: (**a**) 25 cm, (**b**) 30 cm, (**c**) 35 cm, (**d**) 40 cm, and (**e**) 45 cm. Iso-contours of the induced current density in the x-y cross-section at $z = 0$. Boxed results denote the default model height.

As is evident from Figure 12, using the model with larger diameter D positioned within the same stimulating coil has the effect of body being closer to the coil windings. As a result, the higher values of the induced current density are obtained. The relative increase in the induced current density 2 cm from the body surface (the first iso-contours from Figure 12) is 16%, 32%, and 40% for the three models with a larger diameter. In case of smaller diameter model, the relative decrease with respect to default body model is around 20%. The results suggest that, depending on the human body size, in order to obtain the similar value of induced current density, the appropriate size of the stimulating coil should be utilized. Of course, there are other ways to compensate for this such as decreasing the coil current.

4.2.3. Effect of Body Conductivity

The final results obtained for the coaxial position of magnetic coil are related to different conductivity values of homogeneous model, as given in Table 4. The results were obtained at a depth of 1 cm directly under the coil center. The following coil parameters were used: $r = 0.3$ m, $L = 0.4$ m, $I = 1$ A, and $N = 4$ turns.

Table 4. The results using different biological body conductivity σ.

Conductivity σ [S/m]	J [mA/m^2]	E [V/m]
0.3	8.5	0.02833
0.4	11.4	0.0285
0.5	14.2	0.0284
0.6	17.0	0.02833

As expected, the results from Table 4 show that induced current density increases proportionally with increasing conductivity. However, the value of the induced electric field remains constant in all calculations because $J = \sigma \cdot E$.

It should be emphasized that using the homogeneous body conductivity is a great simplification as the human body consists of many tissues with different parameter values. Moreover, there are many uncertainties regarding the exact value of particular tissue parameter, particularly at lower frequencies [36,37]. The uncertainty of the tissue electrical conductivity can be taken into account via statistical approaches such as the polynomial chaos method (PCM) or the stochastic collocation method (SCM). An interested reader could find more details on several examples of the SCM approach applied to modeling biomedical applications including transcranial electrical stimulation (TES) [38] and transcranial magnetic stimulation (TMS) [39].

4.3. Displacement of Magnetotherapy Coil

The final set of results obtained using cylindrical model are related to magnetotherapy coil positioned perpendicular to body model, as depicted in Figure 13.

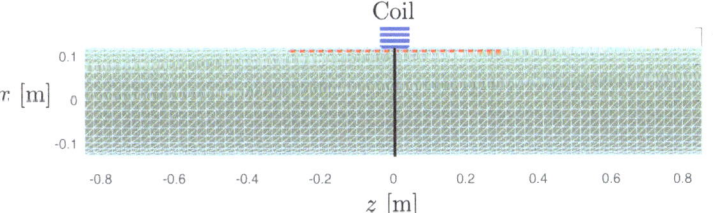

Figure 13. Perpendicular orientation of coil with regard to the human body. The red dashed line denotes observation points 1 cm under the cylinder surface (axial distribution $z = [-30, +30]$ cm), while the full black line ($z = 0$) denotes the cross-section plane where induced current density is also calculated.

The coil is placed at a 1 mm distance from the body, with coil axis perpendicular to the human body axis. The observation points are along the z-axis of the model at 1 cm from the body surface. The default parameters of the human body model are used: $h = 1.75$ m, $D = 30$ cm, and $\sigma = 0.5$ S/m. The results are obtained with following coil parameters: $L = 5$ cm; $r = 3.75$ cm, $N = 4$ turns, $I = 1$ A, and $f = 10$ kHz. The results are presented in Figures 14–16.

The induced current density along the body axis is shown in Figure 14.

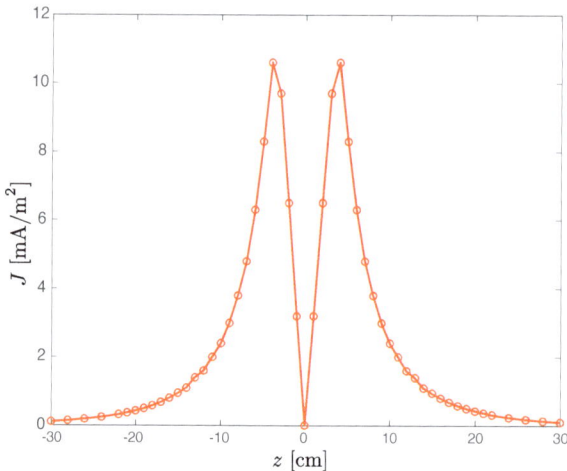

Figure 14. Axial distribution of induced current density directly under coil geometric center. Current density J [mA/m^2] calculated at points 1 cm under the cylinder surface.

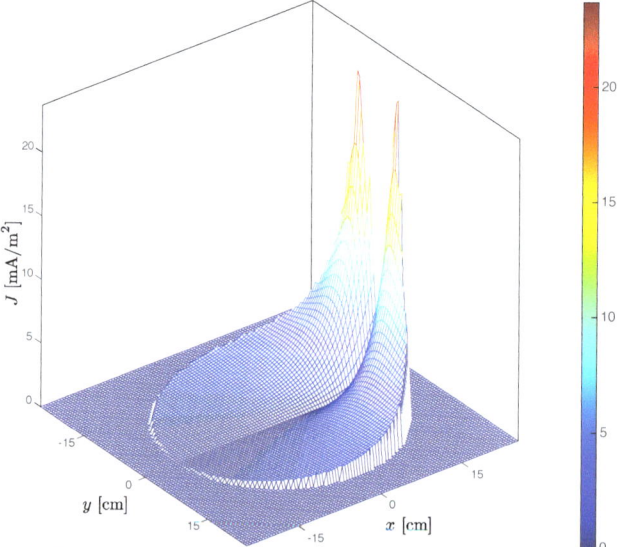

Figure 15. Induced current density J [mA/m^2] at the cross-section $z = 0$ of cylindrical body. The coil (not shown) center located at $x = 15$ cm and $y = 0$ cm.

The results from Figure 14 indicate that at the body center ($z = 0$), while the induced current density and the induced electric field are approximately 0. Moving away from the center along the z-axis (in both directions), these values increase until $z = 4$ cm (and $z = -4$ cm), corresponding to position directly under the coil windings where the induced current density reaches 10.6 mA/m^2, and the induced electric field reaches a corresponding value of 0.0212 V/m. With the increasing distance, both J and E begin to decline exponentially.

The results for the induced current density obtained at the horizontal cross-section ($z = 0$), corresponding to coil axis, are shown in Figure 15.

As is evident from Figure 15, the induced current density along the coil axis is basically nonexistent when the coil is oriented perpendicular with respect to the body. Moreover, a very sharp decline in the induced current density can be noticed, when moving from the model surface. These results indicate that, when using the circular magnetotherapy coil, the highest value of the induced field will be obtained very close to coil windings. Thus, if the ultimate goal is to achieve high values of induced field in a very focused region, a very different coil geometry, such as figure-of-eight, should be considered.

The final numerical results, obtained in x-y cross-section of cylindrical model, at $z = 0$, are depicted in Figure 16.

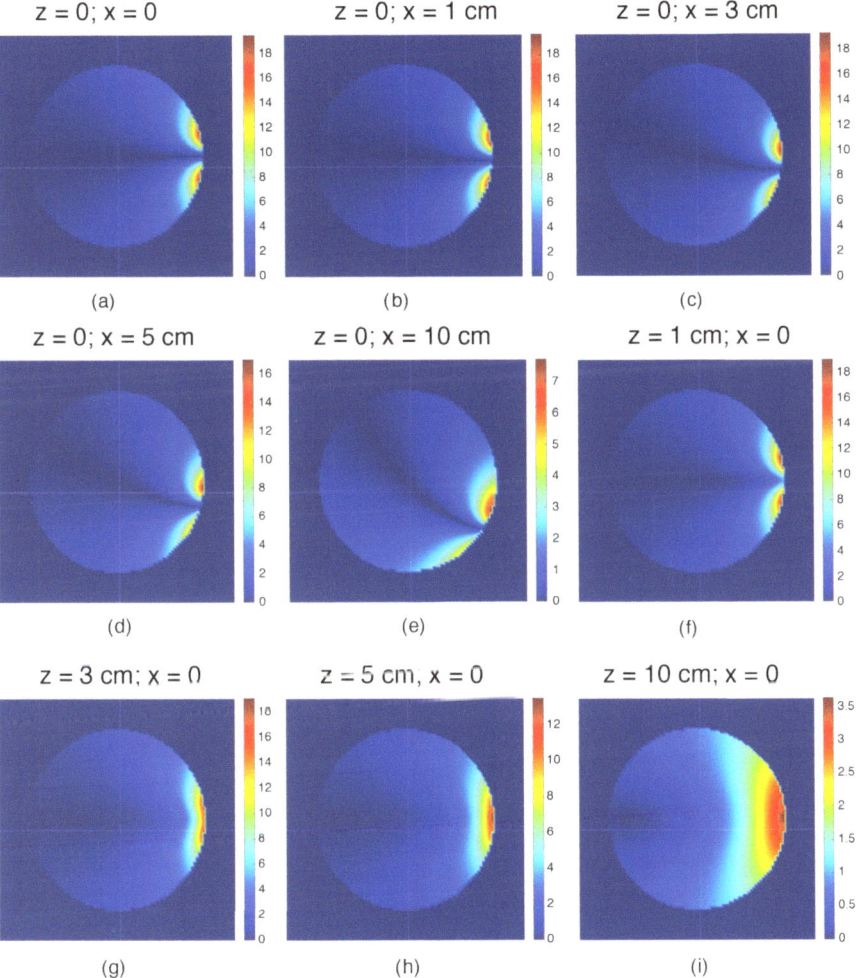

Figure 16. Distribution of induced current density on the cross-section of model. (**a**) The initial position of coil geometrical center ($z = 0$ and $x = 0$). The displacement along the x-axis: (**b**–**e**). The displacement along z-axis (body height): (**f**–**i**). All values in [mA/m^2].

The results shown in Figure 16 illustrate the effect of the perpendicularly oriented coil displacement on the induced current density. The initial position of the coil is with its center at $x = 0, z = 0$, as shown in Figure 14. The coil is displaced with respect to x and z directions by 1 cm, 3 cm, 5 cm, and 10 cm.

As evident from Figure 16b–e, horizontal displacement of coil along x-axis, results in the position with maximum induced current density also being shifted. As already mentioned, the maximum induced value will be under the coil windings. At the point 1 cm below the surface, the obtained induced current density is 4.2 $\mu A/m^2$, 11.2 $\mu A/m^2$, 10.5 $\mu A/m^2$, and 3.5 $\mu A/m^2$ when the coil is moved 1 cm, 3 cm, 5 cm, and 10 cm, respectively.

Compared to this, the vertical displacement of coil along z-axis, as shown in Figure 16f–i, will result in similar values of J at the same point; however, a different distribution of induced current density will be obtained. The coil displacement by 1 cm, 3 cm, 5 cm, and 10 cm, respectively, will result in the corresponding induced current density of 4 $\mu A/m^2$, 10.7 $\mu A/m^2$, 10.1 $\mu A/m^2$, and 3.3 $\mu A/m^2$ at the point 1 cm from the surface. However, in this case, a maximum value of the induced current will be spread over a considerably larger cross-sectional area, i.e., a smoother gradient of the induced current density will be achieved.

5. Conclusions

This paper presented the numerical model for a magnetotherapy device based on the surface integral equation formulation. The numerical solution was carried out using a method of moments technique. The illustrative numerical results for the induced current density and the induced electric field were obtained using a simplified geometry for the human body. The analyses of several magnetotherapy device parameters were carried out, as well as for different values of homogeneous body conductivity, in order to assess their effects on the parameters of interest. The presented numerical approach could easily be extended to more complicated body geometries. Future works will thus be related to tackling an anatomically realistic model of the human body using the proposed approach.

Author Contributions: Conceptualization, methodology, writing—original draft preparation, and supervision: M.C.; formal analysis and investigation: B.S.; writing—review and editing and visualization: M.C. and B.S. All authors have read and agreed to the published version of the manuscript.

Funding: This research received no external funding.

Data Availability Statement: The data presented in this study are available on request from the corresponding author.

Conflicts of Interest: The authors declare no conflicts of interest.

Abbreviations

The following abbreviations are used in this manuscript:

ELF	extremely low-frequency
EMF	electromagnetic field
PEMF	pulsed electromagnetic field
TMS	transcranial magnetic stimulation
SCS	spinal cord stimulation
MOM	method of moments
PCM	polynomial chaos method
SCM	stochastic collocation method
TES	transcranial electrical stimulation

Appendix A

The analytical expression for the induced circular current density due to the normally oriented magnetic flux density can be assessed using the disk human body model, as shown in Figure A1.

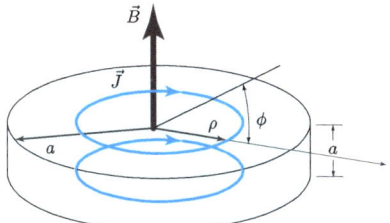

Figure A1. Disk model of the human body [24].

This analytical model has been proposed in [34] to provide rapid estimation of the ELF magnetic field exposure. The disk is assumed to be homogeneous with conductivity σ and radius a. The analytical expression for the current density can be derived using the differential form of Faraday's law, which for the time harmonic fields is given by:

$$\nabla \times \vec{E} = -j\omega \vec{B} \tag{A1}$$

where $\vec{E}$ is the impressed electric field, which is related to the induced current density via:

$$\vec{J} = \sigma \vec{E} \tag{A2}$$

Combining (A1) and (A2), followed by integration over an arbitrary surface S, results in the following:

$$\int_S \nabla \times \vec{J}\, d\vec{S} = -\int_S j\sigma\omega \vec{B}\, d\vec{S} \tag{A3}$$

Using the Stokes' theorem, the left hand side of (A3) can be rewritten as a line integral over curve c bounding the surface S:

$$\oint_c \vec{J}\, d\vec{s} = -j\omega\sigma\vec{B} \int_S d\vec{S} \tag{A4}$$

The expression (A4) can be expanded in the cylindrical coordinates as:

$$\int_0^{2\pi} J_\phi \rho\, d\phi = -j\omega\sigma B_z \int_0^{\rho'} \int_0^{2\pi} \rho\, d\rho\, d\phi \tag{A5}$$

where ω is the angular frequency.

Taking into account the rotational symmetry, the integration results in:

$$J_\phi \cdot 2\pi\rho = -j\omega\sigma B_z \rho^2 \pi \tag{A6}$$

Substituting $\omega = 2\pi f$ in (A6), the following expression for the induced current density inside the human disk model is obtained:

$$|J_\phi| = \sigma\pi\rho f \cdot B_z \tag{A7}$$

From the current density, the total current flowing through the cross-section of the disk, can be simply calculated:

$$I = \int_S \vec{J}\, d\vec{S} = \int_0^a \int_0^{2\pi} \sigma\pi f B_z \rho\, d\rho\, dz = \sigma\pi f B_z \int_0^a \int_0^{2\pi} \rho\, d\rho\, dz = \sigma\pi f B_z \frac{a^3}{2} \tag{A8}$$

References

1. Markov, M.S. Pulsed electromagnetic field therapy history, state of the art and future. *Environmentalist* **2007**, *27*, 465–475. [CrossRef]
2. Bassett, C.; Pawluk, R.; Pilla, A. Acceleration of fracture repair by electromagnetic fields. A surgically noninvasive method. *Ann. N. Y. Acad. Sci.* **1974**, *238*, 242–262. [CrossRef]
3. Kuipers, N.T.; Sauder, C.L.; Ray, C.A. Influence of static magnetic fields on pain perception and sympathetic nerve activity in humans. *J. Appl. Physiol.* **2007**, *102*, 1410–1415. [CrossRef] [PubMed]
4. Yu, S.; Shang, P. A review of bioeffects of static magnetic field on rodent models. *Prog. Biophys. Mol. Biol.* **2014**, *114*, 14–24. [CrossRef] [PubMed]
5. Basford, J.R. A historical perspective of the popular use of electric and magnetic therapy. *Arch. Phys. Med. Rehabil.* **2001**, *82*, 1261–1269. [CrossRef] [PubMed]
6. Brown, C.S.; Ling, F.W.; Wan, J.Y.; Pilla, A.A. Efficacy of static magnetic field therapy in chronic pelvic pain: A double-blind pilot study. *Am. J. Obstet. Gynecol.* **2002**, *187*, 1581–1587. [CrossRef] [PubMed]
7. Carter, R.; Hall, T.; Aspy, C.B.; Mold, J. The effectiveness of magnet therapy for treatment of wrist pain attributed to carpal tunnel syndrome. *J. Fam. Pract.* **2002**, *51*, 38–40. [PubMed]
8. Richmond, S.J. Magnet therapy for the relief of pain and inflammation in rheumatoid arthritis (CAMBRA): A randomised placebo-controlled crossover trial. *Trials* **2008**, *9*, 1–17. [CrossRef] [PubMed]
9. Flamm, B. Magnet therapy: Extraordinary claims, but no proved benefits. *Br. Med. J.* **2006**, *332*, 4.
10. Pipitone, N.; Scott, D.L. Magnetic pulse treatment for knee osteoarthritis: A randomised, double-blind, placebo-controlled study. *Curr. Med. Res. Opin.* **2001**, *17*, 190–196. [CrossRef]
11. Kessler, T.M.; Mordasini, L.; Weisstanner, C.; Jüni, P.; da Costa, B.R.; Wiest, R.; Thalmann, G.N. Sono-electro-magnetic therapy for treating chronic pelvic pain syndrome in men: A randomized, placebo-controlled, double-blind trial. *PLoS ONE* **2014**, *9*, e113368. [CrossRef]
12. Galovic, P.; Celan, D.; Hernja-Rumpf, T. Short term effect of PEMF magnetotherapy on chronic Low back pain. *J. Magn.* **2018**, *23*, 553–558. [CrossRef]
13. Sengupta, S.; Balla, V.K. A review on the use of magnetic fields and ultrasound for non-invasive cancer treatment. *J. Adv. Res.* **2018**, *14*, 97–111. [CrossRef] [PubMed]
14. Paolucci, T.; Pezzi, L.; Centra, A.M.; Giannandrea, N.; Bellomo, R.G.; Saggini, R. Electromagnetic field therapy: A rehabilitative perspective in the management of musculoskeletal pain—A systematic review. *J. Pain Res.* **2020**, *13*, 1385–1400. [CrossRef] [PubMed]
15. Hallett, M. Transcranial magnetic stimulation: A primer. *Neuron* **2007**, *55*, 187–199. [CrossRef] [PubMed]
16. Oakley, J.C.; Prager, J.P. Spinal cord stimulation: Mechanisms of action. *Spine* **2002**, *27*, 2574–2583. [CrossRef] [PubMed]
17. Poljak, D.; Sesnic, S.; Cavka, D.; Titlic, M.; Mihalj, M. The human body exposed to a magnetotherapy device magnetic field. *WIT Trans. Biomed. Health* **2009**, *13*, 203–211.
18. Miaskowski, A.; Krawczyk, A.; Ishihara, Y. Computer modelling of magnetotherapy in orthopedic treatments. *COMPEL Int. J. Comput. Math. Electr. Electron. Eng.* **2010**, *24*, 1015–1021. [CrossRef]
19. Krawczyk, A.; Miaskowski, A.; Łada-Tondyra, E.; Ishihara, Y. Healing of Orthopaedic Diseases by Means of Electromagnetic Field. *Acta Tech. Jaurinensis* **2011**, *4*, 357–364.
20. Cieśla, A.; Kraszewski, W.; Tadeusiewicz, R. Visualization of magnetic field generated by portable coil designed for magnetotherapy. *Przegląd Elektrotechniczny* **2012**, *88*, 127–131.
21. Richter, A.; Ferková, Ž. Physical and energy analysis of therapy applying low-dynamic magnetic fields. In Proceedings of the 2017 IEEE International Workshop of Electronics, Control, Measurement, Signals and Their Application to Mechatronics (ECMSM), Donostia, Spain, 24–26 May 2017; pp. 1–5.
22. Syrek, P. Uncertainty problem as illustrated by magnetotherapy. *Appl. Comput. Electromagn. Soc. J.* **2019**, *34*, 1445–1452.
23. Cvetković, M.; Sučić, B. Magnetotherapy Device Induced Fields in Simplified Human Body Model. In Proceedings of the 2023 8th International Conference on Smart and Sustainable Technologies (SpliTech), Split/Bol, Croatia, 20–23 June 2023; pp. 1–6. [CrossRef]
24. Poljak, D.; Cvetkovic, M. *Human Interaction with Electromagnetic Fields: Computational Models in Dosimetry*; Academic Press: Cambridge, MA, USA, 2019.
25. Makarov, S.N.; Noetscher, G.M.; Nazarian, A. *Low-Frequency Electromagnetic Modeling for Electrical and Biological Systems Using MATLAB*; John Wiley & Sons: Hoboken, NJ, USA, 2015.
26. Cvetković, M.; Poljak, D.; Haueisen, J. Analysis of Transcranial Magnetic Stimulation Based on the Surface Integral Equation Formulation. *Biomed. Eng. IEEE Trans.* **2015**, *62*, 1535–1545. [CrossRef] [PubMed]
27. Luquet, S.; Barra, V.; Lemaire, J.J. Transcranial magnetic stimulation: Magnetic field computation in empty free space. In Proceedings of the 2005 IEEE Engineering in Medicine and Biology 27th Annual Conference, Shanghai, China, 17–18 January 2006; pp. 4365–4368.
28. Dodig, H.; Cvetković, M.; Poljak, D. On the Computation of Singular Integrals Over Triangular Surfaces in R3. *WIT Trans. Eng. Sci.* **2019**, *122*, 95.

29. Cvetković, M.; Lojić Kapetanović, A.; Poljak, D.; Dodig, H. On the Applicability of Numerical Quadrature for Double Surface Integrals at 5G Frequencies. *J. Commun. Softw. Syst.* **2022**, *18*, 42–53. [CrossRef]
30. Kuster, N.; Balzano, Q. Energy absorption mechanism by biological bodies in the near field of dipole antennas above 300 MHz. *IEEE Trans. Veh. Technol.* **1992**, *41*, 17–23. [CrossRef]
31. Rasic, P.; Skiljo, M.; Blazevic, Z.; Doric, V.; Poljak, D. Simulation of human body exposure to high and low frequency wireless power transfer systems using simplified models. In Proceedings of the 2018 3rd International Conference on Smart and Sustainable Technologies (SpliTech), Split, Croatia, 26–29 June 2018; pp. 1–6.
32. King, R.W.; Sandler, S.S. Electric fields and currents induced in organs of the human body when exposed to ELF and VLF electromagnetic fields. *Radio Sci.* **1996**, *31*, 1153–1167. [CrossRef]
33. Hasgall, P.; Di Gennaro, F.; Baumgartner, C.; Neufeld, E.; Lloyd, B.; Gosselin, M.C.; Payne, D.; Klingenböck, A.; Kuster, N. IT'IS Database for Thermal and Electromagnetic Parameters of Biological Tissues, Version 4.1, 22 February 2022. Available online: https://itis.swiss/database (accessed on 17 February 2024).
34. *IEC 62226-2-1:2004*; Exposure to Electric or Magnetic Fields in the Low and Intermediate Frequency Range—Methods for Calculating the Current Density and Internal Electric Field Induced in the Human Body—Part 2-1: Exposure to Magnetic Fields—2D Models. IEC: Geneva, Switzerland, 2004; pp. 1–113.
35. Cassola, V.; Milian, F.; Kramer, R.; de Oliveira Lira, C.; Khoury, H. Standing adult human phantoms based on 10th, 50th and 90th mass and height percentiles of male and female Caucasian populations. *Phys. Med. Biol.* **2011**, *56*, 3749. [CrossRef] [PubMed]
36. Gabriel, C.; Peyman, A.; Grant, E.H. Electrical conductivity of tissue at frequencies below 1 MHz. *Phys. Med. Biol.* **2009**, *54*, 4863. [CrossRef] [PubMed]
37. De Santis, V.; Chen, X.L.; Laakso, I.; Hirata, A. An equivalent skin conductivity model for low-frequency magnetic field dosimetry. *Biomed. Phys. Eng. Express* **2015**, *1*, 015201. [CrossRef]
38. Šušnjara, A.; Verhnjak, O.; Poljak, D.; Cvetković, M.; Ravnik, J. Uncertainty quantification and sensitivity analysis of transcranial electric stimulation for 9-subdomain human head model. *Eng. Anal. Bound. Elem.* **2022**, *135*, 1–11. [CrossRef]
39. Cvetković, M.; Šušnjara, A.; Poljak, D. Deterministic–stochastic modeling of transcranial magnetic stimulation featuring the use of method of moments and stochastic collocation. *Eng. Anal. Bound. Elem.* **2023**, *150*, 662–671. [CrossRef]

Disclaimer/Publisher's Note: The statements, opinions and data contained in all publications are solely those of the individual author(s) and contributor(s) and not of MDPI and/or the editor(s). MDPI and/or the editor(s) disclaim responsibility for any injury to people or property resulting from any ideas, methods, instructions or products referred to in the content.

Article

The Use of Business Intelligence Software to Monitor Key Performance Indicators (KPIs) for the Evaluation of a Computerized Maintenance Management System (CMMS)

Paola Picozzi [1], Umberto Nocco [2], Andrea Pezzillo [1], Adriana De Cosmo [1] and Veronica Cimolin [1,3,*]

[1] Department of Electronics, Information and Bioengineering, Politecnico di Milano, 20133 Milano, Italy; paola.picozzi@polimi.it (P.P.); andrea.pezzillo@mail.polimi.it (A.P.); adriana.decosmo@mail.polimi.it (A.D.C.)
[2] Clinical Engineering Department of ASST Grande Ospedale Metropolitano Niguarda, 20162 Milano, Italy; umberto.nocco@ospedaleniguarda.it
[3] Istituto Auxologico Italiano, IRCCS, S. Giuseppe Hospital, 28824 Oggebbio, Italy
* Correspondence: veronica.cimolin@polimi.it

Abstract: The increasing use of electromedical equipment in hospital care services necessitates effective management of complex devices often unsupported by existing control systems. This paper focuses on developing a pool of evaluation indices for the Clinical Engineering Department (CED) of the ASST Grande Ospedale Metropolitano Niguarda in Milano (Italy), aiming to enhance awareness of the economic value, assess operational units, and optimize maintenance processes. Leveraging business intelligence, this study identifies 18 key performance indicators (KPIs) across logistics, technical, and equipment management categories. An interactive dashboard, implemented using Power BI, facilitates dynamic analysis and visualization of these KPIs, providing insights into the maintenance efficiency and obsolescence of medical devices. It offers a comprehensive framework for ongoing monitoring and decision-making. The results showcase the potential of the developed KPIs and dashboard to enhance operational insights and guide improvements in the healthcare facility's maintenance processes.

Keywords: clinical engineering; business intelligence; computerized maintenance management system; CMMS

Citation: Picozzi, P.; Nocco, U.; Pezzillo, A.; De Cosmo, A.; Cimolin, V. The Use of Business Intelligence Software to Monitor Key Performance Indicators (KPIs) for the Evaluation of a Computerized Maintenance Management System (CMMS). *Electronics* **2024**, *13*, 2286. https://doi.org/10.3390/electronics13122286

Academic Editors: Ilaria Sergi and Teodoro Montanaro

Received: 30 April 2024
Revised: 5 June 2024
Accepted: 7 June 2024
Published: 11 June 2024

Copyright: © 2024 by the authors. Licensee MDPI, Basel, Switzerland. This article is an open access article distributed under the terms and conditions of the Creative Commons Attribution (CC BY) license (https://creativecommons.org/licenses/by/4.0/).

1. Introduction

Currently, there is a monumental digital revolution characterized by the emergence, evolution, and widespread proliferation of digital infrastructures and tools. This transformative shift is reshaping the very paradigms in which individuals exist, operate, and engage in our daily endeavors [1]. The realm of public healthcare, once considered somewhat resistant to rapid technological change, is now fully immersed in the tide of digital transformation and technological innovation, mirroring trends seen across various sectors of society and industry [2–4].

The gradual integration of digital technologies into healthcare settings has become a driving force for advancing care delivery methods, fostering precision and personalization in treatment approaches. Concurrently, it has spurred the implementation of novel organizational and management strategies within clinical structures [5–7]. The transformative impact of digital health is clearly not limited to clinical therapies but also extends to the management of biomedical technologies and the evolution of operational management models within healthcare systems [3,8].

This convergence of digital advancements and healthcare represents a pivotal moment in the industry's evolution, with profound implications for patient care, organizational efficiency, and overall healthcare delivery. Navigating this digital landscape reveals the increasing importance of embracing and harnessing technological innovations to drive positive change and ensure the continued advancement of healthcare services.

In this context, the role of clinical engineering is crucial in the healthcare setting. It is an area of biomedical engineering, defined as the application of engineering principles and technologies to enhance the quality of healthcare services. This includes improving organizational processes, acquiring and managing equipment, and developing or adapting hospital information systems and telemedicine networks [9].

The positive outcomes achieved in terms of economic management and safety quickly led to the widespread adoption of the Clinical Engineering Department (CED) in the United States, Canada, and major European countries. Recognizing its importance, the World Health Organization (WHO) has repeatedly advocated for the establishment of CED in both industrialized and developing countries [10].

The introduction of clinical engineering expertise has resulted in reduced risks associated with technology use in healthcare facilities and facilitated the controlled adoption of new technologies, leading to cost savings. Additionally, clinical engineering oversees maintenance processes and ensures the safe use of medical devices through risk analysis, safety plans, and incident monitoring [9].

Considering the different activities of a CED, equipment data acquire a lot of importance, and it is crucial to keep updated on the status of clinical devices to ensure a high standard of care quality, reduce expenses, and minimize the risk of adverse events for patients and users [11].

The intricacy of electromedical equipment, characterized by its quantity and diversity, presents challenges in managing these devices effectively [12]. To address this growing complexity, CEDs implement management software systems called Computerized Maintenance Management Systems (CMMS) to ensure the safe and efficient management of the hospital's medical equipment [13].

CMMS are software packages that utilize connections to databases containing data related to a company's device support activities to digitize documentation of all activities concerning them [14]. The main functionalities that a CMMS should support, as identified by the WHO, include the following:

- Institutionalizing and interconnecting data within a healthcare technology management program;
- Contributing to the organization and monitoring of inspections and preventive maintenance;
- Tracking repairs;
- Monitoring equipment performance indicators;
- Monitoring clinical engineering staff performance indicators;
- Generating reports for planning training programs;
- Providing libraries of regulatory requirements and safety information;
- Generating documentation suitable for accreditation by regulatory and standard organizations [15].

Utilizing a CMMS offers numerous advantages over traditional paper-based methods, including easier data storage and retrieval, streamlined maintenance management, enhanced patient safety, reduced workload and working time, decreased risk of human error, and improved tracking of medical equipment throughout its life cycle [16–18]. Furthermore, the adoption of a CMMS aligns with the increasing demand across all sectors to gather structured data for processing, analysis, and exchange between operational units.

By collecting and analyzing data related to maintenance activities, CEDs can identify process inefficiencies and address device issues, thereby promoting technological advancement.

In the healthcare context, the continuous growth in data collection has allowed business intelligence (BI)—defined as "the techniques, technologies, systems, practices, methodologies, and applications that analyze critical business data to help a business better understand its business and market and make timely business decisions" [19]—to emerge as an area of study for both professionals and researchers in various sectors. This reflects the breadth and impact of data-related issues faced by contemporary business organizations.

BI solutions enable the collection of information from financial and operational data to make smarter decisions, aiming to improve process efficiency and effectiveness. Successful companies recognize that leveraging business intelligence can provide a competitive advantage by converting data into information and knowledge, answering not only the question "what?" but also "why?" [20].

There are two main types of BI systems: those centered on data and those focused on processes. Data-centered perspectives use BI systems to understand organizational capabilities by collecting, transforming, and integrating data to provide complex and competitive insights, aiming to enhance the timeliness and quality of decision-making. Process-centered perspectives view organizations as sets of well-integrated processes, where BI is used to assimilate information into these processes [21].

Despite the advantages, using BI to solve business problems brings challenges such as data access, structure, and supporting hardware technology.

In the healthcare environment, the challenge lies in converting vast amounts of data into valuable insights and knowledge. BI's ability to add value by gathering data from various sources and combining them in a common repository allows for in-depth analysis and supports decision-making processes.

Furthermore, emerging BI tools can provide answers to key questions more rapidly and potentially with higher quality using analysis and visualization tools [22].

Analysis of data allows for the examination of various situations obtaining relevant information for business support. In healthcare, the use of BI provides important information, particularly on improvement opportunities. The rigorous and systematic approach of these techniques allows for improved investment performance and consequently increases the level of care provided.

The BI operations can pose challenges for any company, but in the healthcare sector, there are additional layers of complexity, such as privacy issues related to sensitive patient data regulated by privacy laws [23].

Sabherwal and Becerra-Fernandez outline four interconnected capabilities of business intelligence: organizational memory, information integration, insight creation, and presentation. These capabilities are crucial for various sectors, with healthcare organizations benefiting significantly [24].

Also, for the CED, it is increasingly essential to have a measurable understanding of the efficiency of the healthcare company's maintenance service.

Despite the widespread use of business intelligence tools in the healthcare sector, few studies apply these tools to the management of electromedical equipment within the context of clinical engineering. Additionally, existing studies define generic indicators that do not allow for a detailed investigation of all the processes carried out by clinical engineering departments. This study aims to define a specific set of indicators tailored to the analyzed facility.

The primary objective of the following study is to develop a pool of evaluation indices capable of allowing analysis of the entire machinery fleet present in the facility, gaining greater awareness of the economic value managed by the structure, and better understanding and evaluating the critical issues of the various existing operational units. In particular, the research was conducted at the Clinical Engineering Department of the ASST Grande Ospedale Metropolitano (GOM) Niguarda in Milano (Italy), where 10 evaluation indices developed according to the ISO 9001:2015 [25] certification system have already been used. However, these do not cover all areas of the facility's work. Therefore, the possibility of expanding this list of indices through an in-depth study of the current standard, its structure, and its needs has been identified.

In addition, another aim of this study was to verify the feasibility of calculating the defined KPI using the data available in the management software system.

Furthermore, visualizing the trend of evaluation indices is essential for making decisions. Simple and intuitive methods allow anyone to grasp complex information and consequently decide how to behave and improve the system.

Therefore, the additional goal of implementing a dashboard to observe and monitor the trend of the detected indices has been defined. BI tools enable thorough and systemic analysis by providing the necessary information to make the best decision.

The ultimate goal is to harness the potential of BI to monitor the trend of the detected indices. These technologies, as will be demonstrated, are essential today to optimize the system to the fullest.

2. Literature Review

A literature review was undertaken to identify existing indicators in the literature and to define new indicators that are more closely aligned with the CED's needs.

An electronic search was conducted on PubMed and Scopus databases. The following words were used to perform the research: "indicator" AND "medical equipment" AND "management".

The following criteria for inclusion were employed in the article selection process:

1. Written in the English language;
2. Full articles written in English, excluding reviews, perspectives, and communications;
3. Full text available;
4. Published from 2014 to September 2023;
5. Reporting the indicators;
6. Focused on the management of electromedical equipment.

Otherwise, the following exclusion criteria were considered:

1. Articles concerning the management of medical devices that were not electromedical equipment;
2. Studies that define a maintenance prioritization index;
3. Papers that report cases of management in critical contexts or situations.

The review's references were checked to find relevant papers that were included in the research.

Article titles and abstracts underwent screening to assess their relevance according to the inclusion and exclusion criteria.

A total of 303 articles was obtained from the electronic databases research previously mentioned, while the number of records identified through snowballing was 19. After duplicate removal, 293 papers remained. The screening of titles and abstracts resulted in the exclusion of 272 items. Among the remaining 21 articles, 16 papers did not meet the inclusion criteria.

Table 1 presents the five papers included in the review together with the indicators used.

Table 1. Literature review's results.

Source	Year	Indicator Used
Bhardwaj, P. et al. [26]	2022	Uptime; downtime; response time; mean time to repair.
Iadanza, E. et al. [12]	2019	Downtime; uptime; mean time to restoration; mean time between failure; class failure ration; global failure rate; age failure rate; negligent actions; "1 day" actions; scheduled maintenance (SM) with failure; scheduled maintenance coverage rate; percentage of no problems found in SM; number of devices per technician; cost of service ratio; internal maintenance cost (% respect to the total maintenance cost); SM cost (% with respect to total cost); corrective maintenance cost (% with respect to total maintenance cost); cost of spare part (% respect to the total maintenance cost).
Gonnelli, V. et al. [27]	2018	Total CED expense as a percentage of total cost of acquisition (cost of acquisition ratio); CM (and SM) expense as a percentage of total CED expense; in-house (and external contracts) expense as a percentage of total CED expense; spare part (and supplies) costs; hourly cost of technicians (internal and external); repair time; uptime; downtime; class failure rate; age failure rate; number of technicians per number of capital devices; number of SM performed per number of capital devices; percentage of SM with problems (i.e., not coded as NPF); "delinquent work-orders" (i.e., not completed within 30 days).
Camila, R. S. et al. [28]	2015	Mean time between failure; mean time to repair; availability.
Oshiyama, N. F. et al. [29]	2013	Number of corrective maintenance events; total time spent on corrective maintenance; corrective maintenance costs.

3. Materials and Methods

In this section, the methods for defining and identifying KPIs are given, and the criteria and tools used to create the dashboard are shown according to Sections 3.1 and 3.2, respectively.

3.1. Indicator Definition

The initial phase involved examining the processes of the clinical engineering structure, along with conducting a literature search [12,26–29] to identify the classes of key performance indicators.

The KPI classes identified are the following:

- Administrative management: Related to the costs of activities. Examples of these indices are the costs related to preventive and corrective maintenance;
- Logistics management: Related to CED's activities as purchase, service, rental, loan donation, spare parts, and accessories, in and out of the warehouse, both from healthcare facilities and from external companies All the indices belonging to this category are time indices. Examples of logistics management indicators are the average arrival time of spare parts or average call closure times;
- Technical management: Related to all activities carried out by technicians on biomedical equipment. They are useful indicators to assess the level of efficiency and coordination of technical staff. Examples of such indices may be "One-Day Action" or "Mean Time To Repair (MTTR)";
- Training: Indicators measuring the level of staff training.;
- Quality: Measures to assess that the management of biomedical equipment is appropriate, effective, safe, and economical;
- Equipment management: Related to the management of all the equipment managed or used by the CI. Examples are downtime and uptime measures.

The latter did not exist prior to the following work but was defined following the study of the facility's needs.

The second step involved outlining the structure of the KPIs. It is crucial that a KPI is defined clearly and unambiguously to ensure it is comprehensive and leaves no room for misinterpretation [29,30]. The requirements for defining a KPI to be at least comprehensive are as follows:

- Name: Name of the KPI, using a standard naming system. The name should be self-explanatory, such as "Mean Time to Repair";
- Number and type: Number associated with the KPI. It is also necessary to indicate to which class it belongs (administrative, logistics, technical, training, quality, equipment management). The two pieces of information can be combined to create an alphanumeric abbreviation identifying the KPI;
- Short definition: Short description of the KPI, similar to a name, e.g., "Average time to repair a device";
- Detailed definition: A more comprehensive description of the KPI, including sources, formulas, possible limitations, and applicability in the organization. The detailed definition should also include the rationale for choosing and adopting the KPI in the decision-making and review process;
- Formula: Mathematical equation of the KPI;
- Numerator: Description of the numerator, including inclusion and exclusion criteria;
- Denominator: Description of the denominator, including inclusion and exclusion criteria. Often, the denominator is the 'total' (to obtain percentage KPIs);
- KPI unit: Format of the KPI result (days, months, or percentage);
- Statistical adjustments: Illustration of statistical techniques used on the dataset to reduce the presence of confounding values (such as outliers often also caused by sampling or transcription errors);

- Reference values (benchmarks): KPI values obtained from external organizations that are similar to the object of study, often indicated as a model for best hospital practice, or from other internal departments that can provide a direct comparison. These are useful for setting a baseline and an ideal target for process improvement.

Therefore, considering the criteria suggested by the standard [31], as well as the literature analyzed and the knowledge and needs in the field, a set of 18 KPIs has been designed, in addition to the 10 already implemented by the structure (Appendix A).

The KPIs identified relate exclusively to the categories of logistics, technical, and equipment management. This is because the indicators already present for the remaining categories comply with the standard and are sufficient for the objective set. Instead, it was decided to investigate technical, logistical, and equipment-related aspects that had been neglected until now in more detail.

The methodology previously reported, together with the process analysis and the literature review, leads to defining the KPI and the methodology for their calculations (Table 2).

Table 2. KPI calculation.

KPI	Formula	Indicator Type
Average downtime in the warehouse	$\dfrac{\textit{Average idle time of the repaired device in the warehouse}}{\textit{Total number of devices repaired in the warehouse}}$	Logistics management type
Receiving spare parts meantime	$\dfrac{\textit{Total turnaround time for arrival of replacement parts}}{\textit{Number of orders}}$	Logistics management type
Mean arrival time	$\dfrac{\textit{Arrival in the warehouse's time} - \textit{opening ticket's time}}{\textit{Number of tickets received}}$	Logistics management type
Percentage of external downtime	$\dfrac{\textit{equipment downtime due to external maintainance}}{\textit{theoretical time of use}}$	Logistics management type
Average time since first intervention	$\dfrac{\textit{time of opening ticket} - \textit{time of the first intervention}}{\textit{Number of close ticket}}$	Technical management
Mean time to repair	$\dfrac{\textit{closure request time} - \textit{maintenance start time}}{\textit{total number of maintenance operations}}$	Technical management
Average request closing time	$\dfrac{\textit{closure request time} - \textit{open request time}}{\textit{total number of corrective maintenance operations}}$	Technical management
Supported devices for technical personnel	$\dfrac{\textit{number of request assigned to each technician}}{\textit{total number of device}}$	Technical management
One-day action	$\dfrac{\textit{maintenance corrective maintenance completed within 24 h}}{\textit{number of maintenance corrective maintenance}}$	Technical management
Negligent actions	$\dfrac{\textit{Number of request open for more than X days}}{\textit{total number of corrective maintenance}}$	Technical management
Average failure time	$\dfrac{\textit{time between two failures}}{\textit{total number of corrective maintenance}}$	Equipment management
Uptime	$\dfrac{\textit{device activity time}}{\textit{theoretical time of use}}$	Equipment management
Uptime for life-saving equipment	$\dfrac{\textit{device activity time}_{\textit{life saving equipment}}}{\textit{theoretical time of use}_{\textit{life saving equipment}}}$	Equipment management
Corrective maintenance downtime	$\dfrac{\textit{downtime due to corrective maintenance}}{\textit{theoretical time of use}}$	Equipment management
Preventive maintenance downtime	$\dfrac{\textit{downtime due to preventive maintenance}}{\textit{theoretical time of use}}$	Equipment management
Inventories that generate request	$\dfrac{\textit{device that generate request(ward, specific device type)}}{\textit{total number of devices (ward, specific device type)}}$	Equipment management
Number of requests over number of devices per hospital wards	$\dfrac{\textit{number of request (specific ward)}}{\textit{total number of devices (specific ward)}}$	Equipment management
Failure rate category	$\dfrac{\textit{number of corrective maintenance for a specific class of devices}}{\textit{total number of corrective maintenance}}$	Equipment management

3.2. Dashboard

Subsequently, a dashboard was developed to visualize the defined KPIs. First, the platform to be used for development was identified.

There are various business intelligence platforms and tools on the market (Power BI, Tableau, Qlik Sense, for example), and the choice of use depends mainly on specific needs, personal preferences, and the technical characteristics sought.

After exploring several possibilities on the market, the choice for the development dashboard for our project fell on the Power BI tool. The choice of this instrument was dictated by the cost-effectiveness of the Microsoft product, the ease of data integration and ease of use, and the moderate amount of data under analysis. The considerations of this choice are reported below:

1. Using the Microsoft ecosystem: If one already uses Microsoft systems, integration with Power BI may be easier. This platform, being proprietary to the US company, is seamlessly integrated with other Microsoft applications, simplifying data sharing and collaboration within the Microsoft environment itself;
2. Ease of use: Power BI's intuitive and user-friendly interface makes the platform a particularly advantageous choice for less experienced users of data analysis;
3. Price: In terms of cost, the Microsoft platform offers a free plan with limited functionality. This allows anyone to enjoy the benefits of business intelligence. Other platforms allow access to the service only through subscriptions of different durations and functionalities. Power BI also has different premium plans;
4. Scalability: The management of large amounts of data is allowed by all platforms. Compared to other platforms, Power BI is considered less scalable for advanced analysis and the needs of large companies;
5. Customization and visualization: In some cases, visualization and customization play a key role in the creation of a dashboard or report. The possibility of having a wide range of visualization tools makes the product more dynamic and intuitive;
6. Analysis capabilities: Visualizations and, above all, advanced analysis capabilities and complex and detailed analyses are essential for large companies;
7. Community and support: BI platforms today have a solid base of users and online communities. The choice may depend on the availability of support resources and the possibility of finding answers to your questions.

Initiating the implementation process for a dashboard involves two primary steps: defining the requisite data and importing it into the application. Power BI offers the flexibility to leverage various data sources such as databases, Excel files, and cloud services. In our context, Excel files downloaded to the ASST GOM Niguarda's CMMS, which is ControlASSET® [32], were used. Although using Excel simplifies data management, it lacks real-time synchronization with the CMMS.

The available dataset comprises three main files:

1. "Maintenance": This file contains details of maintenance activities since January 1, 2022. It includes fields such as "Number", "Description", "Contact", and more;
2. "Equipment": This file provides information on various equipment types and their attributes;
3. "Criticality": This file, containing ISO-related criticality assessments, offers insights into equipment descriptions, functions, damages, and more.

Before importing the data, the header rows were removed to prevent formatting errors post-import. Subsequently, the tables were edited using the "Transform Data" function, performing the following actions:

- In the "Equipment Table", two empty columns were removed and transformed into inventory numbers integers for consistency;
- Similarly, in the "Maintenance Table", an empty column was addressed and ensured data type consistency;
- For the "Criticality Table", data types were verified and standardized values for clarity.

Each page of our dashboard follows a standardized process: starting with key performance indicators (KPIs), new columns were created, if necessary, primary diagrams were generated, dynamic filters were implemented, and, finally, graphical and design refinements were applied.

Detailed implementation focuses on individual pages of our dashboard include the following:

- "Average Request Closing Time": This page calculates the average time to close maintenance requests, visualizing data through line charts and stacked column histograms with dynamic filters for enhanced usability;
- "One-Day Action": This page identifies maintenance actions completed within a day, presenting data through pie and donut charts, accompanied by a detailed table for comprehensive analysis;
- "Mean Time To Repair": Utilizing bar charts, this page evaluates repair times for technicians and equipment types, facilitating data interpretation through dynamic filters;
- "Supported Devices for Technical Personnel": Visualizing maintenance assignments and device statuses, this page provides insights into technician workload and equipment conditions;
- "Negligent Action": By categorizing open calls based on duration and status, this page highlights potential operational inefficiencies, aiding in proactive maintenance management;
- "Number of Requests vs. Installed Devices": This page compares maintenance requests with installed devices per department, offering insights into resource allocation and operational efficiency;
- "Details of Department Requests": Building on the previous page, this section provides detailed breakdowns of maintenance requests per department, facilitating deeper analysis;
- "Criticality": This page focuses on equipment criticality, visualizing device distribution and criticality percentages per operating unit;
- "Obsolescence": Utilizing device lifespan data, this section assesses equipment obsolescence and provides insights into equipment age and distribution.

Each page incorporates specific filters tailored to the data displayed, ensuring a customized and user-friendly experience.

4. Results

This section will showcase all selected KPIs (Table 2), detailing their descriptions, usage, and graphical representation. Furthermore, it will present a retrospective investigation covering the years 2022–2023, allowing numerical calculation of KPI values where sufficient data from the CMMS were available. Following this, the section will provide implementation on dashboards and graphical representation for the mentioned KPIs.

4.1. Logistics Management KPIs

4.1.1. Average Downtime in the Warehouse

The "Average downtime in the warehouse" (Appendix B) indicator evaluates the average time devices spend in a state of repair in the warehouse. Unlike other metrics where technicians return repaired devices to the department, in this case, it is handled by a department operator. Monitoring this indicator is crucial for assessing the efficiency of warehouse department coordination to ensure service continuity. For ASST GOM Niguarda, this indicator is monitored and calculated annually by the logistics area coordinator, with results expressed in days. The value of this indicator contributes to the calculation of total downtime, and any increase requires investigation into which departments are experiencing issues and the underlying causes. Keeping this value as low as possible is a goal of the CED, not just as an efficiency and coordination measure but also because prolonged device downtime causes logistical issues due to limited warehouse space. Currently, data required for calculation are missing from the ControlASSET® management system, specifically information on device retrieval from the warehouse. Therefore, implementation of this indicator on the dashboard will be delayed until the management system is completely renewed.

4.1.2. Receiving Spare Parts Meantime

The "Receiving spare parts meantime" (Appendix B) index evaluates the average time elapsed between the order of spare parts and the arrival of the material. For ASST GOM Niguarda, the established frequency of measurement and calculation is annual and is the responsibility of the logistics area coordinator. The index is expressed in days. Through the calculation of this index, it is possible to assess the efficiency of the supply service provided by the external company. For the analysis to be meaningful, it is important to compare the obtained temporal value with a benchmark, which can be calculated considering the origin site of the materials. Currently, the calculation is not possible due to a lack of useful data in the ControlASSET® management system: information on material arrival is missing. Therefore, the aforementioned index will not be implemented on the dashboard until the complete renewal of the management system used.

4.1.3. Mean Arrival Time

The "Mean Arrival Time" (Appendix B) index assesses the average time from reporting a malfunction until the device arrives in the warehouse for repair. It aids in evaluating warehouse department coordination efficiency for continuous service. ASST GOM Niguarda measures and calculates this annually under the logistics coordinator's supervision, with results in hours. In this case, as well, the lower this index is, the more efficient the service will be. Identifying causes of delays through workflow analysis can optimize processes. However, the lack of necessary data in ControlASSET® prevents current calculation, delaying dashboard implementation until the management system is updated.

4.1.4. Percentage of External Downtime

The "Percentage of external downtime" (Appendix B) indicator measures downtime attributed to external maintenance, especially for contract devices, where downtime tends to be longer due to external servicing. ASST GOM Niguarda monitors and calculates this annually under logistics supervision, with results in hours. The index helps assess external workload volumes and, with high values, prompts analysis for workflow optimization or contract adjustments. However, lacking necessary data in ControlASSET® hinders current calculations, delaying dashboard implementation until system renewal. Keeping this value as low as possible is a CED's goal.

4.2. Technical Management KPIs

4.2.1. Average Time since First Intervention

The "Average time since first intervention" (Appendix B) index evaluates the time between reporting a malfunction and beginning maintenance work. It is divided into two time windows: fault detection to reporting and reporting to intervention. The index helps assess technical staff efficiency and coordination, but the lack of necessary data in ControlASSET® prevents current calculation; thus, it is not implemented in the dashboard. It is calculated in hours and should be as low as possible.

4.2.2. Mean Time to Repair (MTTR)

The KPI "Mean Time to Repair" (Appendix B) assesses the average time taken to repair a device from when the technician starts work until the device is completely restored. This measure is crucial for evaluating the efficiency of the technical department in restoring equipment functionality promptly. ASST GOM Niguarda measures MTTR annually under the supervision of the technical area coordinator, with data extracted from the ControlASSET® management system and expressed in hours. Due to missing "start work time" data, "hours worked" data are utilized for calculation. MTTR is calculated as the ratio of total repair time to total maintenance interventions, aiming to minimize downtime and identify root causes of delays through Root Cause Analysis (RCA). MTTR helps set time objectives for repair and optimizes processes to meet those objectives. Through Power BI implementation, MTTR trends can be visualized by technicians (Figure 1) but also for devices, allowing for analysis and identification of devices exceeding repair time limits. Adjustment of the time window provides insights into MTTR trends over different periods, aiding in continuous improvement efforts within the technical department. This KPI is measured in hours, and it is possible to see that it is dependent on the technician who is in charge of the maintenance. So, this indicator should be similar to every technician and should be around 20 h.

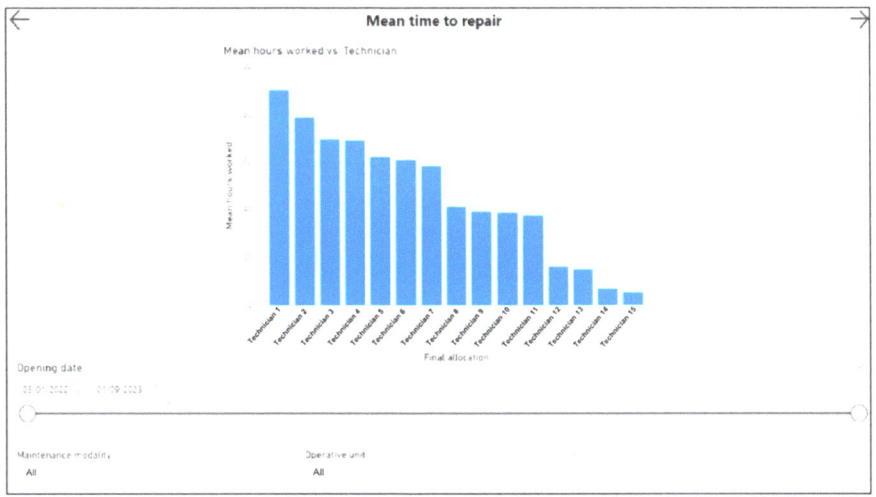

Figure 1. Implementation in Power BI of mean time to repair KPI.

4.2.3. Average Request Closing Time

The KPI "Average requests closing time" (Appendix B) evaluates the average time interval between reporting a fault and restoring the device. It consists of two distinct contributions: "Average time since first intervention", which is the time between fault reporting and maintenance initiation, and "Mean Time to Repair", which is the actual repair duration. ASST GOM Niguarda measures this annually under the supervision of the technical area coordinator, using data from the CMMS and expressing the indicator in hours. The calculation is performed as the difference between the closure time and the start time of maintenance, divided by the total number of maintenance interventions.

Monitoring the index value is crucial, as is aiming to keep it as low as possible. However, it is important to note that long call closure times do not always correspond to long maintenance interventions; calls are often closed after maintenance ends. Therefore, the dashboard implementation allows observation of the "Average requests closing time" for each technician and device type, enabling the technical area coordinator to optimize the process.

Figure 2 presents a column chart showing the monthly number of maintenance requests generated from January 2022 to 1 September 2023, with a dashed line indicating the trend of the index. Despite the relatively high average number of maintenance requests generated, the index value slightly decreased in the first 8 months of 2023 compared to 2022.

The potentials of Power BI enable data filtering by final allocation, internal/external maintenance, maintenance cause, and inventory number. For instance, users can observe the number of faults for a specific inventory within the selected time frame and the average time calls remain open.

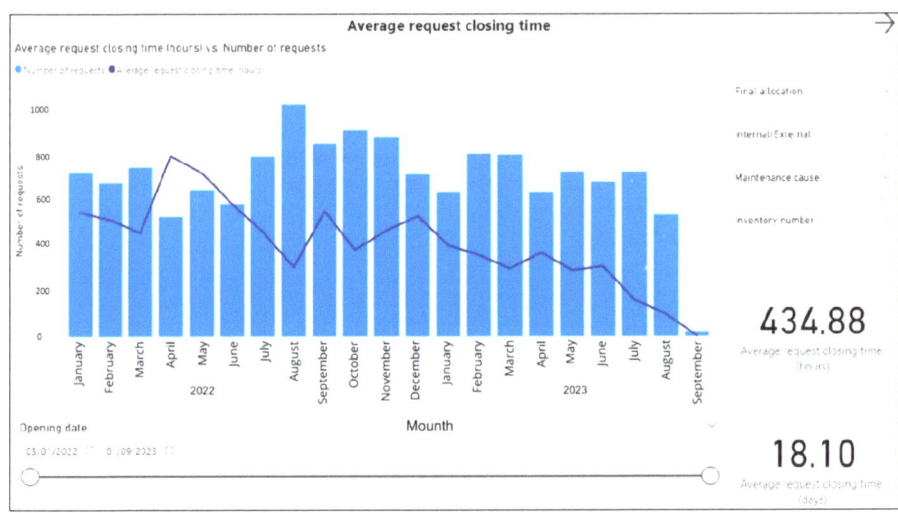

Figure 2. Implementation of average request closing time KPI in Power BI.

Figure 3 provides a practical example of using the index, focusing only on ECG devices to illustrate realistic calculation. The average call closure time for ECG devices is observed to be 9.11 days, aligning with expectations. Peaks in April and May 2022 coincide with director changes during those months. While the overall value of "Average requests closing time" may be unreliable due to impure data, a detailed analysis of individual device classes can already provide valuable insights.

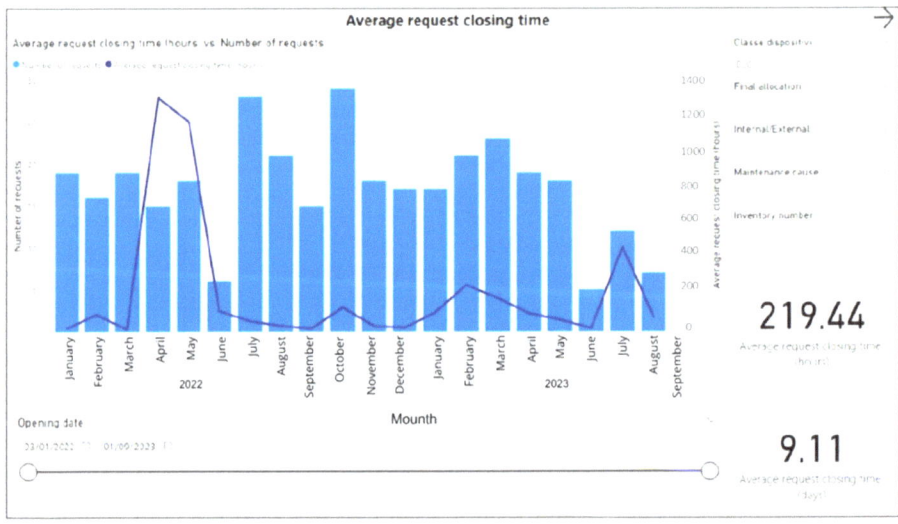

Figure 3. Average request closing time for electrocardiograph device—detailed view in Power BI.

4.2.4. Supported Devices for Technical Personnel

The KPI "Supported devices for technical personnel" (Appendix B) determines the workload supported by specialized technical staff. ASST GOM Niguarda monitors and calculates this index daily under the supervision of the technical area coordinator, using data extracted from the ControlASSET® management system. The index is expressed as a percentage.

Implementing this indicator on a dashboard, as shown in Figure 4, allows for various analyses. The first graph, on the left, is a stacked column chart providing detailed information. Firstly, it shows how many devices each technician is working on based on the number of assigned calls, aiding the technical area coordinator in quickly assigning new calls to technicians. Secondly, it evaluates the number of devices each technician has worked on within a predefined time window.

Overall, the indicator provides a comprehensive overview of the technical staff's activity. In this case, there is not a specific number to reach because the number of devices repaired by the technician depends on the type of malfunction that occurs and on the maintenance time.

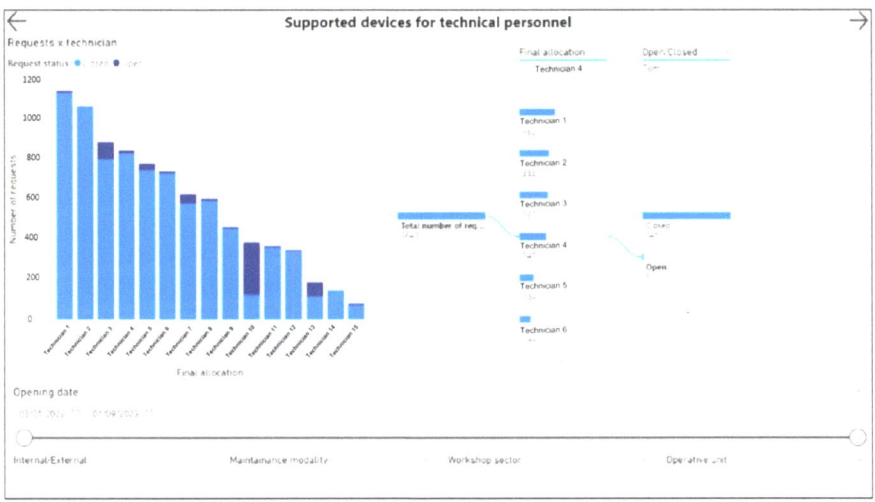

Figure 4. Implementation of supported devices for technical personnel KPI in Power BI.

4.2.5. One-Day Action

The "One-Day Action" (Appendix B) index evaluates the percentage of maintenance tasks completed within 24 h of the occurrence of a fault. It is calculated based on the mean time to repair (MTTR) and is expressed as a percentage. ASST GOM Niguarda monitors and calculates this index annually, and it is managed by the technical area coordinator using data from the ControlASSET® management system. The index aims to minimize machine downtime for service continuity, especially by providing temporary replacements for devices under contract or requiring spare parts. The corresponding dashboard (Figure 5) provides visual representations of call closure percentages. Filters are available for various maintenance parameters. Overall, the index allows for assessing the efficiency and speed of the technical department in handling maintenance tasks, particularly simple interventions completed within 24 h. The goal of clinical engineering is to keep this value high, as the higher it is, the greater the number of devices that can be repaired in a day.

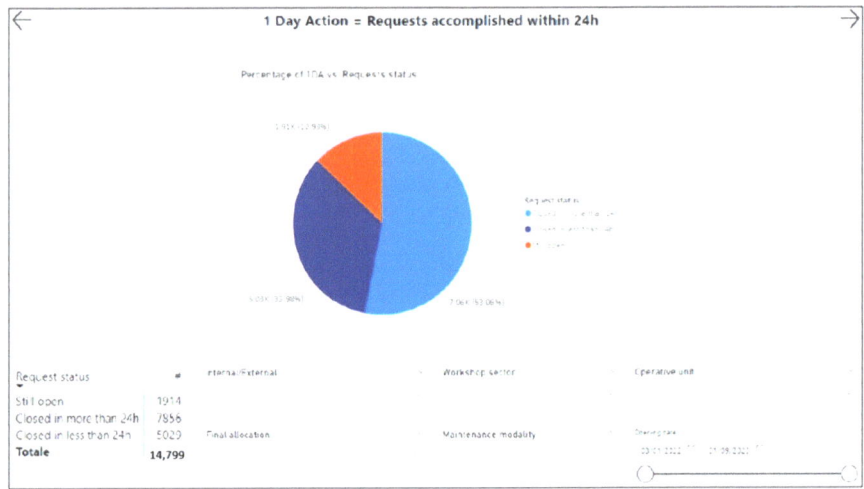

Figure 5. Implementation of one-day action KPI in Power BI.

4.2.6. Negligent Actions

The "Negligent Actions" (Appendix B) indicator evaluates the percentage of procedures not completed within a predetermined assignment period. ASST GOM Niguarda monitors and calculates this index semi-annually, managed by the technical area coordinator using data from the ControlASSET® management system. The index is expressed as a percentage and is calculated by dividing the number of overdue procedures by the total number of maintenance requests within the specified assignment period. The standard assignment period is 30 days, as per the literature. The objective is to minimize this value and analyze the causes of any peaks, considering the type of maintenance tasks. Temporary replacements are provided until the device is fully restored to ensure service continuity. The dashboard (Figure 6) visually represents the percentage of closed and open calls, categorized into assigned and unassigned ones. Additionally, it displays a summary of the distribution of open practices and the days elapsed since the opening date. The analysis of these results highlights the considerable number of open tickets with high resolution times.

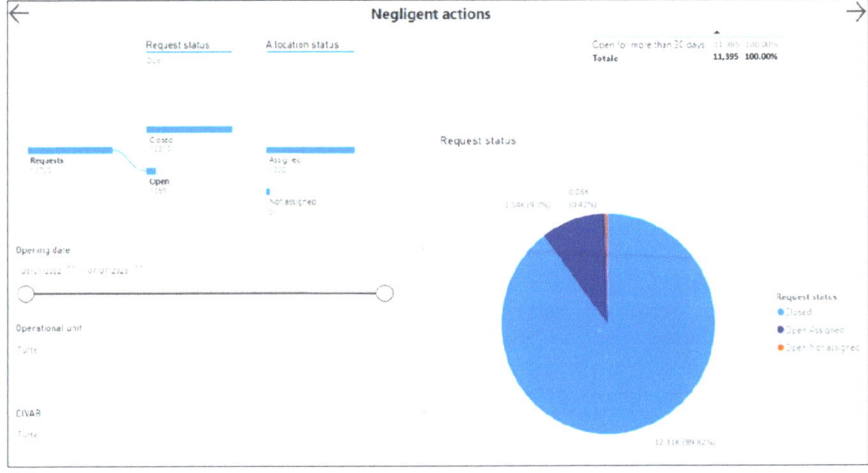

Figure 6. Implementation of negligent actions KPI in Power BI.

4.3. Equipment Management KPIs

4.3.1. Average Failure Time

The "Average Failure Time" (Appendix B) index evaluates the average time between the resolution of a failure and the occurrence of a second one. It serves as a reliability parameter to assess not only the frequency of failures on a device but also the average period of equipment availability.

For ASST GOM Niguarda, the index's detection and calculation frequency is set annually and is managed by the quality group. Data for calculation are extracted from the ControlASSET® management system, and the index is expressed in days. The calculation involves subtracting the date of the opening of a new maintenance request from the date of closure of the previous one and dividing it by the total number of corrective maintenance actions.

The objective is to maximize the "Average Failure Time", meaning to extend the time between two successive failures as much as possible. Calculating and graphically representing this index is essential for monitoring trends over time and investigating the causes of any decrease in its value.

It is expected that the index will be higher for technologies with low technical complexity and lower for devices prone to more frequent failures, such as those with high technical complexity. Additionally, comparing the causes of two successive failures could be useful, especially if there are recurring reasons, allowing for efficient solutions.

Currently, the index is not implemented in the dashboard.

4.3.2. Uptime

The "Uptime" (Appendix B) index measures the actual availability time of a device, expressed as a percentage. ASST GOM Niguarda calculates it annually, managed by the quality group, using data from the ControlASSET® management system. It is computed by dividing the device's uptime by its theoretical usage time. The goal is to maintain a high value to reduce equipment downtime and associated costs. While not currently implemented in the dashboard, special attention is given to life-saving devices, leading to the development of a related indicator called "Uptime for life-saving equipment."

4.3.3. Uptime for Life-Saving Equipment

Particular attention must be paid to 'life-saving' devices. This is why it was decided to implement an indicator that more accurately monitors this type of device.

The index developed is 'Uptime for life-saving equipment' (Appendix B) and bases its principle and use on the 'Uptime' index.

4.3.4. Corrective Maintenance Downtime

The "Corrective Maintenance Downtime" (Appendix B) index evaluates the machine downtime due to corrective maintenance, which is caused by sudden failures rather than scheduled maintenance or electrical checks. ASST GOM Niguarda calculates it annually, managed by the quality group, using data from the ControlASSET® management system. The index is expressed as a percentage and is calculated by dividing the time of corrective maintenance downtime by the theoretical uptime. Currently, the index is not implemented in the dashboard because the classification of devices by risk class will not be available in ControlASSET® until the management system is completely renewed. It is important to keep this KPI as low as possible in order to increment the availability of the electromedical device.

4.3.5. Preventive Maintenance Downtime

The "Preventive Maintenance Downtime" (Appendix B) index evaluates the machine downtime due to scheduled maintenance. ASST GOM Niguarda calculates it annually, managed by the quality group, using data from the ControlASSET® management system. The index is expressed as a percentage and is calculated by dividing the time of preventive maintenance downtime by the theoretical uptime. The "time of machine downtime due to preventive maintenance" refers to the time needed to perform scheduled maintenance, while the "theoretical uptime" is assumed to be 365 days for devices with high criticality and 250 days for other devices. Similar to other indices, this index is not currently implemented in the dashboard pending the complete renewal of the management system. Also, in this case, the KPI should be as low as possible to increase the medical device availability.

4.3.6. Inventories That Generate Request

The "Inventories that generate requests" (Appendix B) index allows for accurately assessing which devices generate the highest number of requests and, therefore, experience a high number of failures. Specifically, it provides observations tailored to each department.

ASST GOM Niguarda calculates this index annually, managed by the quality group, using data extracted from the ControlASSET® management system. The index is expressed as a percentage and is calculated by dividing the number of requests generated by inventory by the total number of devices.

Unlike the "Number of requests over number of devices per hospital wards" indicator, which will be implemented later, this index focuses on identifying which devices frequently encounter failures and how many such devices exist. Additionally, valuable insights can be derived by combining this index with an analysis of device obsolescence. This could lead to the decommissioning of obsolete devices that require frequent maintenance.

Currently, the index is not implemented in the dashboard due to a lack of necessary data for calculation.

4.3.7. Number of Requests over Number of Devices per Hospital Wards

The "Number of requests over number of devices per hospital wards" (Appendix B) index assesses the ratio of maintenance requests opened by each department to the number of devices installed in them. ASST GOM Niguarda calculates this annually, using data from ControlASSET®, expressed as a percentage. The index aids in identifying departments with high maintenance request rates relative to installed devices. Figure 7 displays the dashboard, offering a comprehensive view of departmental data. Detailed analyses help pinpoint causes, especially concerning equipment obsolescence. This index is crucial for promptly addressing maintenance needs and optimizing equipment management.

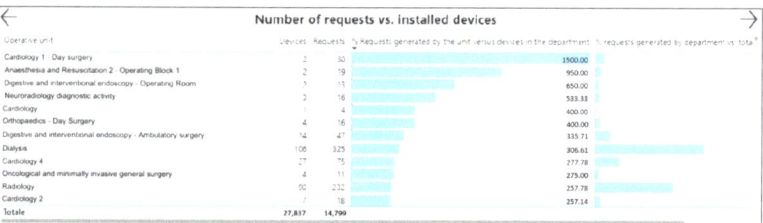

Figure 7. Implementation of number of requests vs. installed devices KPI in Power BI.

4.3.8. Failure Rate Category

The "Failure Rate Category" (Appendix B) indicator is the index of the overall failure rate that considers the specific category of the device. ASST GOM Niguarda calculates this annually, using data from ControlASSET®, and expresses the index as a percentage.

The index is calculated as the number of maintenance interventions per specific device class divided by the total number of maintenance interventions. Devices in a high-risk class are expected to have a higher number of interventions. This indicator should be as low as possible; otherwise, it indicates that the medical device category should be replaced by new ones. An accurate analysis of the index values would enable proper planning of preventive maintenance for high-risk devices, thereby avoiding unexpected failures and service interruptions.

The implementation of the index also allows for investigating the types of failures by device class to prevent systematic breakdowns where they occur. Currently, the index is not implemented on the dashboard due to the absence of device classification by risk class in ControlASSET® until the complete renewal of the management system.

5. Discussion

The identification and implementation of a set of performance indicators allows the Clinical Engineering Department of ASST GOM Niguarda to have a broader operational view of the hospital, with a comprehensive and measurable understanding of the maintenance management of its technological assets, the economic value managed by the facility, and a better understanding and evaluation of the critical issues of the various existing operational units.

The existing indicators within the facility have proven to be of fundamental importance in identifying maintenance processes that have not yet been investigated. Building upon these, along with a thorough study of the existing literature, it was possible to generate a diverse set of 18 KPIs tailored to the facility's needs, considering its size and strategic objectives.

The division of the 18 indices into KPIs for logistics management, technical management, and equipment management has allowed for an overview of processes and activities and has enabled the selection of parameters to monitor in order to identify improvement opportunities useful for achieving the facility's objectives.

In particular, process efficiency indicators such as "One-day action", "Negligent action", or "Mean Time to Repair", along with coordination indicators like those for logistics management, have highlighted the innovativeness of the proposed solution.

The definition of the structure of these indices and their calculation methods will facilitate the easy development of any other indices should new needs or further studies arise. Currently, the segment of economic indices has not been thoroughly explored due to data gaps within the ControlASSET® management system; it is left to the facility to implement these based on the proposed ones.

Moreover, defining benchmarks would make the index monitoring system comprehensive and actionable. As these benchmarks are not present in the literature, given that the indices were adapted to the ASST GOM Niguarda facility, they can be determined through a thorough study of the temporal trends of the indices themselves.

Merely defining KPIs is not sufficient to achieve the objective. Hence, a dashboard has been implemented to allow both graphic and quantitative visualization of individual indicators. This assists the monitoring personnel in conducting an immediate and intuitive analysis of employee occupancy status, process trends, and instant identification of any critical issues. Additionally, the support of filters for maintenance type, technician, year, and department contributes to making the analysis more precise and comprehensive.

The primary constraints of this study stem from the data accessibility within CED of the ASST GOM Niguarda. Specifically, the challenges encountered pertain to the absence of certain data crucial for indicator computation. These data elements are unavailable due to the absence of corresponding fields in the CED's CMMS. Thus, it is necessary to modify the CMMS database structure to encompass a more comprehensive perspective on operational oversight within the department.

Moreover, the existing data are frequently inputted inaccurately by users, resulting in an analysis that may not fully reflect the actual circumstances. Enhanced diligence on the part of users during data input is imperative, which is achievable through heightened awareness of operational management practices. To ensure the integrity of the data, the implementation of a semi-automated data entry system, capturing elements such as time and date, would prove beneficial.

The work carried out has thus contributed to identifying anomalies in the data and gaps in the application itself. Proposals have been provided regarding the inclusion of additional mandatory fields for technicians to fill out and changes to existing fields to enable the calculation of all proposed KPIs.

The primary challenge of data accessibility can be addressed by incorporating specific fields within the management system to collect the necessary data for indicator calculation. Additionally, to resolve this issue, it is essential to directly link the management system's database to the Power BI dashboard. This will enable real-time visualization of the KPIs, eliminating the need to download Excel files from ControlASSET.

Another potential element to consider in future developments is to define thresholds for each indicator. This can be performed based on the analysis of previous years' data and setting thresholds that continuously improve the performance of the service provided by the CED.

Finally, the dashboard has been implemented on Power BI rather than the ControlASSET® application, as the latter is not owned by the facility. Implementing this interactive corporate dashboard on the new application would be the optimal solution and would avoid the need to repeatedly extract data for calculation. This way, calculations could be performed immediately whenever necessary, and they could be accessible to various stakeholders in the maintenance process.

Author Contributions: Conceptualization, P.P., U.N., A.P., A.D.C. and V.C.; formal analysis, V.C.; writing—original draft preparation, P.P. and V.C.; writing—review and editing, P.P., U.N., A.P., A.D.C. and V.C.; supervision P.P., U.N., A.P., A.D.C. and V.C. All authors have read and agreed to the published version of the manuscript.

Funding: This research received no external funding.

Data Availability Statement: Data are contained within the article.

Conflicts of Interest: The authors declare no conflicts of interest.

Appendix A. Description of the Indicators Used in the ASST GOM Niguarda's CED

Process		Indicator	Frequency of Analysis
Administrative management	1	(number of contracts approved within 5 months of signing budget sheet/total number of contracts) × 100	Annually
Logistic management	2	(number of detection of articles under minimum stock/total number of articles in stock with minimum stock) × 100	Annually
	3	(number of articles different from actual stock/total number of articles in stock with minimum stock) × 100	Annually
Technical management	4	(number of operating theatre and intensive care equipment on which safety checks were carried out/total number of operating theatre and intensive care equipment) × 100	Annually
	5	number of intervention sheets assigned to technicians/number of technicians	Annually
	6	number of intervention sheets open for more than 7 days but less than 30 days/number of technicians	Annually
	7	number of action sheets open for more than 30 days/number of technicians	Annually
	8	average first response time of the technician for urgent calls	Annually
Training	9	(number of CI employees who have attended at least one course in a year/total number of employees) × 100	Annually
Quality	10	(number of targets achieved in the year/total targets to be achieved in the year) × 100	Annually

Appendix B. KPI Description

Name	Description	Scope of Measurement (Process, Outcome, Other)	Formula	Numerator—Inclusion Criteria	Numerator—Exclusion Criteria	Denominator—Inclusion Criteria	Denominator—Exclusion Criteria	Units of Measure
			Logistic management Type					
Average downtime in the warehouse	Analysis of the average idle time of a repaired instrument in the warehouse	Process	$\frac{Average\ idle\ time\ of\ the\ repaired\ device\ in\ the\ warehouse}{Total\ number\ of\ devices\ repaired\ in\ the\ warehouse}$	All devices undergoing maintenance in the workshop	All devices not undergoing maintenance in the workshop	Number of devices that underwent maintenance and are idle in the warehouse	All devices in the warehouse that have not undergone maintenance (Inventory)	Days
Receiving spare parts meantime	Analysis of the average time elapsed between the request for spare parts and the arrival of the material	Process	$\frac{Total\ turnaround\ time\ for\ arrival\ of\ replacement\ parts.}{Number\ of\ orders}$	All the orders requesting spare parts	All orders where spare parts are not requested	All orders where spare parts are requested	All orders where spare parts are not requested	Days
Arrival Meantime	Analysis of the average time elapsed between the opening of the ticket and the arrival of the instrument in the warehouse	Process	$\frac{Arrival\ in\ the\ warehouse's\ time-opening\ ticket's\ time}{Number\ of\ tickets\ received}$	All devices requiring workshop maintenance for which the technician does not perform an on-site inspection.	All devices that do not require workshop maintenance or for which the technician performs an on-site inspection.	All maintenance calls for which the technician does not perform an on-site inspection.	All maintenance calls not in the workshop or for which the technician performs an on-site inspection.	Hours
Percentage of external downtime	Analysis of machine downtime due to external maintenance on total machine downtime	Process	$\frac{equipment\ downtime\ due\ to\ external\ maintainance}{theoretical\ time\ of\ use}$	All devices requiring maintenance in the company	All devices that are not sent to the company	All devices requiring maintenance in the company	All devices that are not sent to the company	Percentage

Name	Description	Scope of Measurement (Process, Outcome, Other)	Formula	Numerator—Inclusion Criteria	Numerator—Exclusion Criteria	Denominator—Inclusion Criteria	Denominator—Exclusion Criteria	Units of Measure
			Technical Management					
Average time since first intervention	Analysis of the average time elapsed between the opening of the call and the first intervention	Process	$\frac{time\ of\ opening\ ticket - time\ of\ the\ first\ intervention}{Number\ of\ close\ ticket}$	All devices not under contract	All devices under contract	All tickets for devices not under contract	All tickets for devices under contract	Hours
Mean Time to Repair	Analysis of the average time elapsed between the opening of the call and the first intervention	Process	$\frac{closure\ request\ time - maintenance\ start\ time}{total\ number\ of\ maintenance\ operations}$	All close maintenance request	All open maintenance request	All close maintenance request	All open maintenance request	Hours
Average request closing time	Analysis of average call closure time	Process	$\frac{closure\ request\ time - open\ request\ time}{total\ number\ of\ corrective\ maintenance\ operations}$	All close maintenance request which are not tests	All open maintenance request	All close maintenance request which are not tests	All open maintenance request	Hours
Supported devices for technical personnel	Number of devices supported by a single technician vs. total number of hospital devices	Process	$\frac{number\ of\ request\ assigned\ to\ each\ technician}{total\ number\ of\ device}$	All request assigned to a technician	All request not assigned to a technician	All request assigned to a technician	All request not assigned to a technician	Percentage
One-Day Action	Calculation of the number of interventions carried out in less than 24 h	Process	$\frac{Number\ of\ request\ open\ for\ more\ than\ X\ days}{total\ number\ of\ corrective\ maintenance}$	All open request	All close request	All request	-	Percentage

Name	Description	Scope of Measurement (Process, Outcome, Other)	Formula	Numerator—Inclusion Criteria	Numerator—Exclusion Criteria	Denominator—Inclusion Criteria	Denominator—Exclusion Criteria	Units of Measure
Equipment Management								
Negligent Actions	Average time elapsed between the resolution of one fault and the occurrence of a second fault	Other	$\frac{time\ between\ two\ failures}{total\ number\ of\ corrective\ maintenance}$	All equipment	-	All equipment	-	Percentage
Average Failure Time	Actual device availability time vs. theoretical time of use	Process	$\frac{device\ activity\ time}{theoretical\ time\ of\ use}$	All equipment	-	All equipment	-	Percentage
Uptime	Actual device availability time vs. theoretical time of use referred to life saving equipment	Process	$\frac{device\ activity\ time_{\ life\ saving\ equipment}}{theoretical\ time\ of\ use_{\ life\ saving\ equipment}}$	All life saving equipment	-	All life saving equipment	-	Percentage
Uptime for life saving equipment	Analysis of device unavailability time caused by Corrective Maintenance interventions	Process	$\frac{downtime\ due\ to\ corrective\ maintenance}{theoretical\ time\ of\ use}$	All equipment	-	All equipment	-	Percentage
Corrective Maintenance Downtime	Analysis of device unavailability time caused by Preventive Maintenance interventions	Process	$\frac{downtime\ due\ to\ preventive\ maintenance}{theoretical\ time\ of\ use}$	All equipment	-	All equipment	-	Percentage
Preventive Maintenance Downtime	Analysis of inventories (divided by cost centers) generating maintenance calls	Process	$\frac{device\ that\ generate\ request\ (ward,\ specific\ device\ type)}{total\ number\ of\ devices\ (ward,\ specific\ device\ type)}$	All equipment	-	All equipment	-	Percentage

Name	Description	Scope of Measurement (Process, Outcome, Other)	Formula	Numerator—Inclusion Criteria	Numerator—Exclusion Criteria	Denominator—Inclusion Criteria	Denominator—Exclusion Criteria	Units of Measure
Inventories that generate request	Analysis of how many calls is opened in a given department compared to how many installed have	Other	$\frac{number\ of\ request\ (specific\ ward)}{total\ number\ of\ devices\ (specific\ ward)}$	All equipment	-	All equipment	-	Percentage
Number of requests over number of devices per hospital wards	Failure analysis for each device class	Process	$\frac{number\ of\ corrective\ maintenance\ for\ a\ specific\ class\ of\ devices}{total\ number\ of\ corrective\ maintenance}$	All equipment	-	All equipment	-	Percentage

References

1. Drechsler, K.; Grisold, T.; Gau, M.; Seidel, S. Digital Infrastructure Evolution: A Digital Trace Data Study. Available online: https://www.researchgate.net/publication/364199024 (accessed on 5 June 2024).
2. Limna, P. The Digital Transformation of Healthcare in the Digital Economy: A Systematic Review. *Int. J. Adv. Health Sci. Technol.* **2023**, *3*, 127–132. [CrossRef]
3. Stoumpos, A.I.; Kitsios, F.; Talias, M.A. Digital Transformation in Healthcare: Technology Acceptance and Its Applications. *Int. J. Environ. Res. Public Health* **2023**, *20*, 3407. [CrossRef] [PubMed]
4. Assessing the Impact of Digital Transformation of Health Services Expert Panel on Effective Ways of Investing in Health (EXPH). [CrossRef]
5. Cancela, J.; Charlafti, I.; Colloud, S.; Wu, C. Digital health in the era of personalized healthcare: Opportunities and challenges for bringing research and patient care to a new level. In *Digital Health: Mobile and Wearable Devices for Participatory Health Applications*; Elsevier: Amsterdam, The Netherlands, 2021. [CrossRef]
6. Junaid, S.B.; Imam, A.A.; Balogun, A.O.; De Silva, L.C.; Surakat, Y.A.; Kumar, G.; Abdulkarim, M.; Shuaibu, A.N.; Garba, A.; Sahalu, Y.; et al. Recent Advancements in Emerging Technologies for Healthcare Management Systems: A Survey. *Healthcare* **2022**, *10*, 1940. [CrossRef] [PubMed]
7. Kruk, M.E.; Gage, A.D.; Arsenault, C.; Jordan, K.; Leslie, H.H.; Roder-DeWan, S.; Adeyi, O.; Barker, P.; Daelmans, B.; Doubova, S.V.; et al. High-quality health systems in the Sustainable Development Goals era: Time for a revolution. *Lancet Glob. Health* **2018**, *6*, e1196–e1252. [CrossRef] [PubMed]
8. Abernethy, A.; Adams, L.; Barrett, M.; Bechtel, C.; Brennan, P. The Promise of Digital Health: Then, Now, and the Future Digital Health in the 21st Century. *NAM Perspect.* **2022**, *2022*, 1031478/202206e. [CrossRef]
9. Iadanza, E. Clinical engineering. In *Clinical Engineering Handbook*, 2nd ed.; Academic Press: Cambridge, MA, USA, 2019. [CrossRef]
10. World Health Organization (WHO). *Human Resources for Medical Devices: The Role of Biomedical Engineers*; WHO: Geneva, Switzerland, 2017; pp. 1–234. Available online: https://apps.who.int/iris/bitstream/handle/10665/255261/9789241565479-eng.pdf (accessed on 5 June 2024).
11. Hossain, M.A.; Ahmad, M.; Islam, M.R.; David, Y. Evaluation of Performance Outcomes of Medical Equipment Technology Management and Patient Safety: Skilled Clinical Engineer's Approach. *Glob. Clin. Eng. J.* **2019**, *1*, 4–16. [CrossRef]
12. Iadanza, E.; Gonnelli, V.; Satta, F.; Gherardelli, M. Evidence-based medical equipment management: A convenient implementation. *Med. Biol. Eng. Comput.* **2019**, *57*, 2215–2230. [CrossRef]
13. Bliznakov, Z.; Pappous, G.; Bliznakova, K.; Pallikarakis, N. Integrated software system for improving medical equipment management. *Biomed. Instrum. Technol.* **2003**, *37*, 25–33. [CrossRef]
14. Almomani, H.; Alburaiesi, M.L. Using Computerized Maintenance Management System (CMMS) in Healthcare Equipments Maintenance Operations. 2020. Available online: https://www.researchgate.net/publication/342707011 (accessed on 5 June 2024).
15. WHO. Computerized maintenance. In *WHO Medical Device Technical Series*; WHO: Geneva, Switzerland, 2011; Available online: https://www.who.int/publications-detail-redirect/9789241501415 (accessed on 5 June 2024).
16. Abayazeed, S.A.; Hamza, A.O. Software applications in healthcare technology management: A review. *J. Clin. Eng.* **2010**, *35*, 25–33. [CrossRef]
17. Mobarek, I.; Tarawneh, W.; Langevin, F.; Ibbini, M. Fully automated clinical engineering technical management system. *J. Clin. Eng.* **2006**, *31*, 46–60. [CrossRef]
18. Neven, S.; Rahman, S.A. An Automated Medical Equipment Management System Proposed for Small-Scale Hospitals. *J. Clin. Eng.* **2017**, *42*, E1–E8. [CrossRef]
19. Chen, H.; Chiang, R.H.L.; Storey, V.C.; Robinson, J.M. Special Issue: Business Intelligence Research Business Intelligence and Analytics: From Big Data to Big Impact. Available online: www.freakonomics.com/2008/02/25/hal-varian-answers-your-questions/ (accessed on 5 June 2024).
20. Rouhani, S.; Ashrafi, A.; Ravasan, A.Z.; Afshari, S. The impact model of business intelligence on decision support and organizational benefits. *J. Enterp. Inf. Manag.* **2016**, *29*, 19–50. [CrossRef]
21. Sneed, H.; Verhoef, C. Reengineering the Corporation—A Manifesto for IT Evolution. 2001. Available online: https://www.researchgate.net/publication/2366189 (accessed on 5 June 2024).
22. Yi, Q.; Hoskins, R.E.; Hillringhouse, E.A.; Sorensen, S.S.; Oberle, M.W.; Fuller, S.S.; Wallace, J.C. Integrating open-source technologies to build low-cost information systems for improved access to public health data. *Int. J. Health Geogr.* **2008**, *7*, 29. [CrossRef] [PubMed]
23. Cucoranu, I.C.; Parwani, A.V.; West, A.J.; Romero-Lauro, G.; Nauman, K.; Carter, A.B.; Balis, U.J.; Tuthill, M.J.; Pantanowitz, L. Privacy and security of patient data in the pathology laboratory. *J. Pathol. Inform.* **2013**, *4*, 4. [CrossRef] [PubMed]
24. Sabherwal, R.; Becerra-Fernandez, I. *Business Intelligence Practices Technologies, and Management*; Handbook; John Wiley & Sons: Hoboken, NJ, USA, 2013.
25. ISO 9001:2015. Available online: https://www.iso.org/standard/62085.html (accessed on 5 June 2024).

26. Bhardwaj, P.; Joshi, N.K.; Singh, P.; Suthar, P.; Joshi, V.; Jain, Y.K.; Charan, J.; Ameel, M.; Singh, K.; Patil, M.S.; et al. Competence-Based Assessment of Biomedical Equipment Management and Maintenance System (e-Upkaran) Using Benefit Evaluation Framework. *Cureus* **2022**, *14*, e30579. [CrossRef] [PubMed]
27. Gonnelli, V.; Satta, F.; Frosini, F.; Iadanza, E. Evidence-based approach to medical equipment maintenance monitoring. In *EMBEC-NBC*; Springer: Singapore, 2017. [CrossRef]
28. Camila, R.d.S.; William, C.A.C.; Renan, F.; Renato, G.O. Reliability indicators in the medical equipment management. *IFMBE Proc.* **2015**, *51*, 1566–1570. [CrossRef] [PubMed]
29. Oshiyama, N.F.; Silveira, A.C.; Bassani, R.A.; Bassani, J.W.M. Medical equipment classification according to corrective maintenance data: A strategy based on the equipment age. *Rev. Bras. Eng. Biomed.* **2014**, *30*, 64–69. [CrossRef]
30. Kumar, U.; Galar, D.; Parida, A.; Stenström, C.; Berges, L. Maintenance performance metrics: A state-of-the-art review. *J. Qual. Maint. Eng.* **2013**, *19*, 233–277. [CrossRef]
31. Automation Systems and Integration-Key Performance Indicators (KPIs) for Manufacturing Operations Management-Part 2: Definitions and Descriptions Systèmes D'automatisation et Intégration-Indicateurs de la Performance clé Pour le Management des Opérations de Fabrication-Partie 2: Définitions et Descriptions. 2014. Available online: https://standards.iteh.ai/catalog/standards/sist/8a9efc01-6c74-42a2-ad8f-UNIEN15341:2019 (accessed on 5 June 2024).
32. ControlAsset®. Available online: http://www.ellfsrl.it/i-nostri-prodotti/controlasset (accessed on 5 June 2024).

Disclaimer/Publisher's Note: The statements, opinions and data contained in all publications are solely those of the individual author(s) and contributor(s) and not of MDPI and/or the editor(s). MDPI and/or the editor(s) disclaim responsibility for any injury to people or property resulting from any ideas, methods, instructions or products referred to in the content.

Article

Feature-Based Gait Pattern Modeling on a Treadmill

Woo-Chul Shin [1], Min-Jung Kim [1], Ji-Hun Han [1], Hyun-Sang Cho [2] and Youn-Sik Hong [1,*]

[1] Department of Computer Science and Engineering, Incheon National University, Incheon 22012, Republic of Korea; crepas2@inu.ac.kr (W.-C.S.); alswjdsla47@inu.ac.kr (M.-J.K.); jin4884@inu.ac.kr (J.-H.H.)
[2] R&D Center, CiKLux Inc., Seoul 08585, Republic of Korea; hyunsang.cho@ciklux.com
* Correspondence: yshong@inu.ac.kr

Abstract: In this paper, we present a method of gait analysis on a treadmill based on pressure distribution. We aimed to model the gait patterns of a subject walking at a constant speed on a treadmill based on differences in current consumption. The changes in current consumption were converted into pressure distribution curves, and then specific features were extracted. The extracted features were used to model the walking pattern on a treadmill. To verify the validity of our proposed feature-based gait pattern modeling, we conducted experiments by gender, age, BMI (body mass index), and step-to-step symmetry. The experimental results showed that the heavier the subject, the higher the value of each feature. In particular, our feature point-based gait modeling provides an index that can help determine whether a subject's gait is abnormal, depending on the difference between the features.

Keywords: gait analysis on a treadmill; adapter sensor; feature-based gait pattern modeling; health care; BMI (body mass index)

Citation: Shin, W.-C.; Kim, M.-J.; Han, J.-H.; Cho, H.-S.; Hong, Y.-S. Feature-Based Gait Pattern Modeling on a Treadmill. *Electronics* **2023**, *12*, 4201. https://doi.org/10.3390/electronics12204201

Academic Editor: Hung-Yu Chien

Received: 21 September 2023
Revised: 5 October 2023
Accepted: 6 October 2023
Published: 10 October 2023

Copyright: © 2023 by the authors. Licensee MDPI, Basel, Switzerland. This article is an open access article distributed under the terms and conditions of the Creative Commons Attribution (CC BY) license (https://creativecommons.org/licenses/by/4.0/).

1. Introduction

Gait is a basic human activity and is a key indicator of exercise effectiveness [1] and health status. In particular, in the elderly, factors such as lower-body muscle loss and aging can modify the gait [2] and can lead to falls and limited mobility. In normal adults, a number of orthopedic or neurological conditions can lead to gait disorders [3]. Gait analysis can be used as an indicator to determine the presence of physical abnormalities or diseases.

Sarcopenia, an increasingly recognized geriatric syndrome, causes various dysfunctions, such as decreased walking ability, increased risk of falls, and increased mortality due to weakened lower extremity muscles and decreased physical function [4]. Pieruccini-Faria et al. [5] analyzed gait patterns and brain cognitive abilities in 500 elderly adults and found that gait variability is a strong indicator of problems related to motor control. Middleton [6] stated that gait is one of the vital signs, equivalent to body temperature, pulse, respiration, and blood pressure, and a parameter directly related to life.

As shown in Figure 1, gait can be represented by a gait cycle consisting of a stance phase and a swing phase. In a typical gait cycle, the gait events during are in the following order: heel strike (HS), foot flat (FF), heel rise (HR), toe off (TO), heel strike (HS). The gait cycle maintains a constant pattern unless disturbed by physical abnormalities or the external environment.

Representative research on gait analysis involves installing pressure sensors in the insole of a shoe to determine the pressure distribution or analyzing images of a subject's gait [7,8].

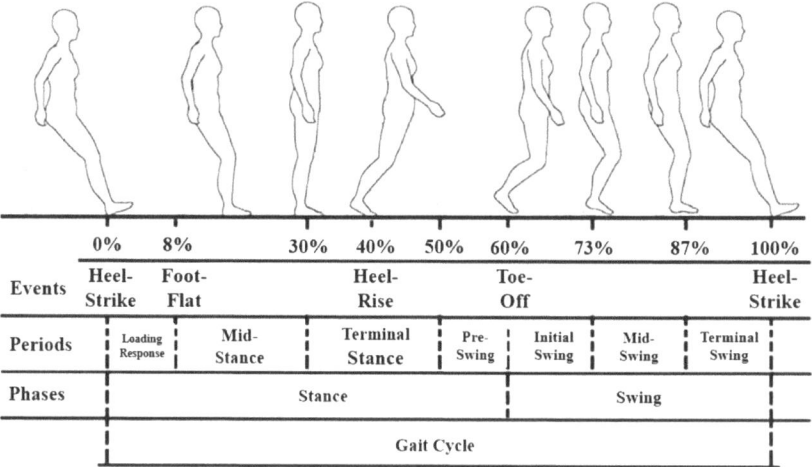

Figure 1. Human gait cycle [7].

Jeong et al. [9] evaluated the gait by embedding a gyro sensor in the insole of a shoe to determine whether the examined subjects walked medially, normally, or externally, according to the foot angle during walking. Bucinskas et al. [10] analyzed gait by embedding three pressure sensors in each shoe insole, for a total of six pressure sensors, to assess gait parameters such as stride size and weight distribution on the feet. The installation of pressure sensors in the insoles requires the production of insoles of multiple sizes for different foot sizes. In addition, there are durability issues related to the pressure sensor embedded in an insole.

Kobsar et. al. [11] used a depth camera to measure vertical oscillation when running on a treadmill and obtained similar results as those achieved with the marker-based standard Vicon system. Potdevin et al. [12] utilized four infrared cameras and two force plates to measure and analyze the asymmetrical gait of subjects through parameters such as MPL and MBL, conducting a classical marker-based gait analysis.

The camera-based gait analysis requires at least four infrared cameras to be installed [13]. In orthopedic or rehabilitation hospitals, gait analysis is sometimes performed on a treadmill. This requires installing cameras to assess the gait as well as pressure sensors at the bottom of the treadmill.

Another form of gait analysis involves building a wearable module with an embedded IMU (inertial measurement unit) sensor [14–16] that is attached to the shank and analyzing roll, pitch, and yaw while walking. IMU sensor-based research analyzes gait by focusing on the angle of foot movement and the stride length. Although IMU sensors are mainly used to analyze gait on flat surfaces, the analysis process can be challenging if the stride length or the foot angle is not consistent; so, most studies require the examined subjects to move at a constant speed. Hutabat et. al. [15] used two IMU sensors attached to the shoes and allowed the examined subjects to adjust their speed on a treadmill to analyze gait changes according to the speed.

Riley et al. [17] performed a gait analysis based on an instrumental treadmill capable of measuring the ground reaction force. The overground walking kinetics were estimated as the subjects walked at their self-selected, comfortable walking speed. During the treadmill gait trials, the subjects walked on two treadmills, so that the heel strike event occurred on the forward treadmill, and the toe off event occurred on the trailing treadmill. The treadmill was set to the average overground walking speed. The authors showed that the treadmill gait is qualitatively and quantitatively similar to the overground gait.

Although not directly comparable to our study, Luessis et al. [18] analyzed the gait of Parkinson's disease (PD) patients using a treadmill with an embedded pressure sensor from Zebris [19]. They found that the insertion of visual elements such as horizontal stripes on the treadmill belt caused changes in key gait parameters such as stride time, stride length, and cadence.

In this paper, we performed gait analysis on a treadmill. First, was we set the walking speed, and the subject walked at the set speed for a certain period of time: then, the pressure distribution on each foot was estimated from the measurement of the pressure applied while walking. We aimed to model the gait patterns of subjects walking at a constant speed on a treadmill based on the differences in current consumption due to pressure differences that occur during different walking states. The changes in current consumption could be converted into pressure distribution curves (envelopes) by preprocessing. From the pressure distribution (average) calculated by superimposing about 50 pressure distribution curves per second, feature points that could model walking patterns were extracted, as shown in Figure 2. The extracted features were used to model the walking patterns on a treadmill. The features that we determined in this paper are related to the walking events shown in Figure 1.

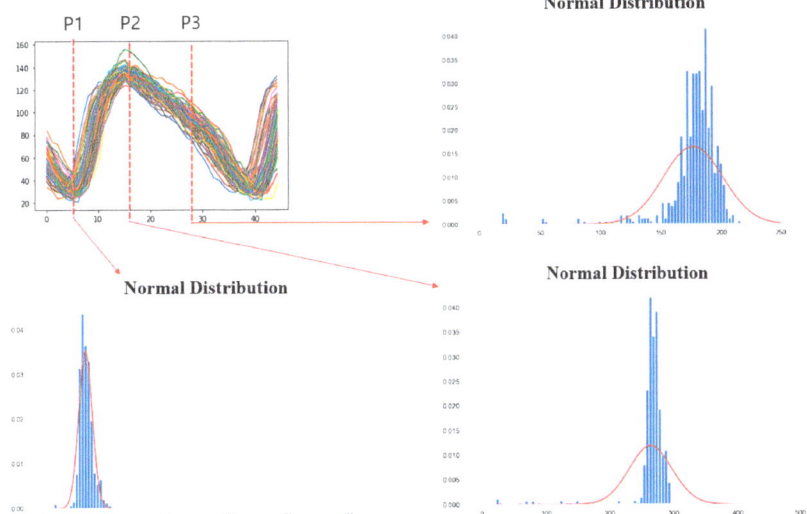

Figure 2. The feature points extracted from the overlapped pressure distribution curves.

In this paper, we implemented an adapter sensor to measure the instantaneous current consumption when walking on a treadmill. Unlike the complex experimental settings used in previous studies, current consumption was simply measured by attaching an adapter to the treadmill.

The paper is organized as follows. Section 1 describes the background of gait analysis and the research needs and discusses the existing studies conducted on the ground and on a treadmill. Section 2 describes the system configured to acquire gait analysis data on a treadmill and the data preprocessing process. Section 3 describes the feature point extraction process from the collected data. Section 4 presents the experimental results to validate the feasibility of our feature-based gait pattern modeling. Finally, Section 5 presents the conclusions and outlooks.

2. System Configuration and Preprocessing

To analyze treadmill walking, an adapter sensor was connected to a treadmill to collect instantaneous changes in current consumption during treadmill walking, as shown in Figure 3. When walking on a treadmill, pressure (load) is applied to the lower part of the treadmill belt, which causes a change in current consumption in the motor that rotates the belt of the treadmill. The adapter sensor measured this change in current consumption.

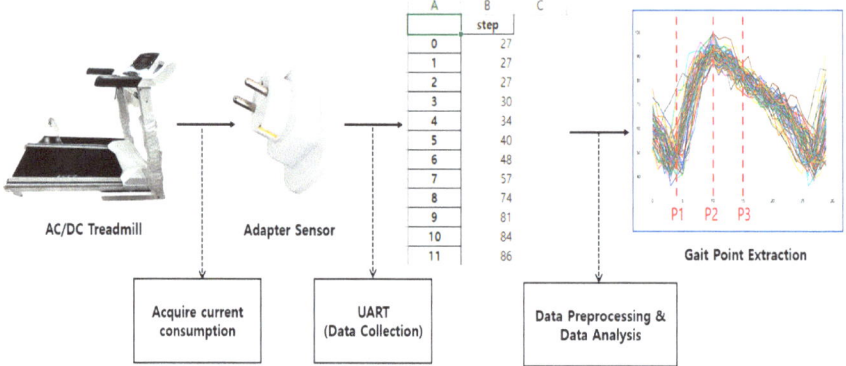

Figure 3. A data flow diagram of the proposed gait analysis system on a treadmill.

The overall flow diagram of the treadmill gait analysis system is shown in Figure 3. The adapter sensor was controlled by an Arduino Nano device. The adapter sensor was connected to the analysis server system via a USB cable, which allowed the raw current consumption changes to be acquired from the server in real time. The collected raw data were preprocessed to extract a pressure distribution curve (envelope), as shown in Figure 3.

The instantaneous current consumption data were converted to numerical data and stored as a text file on the server. The file storage format was compatible with spreadsheet programs such as Excel and could be visualized. After preprocessing, the data files were used for feature point extraction for statistical modeling.

2.1. Data Acquisition Details

When the subject started walking on the treadmill, the instantaneous current consumption data were collected and preprocessed to extract the envelope, as shown in Figure 4. The subject started walking on the treadmill at a preset speed of 4 km/h for 10 min. After a 10 min break, the subject walked at the same speed for another 10 min. A total of two measurements were conducted for the same subject.

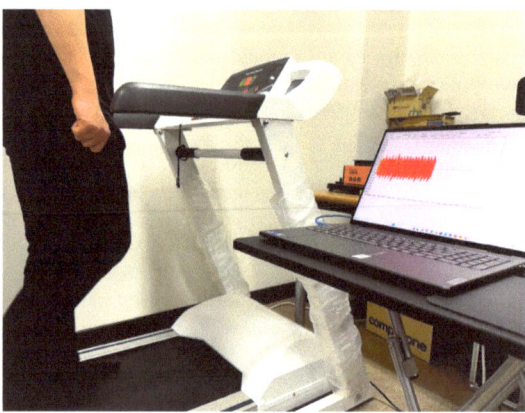

Figure 4. Walking test after attaching the adapter sensor to a treadmill.

Index walking was practiced during the initial gait analysis to help identify the left or right foot on the treadmill. Index walking consisted in taking a long step with the left foot and a relatively short step with the right foot. After about 10 to 15 sessions of index walking, the subject walked normally for 10 min. Figure 5 visualizes the progression of normal walking after the initial 7–8 sessions of index walking.

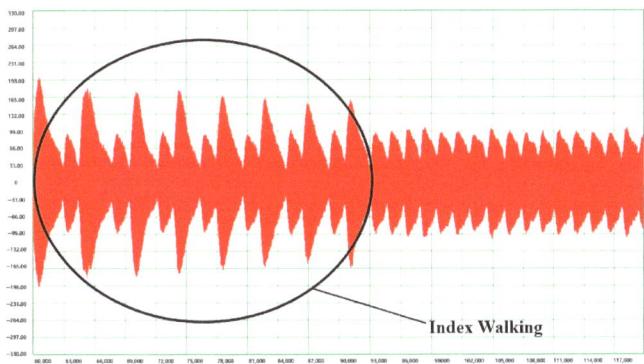

Figure 5. Pressure distribution when walking on a treadmill (includes index walking).

2.2. Data Preprocessing for the Analysis

The collected instantaneous current consumption data were in the form of positive and negative values that were symmetrical; so the raw data could not be used. Therefore, data preprocessing, as shown in Figure 6, was required.

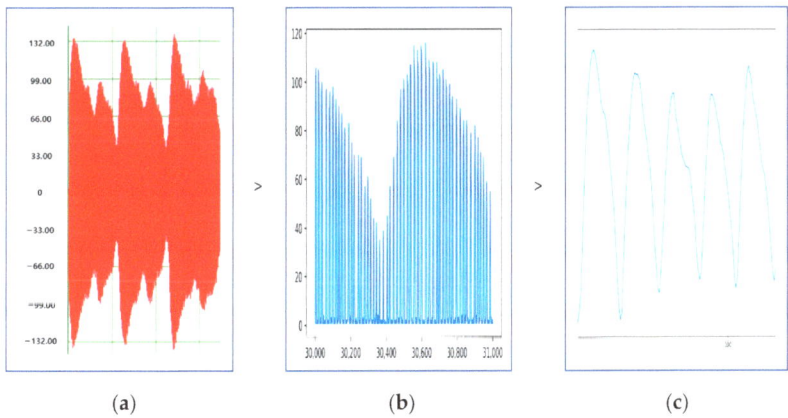

Figure 6. The process of data preprocessing. (**a**) Removal of negative values, (**b**) extraction of envelopes, (**c**) smoothing after applying the Kalman filter.

The raw data of the instantaneous current presented symmetrical positive and negative values, as shown in the graph in Figure 6a. Since the values were symmetrical, if we removed the negative values from the raw data to utilize only the positive values, the graph was transformed, as shown in Figure 6b. Next, we performed envelope extraction, extracting only the endpoints of the graph. After envelopment, the data were extracted and smoothed by applying the Kalman filter [20]. Comparing the data before and after smoothing, we found that the data before smoothing (Figure 6b) were more suitable for gait analysis and discrimination. In the subsequent analysis, only the envelope data in Figure 6b were used.

2.3. Information on the Subjects

Since a stable gait data acquisition requires at least 10 min of continuous walking at a constant speed (4 km/h) on a treadmill, the experiment was conducted on adults with normal walking ability. Data from a total of 19 volunteers were used to compose the dataset for gait analysis. The participating subjects' information is shown in Table 1. Table 1 reports the mean values for the subjects examined, and the values in parentheses indicated the standard deviation (SD).

Table 1. Information on the 19 subjects who participated in the experiments.

	Missing	Overall	Sex	
			Male	Female
No of Subjects		19	12	7
Age, mean (SD)	0	30.7 (9.9)	31.4 (10.3)	29.4 (9.9)
Height, mean (SD)	0	170.5 (9.8)	175.9 (7.9)	161.1 (3.4)

3. Feature Point-Based Gait Pattern Modeling

The instantaneous current consumption data contained 50 data points per second after raw data preprocessing and envelope extraction. The speed of 4 km/h set on the treadmill in this study is close to the average walking speed of an adult. A single stride requires an average of 0.6 to 0.7 s [21] for an adult. Based on this, one gait cycle on the treadmill contained 30 data points, i.e., one envelope consisted of 30 data points, and gait features were extracted from these data points.

Feature points were extracted based on the gait cycle in Figure 1 and the RLA gait model in Figure 7. Although the event occurrence times of the feature points did not perfectly match those of the model, points with similar features were selected.

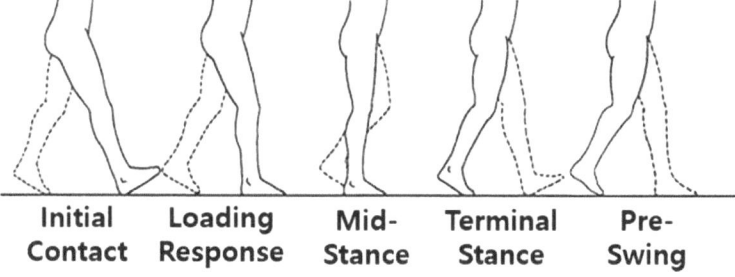

Figure 7. RLA gait model [22].

The feature points extracted from the nested envelopes are shown in Figure 8. One envelope represents one footstep. For the human gait, the main points corresponding to specific events are the heel strike and the toe off points [7,14]. These points correspond to the stance phase of the gait. The foot flat and heel off points are also used for calibration [7]. We extracted two feature points, P1 and P2, as points that had similar behavior to the heel strike and toe off points. The feature point P1 was the point where the foot touches the treadmill, and the stance phase begins. After the first step, one foot touched the treadmill, and the other foot moved away from the treadmill, intersecting with the end of the gait. The feature point P2 was the point where the value of the current consumption was maximized and corresponded to the state just before the transition from mid-stance to terminal stance, when all the pressure was concentrated on one foot. The feature point P3 was extracted based on the point where the value of the current consumption started to decrease. This corresponded to the transition from terminal stance to pre-swing in the gait cycle and coincided with the point when the foot was about to separate from the treadmill. Points with a minimum value after the feature point P2 were excluded because they might overlap with the feature point P1 in the next cycle. The selected feature point P3 was the point where the value of the current consumption started to continuously decrease from the maximum value.

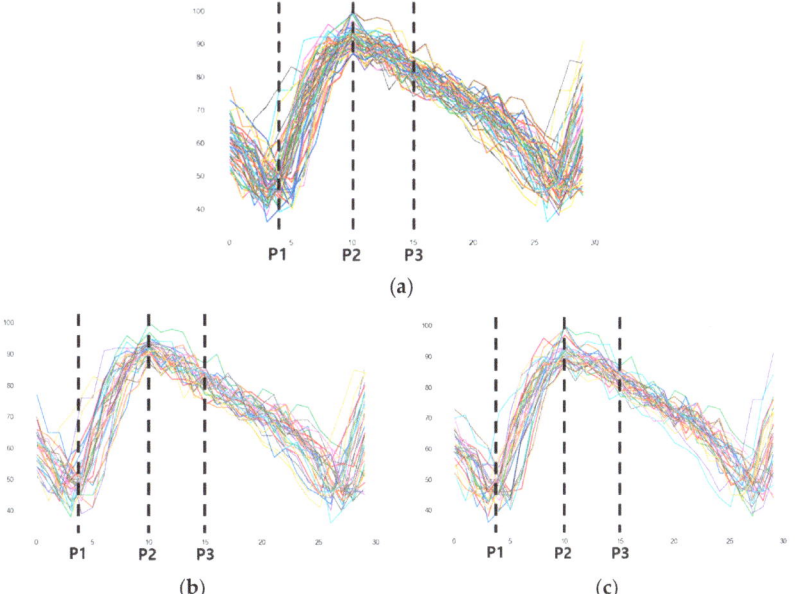

Figure 8. The 3 features extracted from the overlapped envelopes. (**a**) All footsteps, (**b**) left footsteps only, (**c**) right footsteps only.

Figure 8a overlays all footsteps, Figure 8b overlays only the left footsteps, and Figure 8c overlays only the right footsteps.

4. Experimental Results

In this paper, three feature points were extracted based on one step to model the subject's gait pattern. By extracting the feature points for normal gait, a gait pattern standard dataset was built; then, the gait pattern of a subject was compared with that corresponding to the standard dataset to determine if the differences between the feature points were within an acceptable range. By doing so, we expected to determine whether the subject's gait pattern was normal or abnormal. To verify the validity of this modeling, we conducted experiments based on gender, age, and BMI and tested for statistical significance. BMI was included as a comparison indicator because the instantaneous current consumption change of a treadmill is proportional to the pressure applied to the belt. In addition, to determine an abnormal gait, the gait patterns of the left and right feet were compared, i.e., the left and right asymmetrical gait was estimated by comparing differences by gait feature points.

4.1. Feature Point-Based Modeling by Sex

We conducted an experiment to see if there was a significant difference in gait pattern analysis by gender when applying feature point-based gait pattern modeling. To minimize the effect of BMI, we selected four male and four female subjects with a BMI between 20 and 25. In Table 2, SD is the standard deviation, and the feature point values are the mean values, considering all the subjects. The difference for each parameter was obtained by subtracting the female subjects' (F) mean value from the male subjects' (M) minus value.

Table 2. The feature points (avg.) by gender for subjects with BMI between 20 and 25.

	Overall	Sex		Difference = M-F
		Male (M)	Female (F)	
No of subjects	8	4	4	-
BMI, mean (SD)	21.8 (1.6)	22.9 (1.7)	20.6 (0.3)	2.3
P1-mean (SD)	62.3 (5.7)	66.5 (4.4)	58.1 (3.3)	8.4
P2-mean (SD)	95.8 (6.5)	99.3 (6.7)	92.3 (4.6)	7.0
P3-mean (SD)	75.6 (6.7)	78.5 (5.1)	72.8 (7.6)	5.7

The average difference for the feature points according to gender was 8.4 and 7.0 for P1 and P2, respectively, and only 5.7 for P3. Although the difference between genders can be interpreted as significant, we cannot rule out the possibility that it was due to the fact that the BMI of the male subjects (22.9, mean) was about 10% higher than the BMI of the female subjects (20.6, mean).

For comparison, a total of five subjects (three males and two females) with BMIs between 25 and 27 were subjected to gait analysis, and the results are summarized in Table 3. The differences between the male and female values were converted to absolute values. The average difference per feature point was almost similar for P1 and P3 but was 10.5 for P2. Given that P2 had the largest value (mean) of the three feature points, we believe that it changed specifically as the BMI increased. The higher the BMI, the greater the effects on the feature points exerted by physical parameters (height, weight, etc.).

Table 3. The feature points (avg.) by gender for subjects with BMI between 25 and 27.

	Overall	Sex		Difference = M-F
		Male (M)	Female (F)	
No of subjects	5	3	2	-
BMI, mean (SD)	26.0 (0.5)	26.2 (0.5)	25.6 (0.0)	0.6
P1-mean (SD)	66.7 (5.0)	66.4 (5.1)	67.1 (6.9)	0.7
P2-mean (SD)	102.7 (9.5)	106.9 (9.5)	96.4 (6.8)	10.5
P3-mean (SD)	79.4 (4.6)	78.9 (1.6)	80.2 (8.7)	1.3

4.2. Feature Point-Based Modeling by Age

The BMI was found to have a significant effect on the feature points in comparison to the gender. We then analyzed the effect of age and BMI on the feature points. For this purpose, a linear regression analysis was performed using BMI and age as dependent variables, and the results are summarized in Table 4. It can be seen that the BMI had a significant effect on all three characteristic points. In particular, an increase in BMI had the effect of increasing the P2 value by more than three units. Additionally, the p values for all three feature points were found to be <0.05, indicating significant differences. On the other hand, there was almost no change in the characteristic points according to age.

Table 4. Changes in the coefficients for the feature points according to age and BMI.

	P1 Mean Coef	P1 Mean p-Value	P2 Mean Coef	P2 Mean p-Value	P3 Mean Coef	P3 Mean p-Value
Age	−0.008	0.949	−0.263	0.131	0.136	0.391
BMI	1.602	<0.001	3.036	<0.001	1.735	<0.001

4.3. Feature Point-Based Modeling by BMI

Based on the analysis results reported in the previous section, we excluded the factors of age and gender and conducted a gait analysis by feature point based on BMI. The subjects were divided into three groups according to their BMI: normal (20 to 25), overweight (25 to 30), and obese (30 or more), and the experimental results are summarized in Table 5.

Table 5 shows the comparison of the subjects' feature point averages by BMI. Difference is the difference between the maximum and the minimum values of each feature point. It can be seen that, as the BMI increased, the value of each feature point also increased.

Table 5. Classification of the feature points (avg.) by BMI.

	Overall	BMI Group			Difference (Max)
		20~25	25~30	30~	
No of subjects	18	8	6	4	-
BMI, mean (SD))	26.1 (5.8)	21.8 (1.6)	26.6 (1.4)	35.7 (1.9)	-
P1-mean (SD)	67.8 (10.5)	62.3 (5.7)	66.3 (4.5)	84.7 (2.6)	13.9
P2-mean (SD)	105.9 (18.2)	95.8 (6.5)	104.2 (9.2)	135.4 (8.2)	39.6
P3-mean (SD)	84.6 (12.1)	75.6 (6.7)	78.9 (4.3)	101.4 (4.3)	25.8

In order to visually confirm the results reported in Table 5, the feature points for each BMI group are displayed in Figure 9 as a boxplot. As can be seen in Figure 9, the values of the feature points showed an upward trend as the BMI increased.

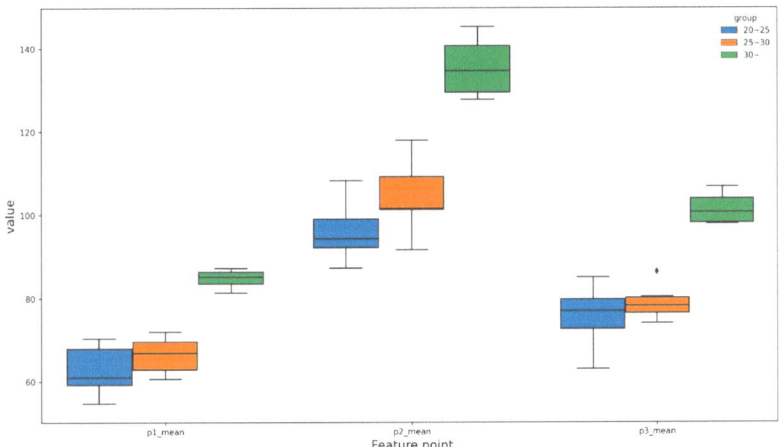

Figure 9. Visualization of each feature point according to the BMI in a boxplot.

The peculiarity is that the boxplot shape of the feature point P3 for the subjects in the BMI 25–30 group and of the feature point P1 for the subjects in the BMI 30+ group was very narrow. This small variation indicated that the gait patterns of the BMI 25–30 group and the BMI 30+ group were similar at a particular feature point.

According to the Kruskal–Wallis test [23], the BMI was found to be significant as a dependent variable, with a p value of 0.008. For further analysis, we performed a univariate regression and found that the effect of BMI on the feature points was significant. The BMI was separated into three variables, i.e., normal weight (BMI_normal), overweight (BMI_overweight), and obese (BMI_obese); normal-weight BMI was the control group, and OLS regression was performed to statistically determine the impact on each feature point value. The results for the entire population were also added to the table, indicated as BMI_continuous before separating the groups by BMI.

As shown in Table 6, the results of the multivariate analysis for the three groups divided based on the BMI were different from the results of the univariate analysis (Table 5). BMI_normal was the control group, with no numerical data. For the feature point P1, the difference between normal and overweight subjects was not significant, but the difference between normal and obese subjects was significant. For the feature point P2, the differences for both overweight and obese cases compared to normal subjects were statistically significant. For the feature point P3, we observed the same as for P1, i.e., the difference between normal and obese subjects was significant, but the difference between normal and overweight subjects was interpreted as not significant. The value of P1 increased by 3.113 in the case of overweight subjects compared to normal subjects and increased by 19.834 in the case of obese subjects. P2 showed the highest increase by group, with a 10.656 increase for overweight subjects compared to normal subjects and a 37.523 increase for obese subjects. P3 showed a very small increase (0.156) for overweight subjects compared to normal subjects and a very large increase (22.569) for obese subjects.

Table 6. The multivariate analysis of the feature points by BMI.

	P1 Mean Coef	P1 Mean p-Value	P2 Mean Coef	P2 Mean p-Value	P3 Mean Coef	P3 Mean p-Value
BMI_continuous	1.466	<0.001	2.809	<0.001	1.708	<0.001
BMI_normal	-	-	-	-	-	-
BMI_over	3.113	0.322	10.656	0.034	0.156	0.964
BMI_obesity	19.834	<0.001	37.523	<0.001	22.569	<0.001

In summary, the higher the BMI, the higher the value of the feature points extracted from the gait analysis. Therefore, the normal gait of a person with a high BMI should be modeled based on the increased feature point values.

4.4. Feature Point-Based Modeling by BMI for Left and Right Footsteps

The adult gait typically exhibits a symmetrical pattern of left and right stepping [24]. However, there are some adults who have asymmetrical gait patterns even though they do not have orthopedic or neurological conditions. A difference in the gait pattern between the left and the right foot can still be considered normal if there is no specific medical condition that impairs the gait. Therefore, we need criteria to determine if an asymmetrical gait is abnormal.

To determine the difference between left and right gait, the difference between the values of each feature point for left and right gait was calculated from the collected data. The figures shown in Table 7 are the differences (absolute value) for each feature point for the subjects' left and right gait. Also shown in Table 7 is the BMI, which affected the feature points.

For most subjects, there was no difference in the gait pattern between the two feet. The average difference between the left and the right gait for all subjects per feature point was 0.69 for P1, 0.32 for P2, and 0.38 for P3. In particular, subjects 7, 10, and 16 showed very little difference between their left and right gait, suggesting that they had a very symmetrical gait, with no balance shift to one side.

On the other hand, for subject 11, the difference (5.8) was large for P1, the point where both feet step out. Compared to the averages for each feature point of the other subjects, we can see that the difference between the mean values of P1 for the left and right footsteps for subject 11 was very large. In other words, a distinct asymmetric gait pattern was extracted from subject 11.

We also compared whether the probability of asymmetrical gait was higher in the obese group, because subject 11 was in the obese group, with a BMI of 30 or more. When we restricted the data to subjects in this experimental group, we could not conclude that asymmetrical gait occurred only in the obese group. In particular, the difference for the gait point P1 was more than 1.0 even in the case of subject 1, who was underweight. Therefore, we can assume that the asymmetrical gait is not related to the BMI.

Table 7. Differences (absolute value) between each feature point for left and right footsteps.

Subject	P1 Diff	P2 Diff	P3 Diff	BMI
1	1.10	0.55	0.29	20.32
2	0.66	0.08	0.11	23.37
3	0.11	0.38	0.13	20.96
4	0.73	0.76	0.02	25.77
5	0.41	0.58	0.01	32.97
6	0.41	0.07	0.07	25.64
7	0.06	0.05	0.01	19.43
8	0.08	0.85	0.19	26.23
9	0.55	0.00	1.07	22.48
10	0.33	0.17	0.46	20.83
11	5.08	0.03	0.12	36.75
12	0.77	0.09	0.40	26.7
13	0.18	1.10	1.06	29.4
14	0.11	0.04	0.06	36.93
15	0.65	0.03	0.40	20.75
16	0.29	0.07	0.05	20.44
17	1.11	0.14	0.02	36.2
18	0.15	0.63	0.17	25.64
19	0.38	0.41	0.71	24.84
Mean	0.69	0.32	0.28	26.43

For the other subjects excepting subject 11, the feature point difference between left and right gait was up to 1.11 for P1, 1.10 for P2, and 1.07 for P3. If the normal gait is evaluated by the change in current consumption on a treadmill, the acceptable range of the feature point difference between left and right gait can be estimated to be within ±2.0.

5. Conclusions

The treadmill gait analysis has the advantage that the subject walks at a certain preset speed, and the pressure distribution of each foot can be inferred by measuring the pressure applied during walking. The treadmill gait cycle begins at the heel strike event, with a sharp increase in pressure from the mid-stance to the terminal-stance, and ends with a decrease in pressure just before the toe off event. A similar pressure distribution curve was obtained when a self-made adapter sensor was attached to the treadmill to acquire and visualize the current consumption during walking.

To verify the validity of analyzing treadmill gait patterns by extracting feature points, we conducted experiments based on gender, age, and BMI. First, we found that the feature points differed by gender, but the impact of the BMI was greater than that of gender. There were no significant differences in the feature points associated with age. Based on the BMI, the gait analysis was conducted on three groups: normal, overweight, and obese. For the obese group with a BMI of 30 or more, the mean value of each feature point increased significantly compared to the normal weight and overweight groups. However, the values of feature point P1 were almost similar: 62.30 ± 5.70 for the normal-BMI group, 66.30 ± 4.50 for the overweight group, and 84.70 ± 2.60 for the obese group. For adults with normal gait the value of P1 was almost unchanged in groups with similar BMI.

We conducted an experiment to determine whether the walking patterns of the left and right feet were symmetrical. Although we could not determine whether the asymmetry in the left and right gait patterns was due to musculoskeletal disorders, we found that feature point modeling could detect abnormal patterns. It is expected that if a difference outside the acceptable error range appears for a feature point value, it can provide an indicator to determine whether a subject has a gait abnormality.

Author Contributions: Conceptualization, Y.-S.H.; methodology, Y.-S.H. and W.-C.S.; software, W.-C.S. and H.-S.C.; validation, Y.-S.H., W.-C.S. and H.-S.C.; formal analysis, W.-C.S. and M.-J.K.; investigation, W.-C.S., M.-J.K. and J.-H.H.; resources, W.-C.S. and H.-S.C.; data curation, W.-C.S. and J.-H.H.; writing—original draft preparation, W.-C.S.; writing—review and editing, W.-C.S. and Y.-S.H.; visualization, W.-C.S. and M.-J.K.; supervision, Y.-S.H.; project administration, H.-S.C.; funding acquisition, Y.-S.H. All authors have read and agreed to the published version of the manuscript.

Funding: This research was partially funded by Incheon National University, grant number 2022-0221.

Institutional Review Board Statement: The study was conducted in accordance with the Declaration of Helsinki and approved by the Institutional Review Board of Incheon National University (7007971-202303-004, 18 May 2023).

Informed Consent Statement: Not applicable.

Data Availability Statement: All data used in this paper are dependent on the sensors used and the measurement environments. The measurement values of each sensor used in our experiments will be provided upon request by e-mail.

Conflicts of Interest: The authors declare no conflict of interest.

References

1. Ramos, A.M.; Marcos-Pardo, P.J.; Vale, R.G.d.S.; Vieira-Souza, L.M.; Camilo, B.d.F.; Martin-Dantas, E.H. Resistance Circuit Training or Walking Training: Which Program Improves Muscle Strength and Functional Autonomy More in Older Women? *Int. J. Environ. Res. Public Health* **2022**, *19*, 8828. [CrossRef] [PubMed]
2. Jayakody, O.; Breslin, M.; Ayers, E.; Verghese, J.; Barzilai, N.; Milman, S.; Erica, W.; Blumen, H.M. Relative trajectories of gait and cognitive decline in aging. *J. Gerontol. Ser. A* **2022**, *77*, 1230–1238. [CrossRef] [PubMed]
3. Lin, C.H.; Wang, F.C.; Kuo, T.Y.; Huang, P.W.; Chen, S.F.; Fu, L.C. Early detection of Parkinson's disease by neural network models. *IEEE Access* **2022**, *10*, 19033–19044. [CrossRef]
4. Kim, K.M.; Kang, H.J. Effects of resistance exercise on muscle mass, strength, and physical performances in elderly with diagnosed sarcopenia: A systematic review and meta-analysis. *Exerc. Sci.* **2020**, *29*, 109–120. [CrossRef]
5. Pieruccini-Faria, F.; Black, S.E.; Masellis, M.; Smith, E.E.; Almeida, Q.J.; Li, K.Z.H.; Bherer, L.; Camicioli, R.; Montero-Odasso, M. Gait variability across neurodegenerative and cognitive disorders: Results from the Canadian Consortium of Neurodegeneration in Aging (CCNA) and the Gait and Brain Study. *Alzheimer's Dement.* **2021**, *17*, 1317–1328. [CrossRef] [PubMed]
6. Middleton, A.; Fritz, S.L.; Lusardi, M. Walking speed: The functional vital sign. *J. Aging Phys. Act.* **2015**, *23*, 314–322. [CrossRef] [PubMed]
7. Chatzaki, C.; Skaramagkas, V.; Tachos, N.; Christodoulakis, G.; Maniadi, E.; Kefalopoulou, Z.; Fotiadis, D.I.; Tsiknakis, M. The Smart-Insole Dataset: Gait Analysis Using Wearable Sensors with a Focus on Elderly and Parkinson's Patients. *Sensors* **2021**, *21*, 2821. [CrossRef] [PubMed]
8. Li, Y.; Zhang, P.; Zhang, Y.; Miyazaki, K. Gait Analysis Using Stereo Camera in Daily Environment. In Proceedings of the 2019 41st Annual International Conference of the IEEE Engineering in Medicine and Biology Society (EMBC), Berlin, Germany, 23–27 July 2019; pp. 1471–1475. [CrossRef]
9. Jeong, K.; Lee, K.-C. Artificial Neural Network-Based Abnormal Gait Pattern Classification Using Smart Shoes with a Gyro Sensor. *Electronics* **2022**, *11*, 3614. [CrossRef]
10. Bucinskas, V.; Dzedzickis, A.; Rozene, J.; Subaciute-Zemaitiene, J.; Satkauskas, I.; Uvarovas, V.; Bobina, R.; Morkvenaite-Vilkonciene, I. Wearable Feet Pressure Sensor for Human Gait and Falling Diagnosis. *Sensors* **2021**, *21*, 5240. [CrossRef] [PubMed]
11. Kobsar, D.; Osis, S.T.; Jacob, C.; Ferber, R. Validity of a novel method to measure vertical oscillation during running using a depth camera. *J. Biomech.* **2019**, *85*, 182–186. [CrossRef] [PubMed]
12. Potdevin, F.; Gillet, C.; Barbier, F.; Coello, Y.; Moretto, P. The study of asymmetry in able-bodied gait with the concept of propulsion and brake. In Proceedings of the 9th Symposium on 3D Analysis of Human Movement, Valenciennes, France, 28–30 June 2006.
13. Lee, D.; Soon, J.; Choi, G.; Kim, K.; Bahn, S. Identification of the Visually Prominent Gait Parameters for Forensic Gait Analysis. *Int. J. Environ. Res. Public Health* **2022**, *19*, 2467. [CrossRef] [PubMed]
14. Gujarathi, T.; Bhole, K. Gait Analysis Using Imu Sensor. In Proceedings of the 2019 10th International Conference on Computing, Communication and Networking Technologies (ICCCNT), Kanpur, India, 6–8 July 2019; pp. 1–5. [CrossRef]
15. Hutabarat, Y.; Owaki, D.; Hayashibe, M. Seamless Temporal Gait Evaluation during Walking and Running Using Two IMU Sensors. In Proceedings of the 2021 43rd Annual International Conference of the IEEE Engineering in Medicine & Biology Society (EMBC), Mexico, 1–5 November 2021; pp. 6835–6840. [CrossRef]
16. Lou, Y.; Wang, R.; Mai, J.; Wang, N.; Wang, Q. IMU-Based Gait Phase Recognition for Stroke Survivors: Preliminary Results. In Proceedings of the 2018 IEEE 8th Annual International Conference on CYBER Technology in Automation, Control, and Intelligent Systems (CYBER), Tianjin, China, 19–23 July 2018; pp. 802–806. [CrossRef]

17. Riley, P.O.; Paolini, G.; Della Croce, U.; Paylo, K.W.; Kerrigan, D.C. A kinematic and kinetic comparison of overground and treadmill walking in healthy subjects. *Gait Posture* **2007**, *26*, 17–24. [CrossRef] [PubMed]
18. Luessi, F.; Mueller, L.K.; Breimhorst, M.; Vogt, T. Influence of visual cues on gait in Parkinson's disease during treadmill walking at multiple velocities. *J. Neurol. Sci.* **2012**, *314*, 78–82. [CrossRef] [PubMed]
19. Dynamic Gait Analysis on the Treadmill. Available online: https://www.zebris.de/en/medical/dynamic-gait-analysis-on-the-treadmill (accessed on 13 September 2023).
20. Borrero, J.D.; Mariscal, J. Predicting Time SeriesUsing an Automatic New Algorithm of the Kalman Filter. *Mathematics* **2022**, *10*, 2915. [CrossRef]
21. Qiao, L.; Button, K.; Al-Amri, M. The effect of virtual reality environment on spatial-temporal gait parameters during self-paced treadmill walking. *Gait Posture* **2021**, *90*, 192–193. [CrossRef]
22. Stance Phase of Gait. Available online: https://clinicalgate.com/assessment-of-gait/ (accessed on 13 September 2023).
23. Chen, Z.; Ma, M.; Li, T.; Wang, H.; Li, C. Long sequence time-series forecasting with deep learning: A survey. *Inf. Fusion* **2023**, *97*, 101819. [CrossRef]
24. Handžić, I.; Reed, K.B. Perception of gait patterns that deviate from normal and symmetric biped locomotion. *Front. Psychol.* **2015**, *6*, 199. [CrossRef] [PubMed]

Disclaimer/Publisher's Note: The statements, opinions and data contained in all publications are solely those of the individual author(s) and contributor(s) and not of MDPI and/or the editor(s). MDPI and/or the editor(s) disclaim responsibility for any injury to people or property resulting from any ideas, methods, instructions or products referred to in the content.

MDPI AG
Grosspeteranlage 5
4052 Basel
Switzerland
Tel.: +41 61 683 77 34

Electronics Editorial Office
E mail: electronics@mdpi.com
www.mdpi.com/journal/electronics

Disclaimer/Publisher's Note: The title and front matter of this reprint are at the discretion of the Guest Editors. The publisher is not responsible for their content or any associated concerns. The statements, opinions and data contained in all individual articles are solely those of the individual Editors and contributors and not of MDPI. MDPI disclaims responsibility for any injury to people or property resulting from any ideas, methods, instructions or products referred to in the content.

www.ingramcontent.com/pod-product-compliance
Lightning Source LLC
LaVergne TN
LVHW072355090526
838202LV00019B/2555